.

Converts to Civil Society

STUDIES IN
WORLD CHRISTIANITY

The Nagel Institute for the Study of World Christianity
Calvin College

Joel A. Carpenter
Series Editor

OTHER BOOKS IN THE SERIES

The Making of Korean Christianity
Sung-Deuk Oak

Converts to Civil Society

Christianity and Political Culture in Contemporary Hong Kong

Lida V. Nedilsky

BAYLOR UNIVERSITY PRESS

Cover Design by Natalya Balnova
Cover Image: Rally at Star Ferry Pier, Tsim Sha Tsui. Photograph by Lida
    V. Nedilsky, 1998.

Library of Congress Cataloging-in-Publication Data

Nedilsky, Lida V.
 Converts to civil society : Christianity and political culture in contempo-
rary Hong Kong / Lida V. Nedilsky.
 239 pages cm. — (Studies in world christianity)
 Includes bibliographical references and index.
 ISBN 978-1-4813-0032-2 (hardback : alk. paper)
 1. Christianity—China—Hong Kong. 2. Christianity and politics—
China—Hong Kong. 3. Religion and civil society—China—Hong Kong. 4.
Civil society—China—Hong Kong. I. Title.
 BR1295.H6N43 2014
 261.7095125—dc23
                                                          2013045457

Printed in the United States of America on acid-free paper with a minimum
of 30% post-consumer waste recycled content.

For Mykola, Orest, and James

Series Foreword

It used to be that those of us from the global North who study world Christianity had to work hard to make the case for its relevance. Why should thoughtful people learn more about Christianity in places far away from Europe and North America? The Christian religion, many have heard by now, has more than 60 percent of its adherents living outside of Europe and North America. It has become a hugely multicultural faith, expressed in more languages than any other religion. Even so, the implications of this major new reality have not sunk in. Studies of world Christianity might seem to be just another obscure specialty niche for which the academy is infamous, rather like an "ethnic foods" corner in an American grocery store.

Yet the entire social marketplace, both in North America and Europe, is rapidly changing. The world is undergoing the greatest transregional migration in its history, as people from Africa, Asia, Latin America, and the Pacific region become the neighbors down the street, across Europe and North America. The majority of these new immigrants are Christians. Within the United States, one now can find virtually every form of Christianity from around the world. Here in Grand Rapids, Michigan, where I live and work, we have Sudanese Anglicans, Adventists from the Dominican Republic, Vietnamese Catholics, Burmese Baptists, Mexican Pentecostals, and Lebanese Orthodox Christians—to name a few of the Christian traditions and movements now present.

Christian leaders and institutions struggle to catch up with these new realities. The selection of a Latin American pope in 2013 was in some respects the culmination of decades of readjustment in the Roman Catholic Church. Here in Grand Rapids, the receptionist for the Catholic bishop answers the telephone first in Spanish. The worldwide Anglican communion is being fractured over controversies concerning sexual morality and biblical authority. Other churches in worldwide fellowships and alliances are treading more carefully as new leaders come forward and challenge northern assumptions, both liberal and conservative.

Until very recently, however, the academic and intellectual world has paid little heed to this seismic shift in Christianity's location, vitality, and expression. Too often, as scholars try to catch up to these changes, says the renowned historian Andrew Walls, they are still operating with "pre-Columbian maps" of these realities.

This series is designed to respond to that problem by making available some of the coordinates needed for a new intellectual cartography. Broad-scope narratives about world Christianity are being published, and they help to revise the more massive misconceptions. Yet much of the most exciting work in this field is going on closer to the action. Dozens of dissertations and journal articles are appearing every year, but their stories are too good and their implications are too important to be reserved for specialists only. So we offer this series to make some of the most interesting and seminal studies more accessible, both to academics and to the thoughtful general reader. World Christianity is fascinating for its own sake, but it also helps to deepen our understanding of how faith and life interact in more familiar settings.

So we are eager for you to read, ponder, and enjoy these Baylor Studies in World Christianity. There are many new things to learn, and many old things to see in a new light.

Joel A. Carpenter
Series Editor

Contents

Acknowledgments

When I was still a student, a friend both senior and wiser told me that if for no other reward than my education I should be grateful for my years of academic work. That education has taken me to Shanghai and Taichung and Hong Kong, Berkeley and San Diego, Chicago and London. It has introduced me to numerous and diverse teachers, given me languages with which to comprehend strangers and forge friendships, and offered me new ways to connect with family members and students.

That education, while generous, cannot compare to the generosity of individuals I have known across the years. I am indebted to Richard Madsen, Kathy Mooney, Dan Bays, Rhys Williams, Joseph Lee, S. K. Cheung, and Lenore Knight Johnson. As my mentors and friends, these individuals instruct and inspire me. Lily Chan Szeto, Wong Hau-Kum, and Carol Cheung—each cultivates my appreciation of the Chinese language. And the Hong Kong NGO founders, members, and staff—to whom I assign pseudonyms reflecting their qualities of wisdom and compassion, joy and courage—make learning the deepest endeavor. They are the reason I keep going back to Hong Kong.

I have also known the generosity of institutions. FLAS and NSEP fellowships, professional encouragement and financial support from the University of California, San Diego, and the hospitality of Hong Kong Shue Yan University and the Chinese University of Hong Kong have aided my efforts to understand the significance of Christianity in Hong Kong. At North Park University, Chicago, I have benefited from funds awarded me by the Professional Development Committee and Dean

Charles I. Peterson, as well as a full-year sabbatical granted by its Board of Trustees.

At Baylor University Press, the enthusiastic responses of Carey Newman and Joel Carpenter have left a lasting impression that sustains my effort still, while the expert direction of Gladys Lewis has boosted my confidence as she has improved my communication. Two anonymous readers offered feedback like old friends in conversation with me. They seemed entirely aware of what I needed to hear.

And at the intimate level of day to day, I have enjoyed the constancy of my family. Collaborations with Bohdan V. Nedilsky, my brother, invigorate and stretch me. Relaxing visits and conference stopovers with my parents, Sofron and Christina Nedilsky, as well as my sister, Kalyna Nedilsky, fortify me. But through everyday struggles and gradual developments it is James, Orest, and Mykola Sison who know me and my work. I am most grateful to them.

Introduction

Distance affects perception. That which appears as one thing turns out upon closer proximity and scrutiny to be quite different. Sir David Attenborough, English broadcaster and naturalist, has remarked on this tendency in the natural world. In his intimate investigation of the microcosmos of insects, "Life in the Undergrowth," what appears to be a cloud of smoke is instead a swarm of midges moved by the actions of every single one.[1] This thrill of discovery not only has fueled scientific investigation but also has inspired Attenborough's particular style of communicating those discoveries to a wider public. When viewers venture to follow Sir David's lead through his rich documentary films, they enjoy a similar sense of wonder and appreciation for the fine details evident in nature if they only get close enough to see exactly what is in front of them.

In the social world as in the natural world, scholars provide the chance to appreciate and discover alongside them. Perhaps the first thrilling view of ourselves is recognition that we are not unique and alone in our experience of the social world. Instead, with the help of sociologists and political scientists, people appear as stable members of groups. Institutions such as religion, education, family, and polity contain people as if in vessels working to form them into comparable and predictable persons.

Seeing the world in terms of groups shouldn't mean we fall into the trap of ascribing to them a staying power and control that is in fact

---

[1] David Attenborough, "Life in the Undergrowth," series producer Mike Salisbury, 2/Entertain, BBC video, London, 2006.

2 — Converts to Civil Society

negotiated in modern society by their individual members. And yet, in enjoying the work of scholars of religion, for instance, we may come to confuse faith tradition, church, or congregation with the believers whose choices infuse the collective with purpose and consequence. In appreciating what scholars of democratic politics write, we may confuse voting rights with the varied practices of politically competent citizens whose everyday actions guard against tyranny. And in wondering about the involvement of religious people in politics and public life, we may assume that particular religious traditions beget particular political traditions. *Converts to Civil Society*, in seeking to account for the development of civil society in Hong Kong at the turn of the twenty-first century, restores attention to the personal and seemingly unique. Breaking away from the vessel approach to studying religion and politics, it focuses on the often overlooked individuals whose commitment to personal development structures society.

In Hong Kong's free market culture, membership options and purveyors of religious development are available in abundance. *Converts to Civil Society* draws us deeply into this rich social marketplace. Our journey of discovery begins with the stories of individuals involved at the intersections of church and state. From 1997 to 2008, from anticipating Hong Kong's return to Chinese sovereignty to experiencing it, I have followed and documented in over eighty interviews these individuals' development. Whether born into Catholic or Protestant families, religious or secular households, these Hong Kong people share an important common narrative: they tell the story of choosing faith. Conversion is a common occurrence, and with it comes an array of memberships. Across their lives, and across the spheres of family, fellowship, church, organizational membership, and workplace, individuals break and forge bonds, enter and exit commitments, and enable others to choose for themselves as well.

In following the movements of individuals, *Converts to Civil Society* provides the necessary vantage to see that what appears to be a stable, steady minority of 10 percent Christian faithful is instead a moving, individuated mass of converts not totally unlike Attenborough's midges. These independent movements not only invigorate and shape religious community in Hong Kong but also, taken together, establish a common experience of religious engagement that enlivens wider public life.

While private commitments to fellowship, church, organization, workplace, and family each predictably challenge the individual convert to develop within faith, Hong Kong's return to Chinese sovereignty threatens the entire project with unpredictability. Political development joins religious development as an essential quest. Membership choices on offer through organizations and churches, courses and careers must satisfy this political need, too. Consequently, the movement that comes with breaking and forging still more social bonds becomes normal, unremarkable, and, for some, unnoticeable.

Much as Attenborough's midges appear as smoke, converts to civil society in Hong Kong can appear as the steady 10 percent of a Christian minority contained within a religious category as if held within a vessel. This impression could not be further from the truth. When we experience a closer look, when we place the details of everyday practices associated with independent movement and shared culture at the forefront, the true nature of these converts reveals itself. We discover a source of vitality in Hong Kong's public life with lessons for other societies, including our own. While difficult to recognize with the naked eye, *Converts to Civil Society* shows us that it is individual acts not only of entering but also of exiting commitments that form a vibrant civil society. Whether because of a marketplace of options, tolerance of the state, or norms of the wider society, wherever people are free to join or quit, they are free to govern themselves according to the ideals of democracy.

−1−

A Question of Competence

Statue Square on a typical Sunday with Legislative Council building in background, Central (photograph by Lida V. Nedilsky, 1998)

Statue Square, June 30, 1997: On the eve of Hong Kong's return to Chinese sovereignty, rain fell intermittently throughout the day, keeping many people off the streets and out of the parks. Hardly unusual for a holiday, residents of the city packed themselves inside the shopping arcades instead. But this public holiday marked the end of 156 years of British colonial rule and the beginning of a negotiated union with the People's Republic of China (PRC). At the stroke of midnight on July 1, Britain would formally hand over the territory of Hong Kong to its new ruler. Administrative bodies like the rural lineage organizations as well as metropolitan government councils planned festivities in venues throughout the territory: from Peking and Cantonese operas to the world's largest karaoke sing along, from a pan-Asian food festival to the Carnival of Unity. By evening the pouring rain had put a very real damper on things. The fireworks display, which had promised to mark the joy of the occasion, was barely visible, blocked by dark, heavy clouds that seemed to lower the ceiling on a sky already cramped by high-rises.

Despite the bad weather, immediately following the harbor-front fireworks people milled about Statue Square in the section of town known as Central. Distinct from official government bodies and their activities, organizers from a coalition of some thirty nongovernmental organizations (NGOs) made final preparations there in Statue Square for what they billed as the Alternative Handover (*lihngnoih wùihgwài*). It could not really be called a celebration, since the organizers agreed not to demand coalition partners' unanimous endorsement of Hong Kong's political fate. Celebration implied cause for rejoicing, and not everyone was pleased with the prospect of becoming a special administrative region (SAR) of China. While guaranteed fifty years of autonomy, Hong Kong people knew well enough from the events in Tiananmen Square not ten years back how tenuous was any political freedom given by the Chinese Communist Party leadership in Beijing. It was on the morning of June 4, 1989, that People's Liberation Army tanks rolled into the central square of the nation's capital to crush demonstrations for democracy. Removed from the violence by time as well as physical distance, one amateur Hong Kong cartoonist suggested on June 30, 1997, let it rain on the SAR's Handover parade! "*Wùihgwài lo*," ran the caption under the stormy scene. "*Yùhgwó lohk daaih yúh, jauh hóuwo!*"[1] ("It's the Handover, mind you. If there's a heavy rain, that's just fine!")

---

[1] True to the documented language of Hong Kong, all translations are from

Partners in the Alternative Handover, while not required to pass uniform judgment on the occasion, had to sign on to the idea of pluralism. Hong Kong was a place of diverse people with different ways of being and types of experience. Like the participating organizations assembled alongside each other in Statue Square, Hong Kong society was made up of professionals and laborers, students and teachers, the nonreligious and the religious faithful. Whether a formal group or a solitary individual, each participant was entitled to an opinion about Hong Kong's return to the motherland. Such tolerance was impossible for some. At least one organization, an ally in similar joint actions, refused to accept this condition. In declining to join the Alternative Handover, its spokesperson explained that participating could compromise the group's potential to negotiate with authorities in post-Handover Hong Kong. Its members set up their own, separate stage immediately northeast of Statue Square and adjacent to the Legislative Council building, Hong Kong's parliament.

At 9:00 p.m fewer than one hundred people sat on plastic liners strewn upon the wet pavement, waiting for the three-hour show to begin. But as foot traffic through the area got heavier, more people settled into the square. Karen, a seasoned organizer, dressed in a transparent slicker, handed out programs for the evening's activities, including song lyrics for the usual sing-along. To give people in the back a view of the stage, another organizer, stationed at the microphone, asked new arrivals to take a seat. This request to sit down brought chuckles from the crowd, since the gathering was meant to enable citizens of Hong Kong to stand up and be counted, as the old Maoist expression goes. Under a banner with the words "Let's Work Together to Build a Better Tomorrow," radio and street personality Queenie strummed a guitar and led the audience through verses as she often did at public gatherings of this sort: "Who says I should be afraid? / Who says I have no worry / That I am simply a money-making gadget / Devoid of a name, a soul, a face, a voice . . . ?"[2]

By 11:00 p.m., well into the program, the entire square was packed. Perhaps a thousand participants filled the space on the pavement, along

---

Cantonese, and all transliterations of Cantonese are standard Yale Romanization according to Chik Hon Man and Ng Lam Sim Yuk, eds., *Chinese-English Dictionary* (Hong Kong: Chinese University Press, 1989).

[2] Lyrics from the Alternative Handover song "Who Says?" Translated in *Network '97* newsletter, July 1997.

the ledges of the fountains, and up against the stage. The mass of people included Rachel and her friends, members of one of the Catholic organizations among the many faith-based NGOs in the Alternative Handover coalition. As they greeted midnight with candles and a countdown, the small group passed a bottle of red wine (a gift from an empathetic priest) among themselves, sharing gulps. Then Jefferson, an event organizer made up in lipstick to playfully obscure his gender identity and accentuate his expressive mouth, distributed hand signs and unfurled a huge banner prepared for the occasion. All assembled commenced an unapproved (and thus adrenaline-spiked) march around the Legislative Council building, symbol of local governance. It was toward the Legislative Council as parliament that most people looked to judge whether they as citizens of a special place stood a chance of realizing the promise of Hong Kong people ruling Hong Kong.

A QUESTION OF COMPETENCE

While organizers sought the space with parliament as backdrop, it is the square and not the Legislative Council building that is the potent symbol of political development and possibility in my account of Hong Kong's democratic culture, *Converts to Civil Society*. This is a book about how the experience of Christianity in one former British colony created the conditions that permit a sphere of free association to thrive in Hong Kong today. Through distinct religious channels, individuals developed the skills necessary to extend beyond their private religious selves and take a place in the public square. This is the experience of a minority, in Hong Kong as elsewhere in the world. Yet, as presented in Statue Square, a minority experience can influence the wider Hong Kong society. Of the one thousand people who lingered however briefly or intently at Statue Square in the midnight hour of June 30, 1997, only a fraction were core organizers and committed supporters. A few, including Karen, Queenie, Rachel, and Jefferson, met regularly or directed others as key actors in their respective organizations during the weeks leading up to the Alternative Handover.[3] They collaborated on plans to involve

---

[3] To preserve anonymity, I have changed the names and obscured the particular details of individuals featured in this qualitative study. Moreover, as is the fashion in Hong Kong, I use Anglicized names and nicknames for those under thirty, who generally use English names regardless of their particular social circle. I have given alternative Chinese surnames to those of an older generation, as English names are not typically used among this group.

a wider pool of participants in marking a turning point in Hong Kong's political journey. Statue Square, positioned as it is at a key confluence of subway exits, bus stops, and a ferry terminal in Central, Hong Kong, practically guaranteed inclusion of some uninitiated participants. At the same time that Statue Square invited entry, it also allowed the uncommitted an easy exit. This dynamic of presenting Hong Kong people with a simple choice—should I stay or should I go?—may seem mundane. But the possibility of choosing one's terms of membership, as social scientists have pointed out, reveals much about a society and its political culture.

Statue Square the night before Hong Kong's Handover represents civil society by drawing together those who chose to participate in reflection, dialogue, and exchange. Civil society is an abstract concept, but the most tangible evidence for it associates with an open space that collects without containing. Whether sphere or square, it is the space for free association. Here private individuals assemble and negotiate their relationships with each other.[4] By assessing and discussing their similarities as well as differences, people learn how to negotiate with each other. In aggregate, they also develop the potential to deal with the state civilly, if critically. In summary, they learn to govern themselves. Recognizing a shared future, those who fill this space as free individuals bound together by choice and interdependence can work together to defend democracy. How? By using those same skills needed to negotiate between themselves in the way that responsible citizens check the authoritarian tendencies that are the temptation of any locus of power, even within a functioning democracy.

Civil society requires that people voluntarily enter and exit their associations, just as pedestrians freely enter and exit a space like Statue Square. So while they develop socially and politically through their engagement with civil society, people must already come with the skills needed to be free.[5] The most basic of these skills is the ability to act as an individual even when a member of a group. This seeming paradox of individual agency despite submission to the group was a fascination of sociologist Georg Simmel. Writing at the turn of the twentieth century,

---

[4] See Alexis de Tocqueville, *Democracy in America*, ed. J. P. Mayer, trans. George Lawrence (New York: Harper Collins, 1969); and Jürgen Habermas, *The Structural Transformation of the Public Sphere: An Inquiry into a Category of Bourgeois Society*, trans. Thomas Burger (Cambridge, Mass.: MIT Press, 2000).

[5] See Adam B. Seligman, *The Idea of Civil Society* (Princeton: Princeton University Press, 1995).

Simmel argued that the individual, in fact, arose from association—voluntary association, that is.[6] When conditions of diversity prevail, such as are found in modern cities, people are presented with the possibility of choosing whether or not to join with others. This one factor, choice, alters the nature of their affiliation.

Based on choice, voluntary association is dynamic. In place of those categories of clan or trade or religion, to which people were a century ago born or delegated and thus resigned, individuals today generally achieve membership on their own terms. For example, in their social affiliations they find their own life partners, write their own marriage vows, or sign marriage contracts drafted by their own lawyers. Once they become members, people negotiate their association with others, weighing the benefits of submitting to the group with the competing benefit of self-assertion and the cost of internal conflict. They may, for instance, uphold or change what it means to be a member. In their professional affiliations or careers they choose for themselves, they introduce new policies or procedures. Or, as free agents of their memberships, they may simply leave the bounds of any given group. In their religious affiliations they can shop around for a church that better suits them, take up Buddhist meditation in place of prayer, or convert to Judaism.

Choice does not weaken the bonds of membership. With the potential to exit, the reverse also holds: the potential to commit. Once on a chosen pathway, the choice among diverse collectives represented by civil society provides experience on a personal level, making it possible to hold tenaciously and passionately to one's course. Michael Walzer, philosopher and thoughtful observer of social life, posits,

> I can imagine individuals choosing spouses, say, and jobs or professions in a world without much associational pluralism. But any more extended version of free choice would not be available; civil society makes it possible to choose not only among possible individual lives but also among complex "forms of life"—and then, so to speak, to keep on choosing.[7]

---

[6] Georg Simmel, "The Web of Group-Affiliations," in *Conflict & The Web of Group Affiliations*, trans. Kurt H. Wolff and Reinhard Bendix (New York: Free Press, 1955).

[7] Michael Walzer, "Equality and Civil Society," in *Alternative Conceptions of Civil Society*, ed. Simone Chambers and Will Kymlicka (Princeton: Princeton University Press, 2002), 37.

Any danger of greedy institutions that commitment might suggest, Walzer argues, is tempered by freedom.[8] A single affiliation cannot exercise exclusive control, for, as Walzer indicates, the experience of choosing commits an individual to a pathway rather than to an end. Choosing points the individual to the realization that life concerns not only choices about specific narrow partnerships but also choices about comprehensive and multiple ways of being and doing.

That agency lies in the individual who is free to come and go raises another important consideration: the portability of the terms and skills of affiliation of the individual that move with that person. This seems plain enough for the casual observer. But for the social scientist, it can be a daunting task to accommodate the reality that the individual, as the song at Hong Kong's 1997 Alternative Handover goes, has a name, a soul, a face, a voice. And feet! The practical problem of at once locating the person in something as abstract as civil society and then keeping up with the individual on his or her real path has often meant privileging a single organization, a particular association, as the vessel of civil society. Inspecting the vessel that contains individuals, whether a club or professional organization, a place of worship or recreation or instruction, reveals much about practices useful in mediating between the individual and the group, the group and the state. As examinations of the religious renaissance in another Chinese society, Taiwan, show, lessons in civility can be introduced and maintained in temples, charities, and religious study groups.[9] Yet studies of associational life, notably research into modern religious experience in the United States, teach us that membership is not constant.[10] Moreover, while institutional lenses reveal certain aspects of culture, such as group norms of civil behavior, precious understanding is lost about the dynamics of modern membership if we fail to

[8] Walzer, "Equality and Civil Society," 37. Walzer references Lewis A. Coser, *Greedy Institutions: Patterns of Undivided Commitment* (New York: Free Press, 1974).

[9] See Robert P. Weller, *Alternate Civilities: Democracy and Culture in China and Taiwan* (Boulder, Colo.: Westview Press, 1999); and Richard Madsen, *Democracy's Dharma: Religious Renaissance and Political Development in Taiwan* (Berkeley: University of California Press, 2007).

[10] See Robert N. Bellah, Richard Madsen, William M. Sullivan, Ann Swidler, and Steven M. Tipton, *Habits of the Heart: Individualism and Commitment in American Life* (New York: Harper & Row, 1985); and Wade Clark Roof, *The Spiritual Marketplace: Baby Boomers and the Remaking of American Religion* (Princeton: Princeton University Press, 1999).

acknowledge the culture of individualism itself that fuels the search for association at the same time it allows individuals to devise their own trajectories.

Just like the unnamed participants who gathered at Statue Square, Karen, Queenie, Rachel, and Jefferson each found her or his own separate way to the Alternative Handover. By documenting their individual paths both to the square and beyond it, by breaking out of the confining notions of membership, *Converts to Civil Society* reveals what skills of freedom they brought with them along with individual agency and where they learned such skills. Like other modern, urban people, individuals in Hong Kong are in constant motion. They are not limited to a street corner or enclave, a church building or congregation. Moreover, these individuals carry within them accumulated, predominant competences.

THE NO-COMPETENCE VOTE

Hong Kong's transition from British colony to Chinese SAR at the close of the twentieth century raised serious questions about the future of democracy, of citizen rights, and of popular agency in the territory. Could Hong Kong people be entrusted with the direct election of their political representatives and leaders? Were they adequately prepared to sustain, let alone defend, democracy with the few skills they had? Were they politically competent?

From the early 1980s, Britain and China were the key powers negotiating Hong Kong's political future. With British and Chinese diplomats hammering out a vision, and Hong Kong people generally limited to the role of onlookers, the negotiated change in sovereignty commonly known as the Handover (*wùihgwài*) had a passive ring to it.[11] At the time of the Handover on July 1, 1997, democratization was as yet incomplete. Under the last two British governors, David Wilson and Christopher Patten, Hong Kong was on a timeline moving gradually toward a more representative government housed in the Legislative Council building. But Hong Kong's citizenry had only begun directly electing legislators

[11] An exception, argues Kevin Lane, is the initial push by Hong Kong businessmen to secure answers from Governor Murray MacLehose about the legal implications associated with the 1997 expiration of Britain's lease on the territory. Only then did representatives of the British government approach Deng Xiaoping, beginning negotiations of Hong Kong's return to Chinese sovereignty. See Kevin Lane, *Sovereignty and the Status Quo* (Boulder, Colo.: Westview Press, 1990).

in September 1991, with nearly 40 percent of the electorate going to the polls to vote on a mere eighteen out of a possible sixty seats.[12] The elections of September 1995 saw just two more seats added to the pool open to direct election by the general population, with the remaining forty legislators determined by select groups.[13] How could Hong Kong realize the promise of Hong Kong people ruling Hong Kong and maintain its distinction from communist China under the one country, two systems (*yātgwok léuhngjai*) model? How could its citizens be ready to build democracy if they lacked a history of democratic governing institutions? Hong Kong historian Ming K. Chan called this failure to institutionalize electoral democracy "the darkest legacy of British rule."[14] As people gathered in Statue Square, the independence of the Legislative Council was more hope than reality.

Electoral politics is not the only factor, however, for judging a democracy. While the occasional casting of votes to choose among a competitive pool of candidates may be the single litmus test used today, more basic, everyday actions and skills also serve to indicate that a culture is democratic. Civil society grounded in everyday practices connecting private individuals with a public sphere is the more established institution of democracy in Hong Kong. But how to explain civil society's roots in a society, it can be effectively argued, that lacks the norms compatible with the freedom to commit?[15] According to the perspective

---

[12] Ming K. Chan, "Hong Kong: Colonial Legacy, Transformation, and Challenge," in *The Annals of the American Academy of Political and Social Science, The Future of Hong Kong*, ed. Max J. Skidmore (September 1996): 21. Before this, the only other experience with direct elections was that of 1988 for the district boards.

[13] Chan, "Hong Kong," 21.

[14] Chan, "Hong Kong," 15.

[15] Hong Kong sociologist Lau Siu-Kai shaped the discussion early with his publications in the 1980s, Lau Siu-Kai, "Utilitarianistic Familism: The Basis of Political Stability," in *Social Life and Development in Hong Kong*, ed. Ambrose Y. C. King and Rance P. L. Lee (Hong Kong: Chinese University Press, 1981); Lau Siu-Kai, "Social Change, Bureaucratic Rule, and Emergent Political Issues in Hong Kong," *World Politics* 35, no. 4 (1983); and Lau Siu-Kai and Kuan Hsin-Chi, *The Ethos of the Hong Kong Chinese* (Hong Kong: Chinese University Press, 1988). For scholarly works drawing on Lau's argument for insight into emigration, social welfare, and education, see Khun Eng Kuah, "Negotiating Emigration and the Family: Individual Solutions to the 1997 Anxiety," in *The Annals of the American Academy of Political and Social Science, The Future of Hong Kong*, ed. Max J. Skidmore (September 1996); Catherine Jones, *Promoting Prosperity: The Hong Kong Way of Social Policy* (Hong Kong: Chinese University Press, 1990); and Gerard Postiglione, "The

that Hong Kong people possess a distinct ethos, the private, material interests of the immediate family and of the calculating individual guide Hong Kong people in their decision making. Such an ethos leaves individuals and groups outside the family, including the wider society, with little consideration in the calculation of actions. Moreover, individuals, groups, and the wider society are used in a highly instrumental manner, important only so far as they further private interests of a material kind. Under such circumstances it would be extremely difficult if not impossible to establish civic culture from the ground up. Rather than an open square, compartmentalization of family units within honeycomb-style apartments of claustrophobic proportion would seem the apt way of concretizing the abstract barriers structuring Hong Kong society.

But looking at the people and events unfolding on the eve of reunification with China, one could detect signs of a viable civil society unaccounted for by the Hong Kong ethos perspective. At a significant historical junction, the gathering at Statue Square signaled that at least up until the return to Chinese sovereignty a space existed into which people flowed freely associating, freely expressing. Statue Square on June 30, 1997, served as both ordered and unordered forum. Not only did it contain a stage set with scripted performances by a select cast, including politicians, student leaders, labor leaders, religious figures, performance artists, and audience members, it also offered scheduled moments of improvisation. Along with the open-mic session facilitated by a local radio and television talk show host, the square provided a wide open area less subject to control. There, at least one individual distributed written materials both cryptic and menacing, a man hoisted the flag of the People's Republic of China and raised a brief ruckus, and the composition of the audience shifted with the passing interests of individuals and their friends. Ordinary Hong Kong people who simply

Decolonization of Hong Kong Education," in *The Hong Kong Reader: Passage to Chinese Sovereignty*, ed. Ming K. Chan and Gerard A. Postiglione (New York: M. E. Sharpe, 1996), respectively. For dissenting views on political culture, see Michael E. Degolyer and Janet Lee Scott, "The Myth of Political Apathy in Hong Kong," in *The Annals of the American Academy of Political and Social Science, The Future of Hong Kong*, ed. Max J. Skidmore (September 1996); Stephen Chiu Wing-Kai and Lui Tai-Lok, eds., *The Dynamics of Social Movement in Hong Kong* (Hong Kong: Hong Kong University Press, 2000); and Lam Wai-Man, *Understanding the Political Culture of Hong Kong: The Paradox of Activism and Depoliticization* (New York: M. E. Sharpe, 2004).

showed up lingered in the square long enough to contribute their voices in song, following the lyrics attached to their photocopied programs. At a moment when a city of 7.1 million people melded with a Chinese nation of 1.3 billion, here was a reminder that diverse and complex individuals figured in the equation.

How to Investigate Competence

Because signs of a viable civil society run deeper than the assembly at Statue Square, this is a book about everyday practices that find application in less frequent public gatherings. For Hong Kong people to assemble as they did in the first place, they must have already established competence. Where does one look for those foundations? Others have made the case that civil society links the private individual to the abstract collective. These studies have not been so much about individuals as about individualism gradually developed, refined, and realized within a particular institution. Such works are instructive on a number of levels. First, they take individualism as a norm that is practiced, ultimately for a significant end. Second, choice itself is understood as a practiced skill. Only in developing the ability to choose can the individual keep choosing groups, forging commitments, and conceiving the portable skills that travel with the individual. Third, as largely historical research, such works prompt investigation that is situated in place, time, and culture. Taken together, these legacies in social research challenge today's social scientist to study a specific era for particular circumstances or features that foster recognizable practices.

Two particular situations afforded middle-class people of seventeenth- and eighteenth-century British, French, and German society the chance to enter voluntarily and develop a sense of self: the conjugal bourgeois household, and the clubs, coffeehouses, and salons or associational forms popular at the time.[16] Within these eighteenth-century spaces, people with disposable income and requisite literacy read novels and newspapers. In the home, with family members they considered the themes of subjectivity, self-knowledge, and empathy that featured in their romantic novels. At the coffeehouse, with neighbors and strangers they debated local matters that featured in whatever they were reading.

Competence in judgment necessary for such reflection and dialogue was a matter of practiced autonomy. People gradually learned that as

[16] Habermas, *Structural Transformation*, 45.

individual consumers of the written word they had a rightful place in determining the meaning of topics like art, literature, and philosophy, not to mention politics, that had once been the strict concern of church and state authorities. Moreover, the act of judging a debate according to the quality of the argument rather than the status of the person generalized and entrenched the ideal of the individual into a norm.[17] As in the context of the bourgeois family, human intimacy within the coffeehouse evoked the illusion of freedom, liberating participants in this space to achieve the full potential of debate possible only among people sharing a common role as critics. Bourgeois society of the eighteenth century, practiced in reading, debating, and judging, thus produced a certain form of public sphere, one passionately concerned with personal development but performed for an audience.

Arguably, the roots of individualism, and so civil society, go back far beyond the eighteenth century to the formation of the early church.[18] The practice of breaking and making social bonds crucial for realizing individualism characterized the church in late antiquity, in the Renaissance of the twelfth century, and in the Protestant Reformation of the sixteenth century.[19]

The early church represented community redefined. Not a community of kin, it was instead one made up of voluntary members, believers in a new order. Not based on Jewish tradition, Christian community was instead forged through choice and the commitment of individual fidelity to a new group and its laws. In later periods, the making and breaking of social bonds would continue, but with new and greater variety. In the twelfth century, for example, private forms of self-expression (some, like the autobiography and confessional literature, rooted in religious tradition) emerged, with new orders differentiating among clerics as well as

[17] Craig J. Calhoun, "Introduction," in *Habermas and the Public Sphere*, ed. Craig J. Calhoun (Cambridge, Mass.: MIT Press, 1992), 22.

[18] Adam B. Seligman, "Individualism as Principle: Its Emergence, Institutionalization, and Contradictions," *Indiana Law Journal* 72 (1997); and Adam B. Seligman, "Between Public and Private: Towards a Sociology of Civil Society," in *Democratic Civility*, ed. Robert W. Hefner (New Brunswick, N.J.: Transaction Publishers, 1998).

[19] It is not fundamentally through Christianity's particular promise of individual salvation resting on a personal relationship to God that we have arrived at Christian individualism. It has been the changing nature of group affiliations over hundreds of years that eventually brought individualism into every arena of human life. Seligman, "Between Public and Private," 93, 99.

among knights, craftsmen, virgins, and widows to further elevate conceptions of individual self and individual agency. And in the sixteenth century, Christians broke from state churches and drew up covenants, blueprints for reorganizing their collective, religious lives. All this breaking and forging, classifying and evaluating of orders, lives, and callings produced a highly differentiated and intentional society. Where there were options, an increasingly private individual exercised his or her conscience as well as agency in matters of love, friendship, and confession, until by the eighteenth century the moral individual shed the religious cloak.[20]

Yet religion persists as a voluntary association, with members of religious associations drawing on their own arsenals as they engage the public sphere. While these associations have resources such as phone lists, treasuries, and meeting rooms just like any other organization, they also lay claim to a special set of cultural resources that defines them as religious groups, and through which these groups can take political action.[21] Resources include recognizable symbols like the cross or sword, or moral authority derived from texts like the Bible or the Koran as well as from histories of exile or genocide.[22] These can be harnessed for presenting private interests to the wider public. Tools introduced in a faith community, moreover, form the basis of distinct subcultures that unify and give continuity to the worlds of work, prayer, and family. In other words, people produce their life forms by acting out membership in a group. By isolating what religious people do in living out their lives that encourages a conception of individualism and, at the same time, public or common concern, we can see the spillover effects that impact individuals as more than believers, and impact more than the believers themselves.

Three examples of practices secured from observation-based studies of contemporary religious life illustrate the result. In these cases, oral

[20] Seligman, "Between Public and Private," 99.

[21] Rhys H. Williams and N. J. Demerath III, "Cultural Power: How Underdog Religious and Nonreligious Movements Triumph against Structural Odds," in *Sacred Companies: Organizational Aspects of Religion and Religious Aspects of Organizations*, ed. N. J. Demerath III, Peter Dobkin Hall, Terry Schmitt, and Rhys H. Williams (Oxford: Oxford University Press, 1998).

[22] For demonstration and explanation of how these same tools are used for uncivil and violent religious ends, see Mark Juergensmeyer, *Terror in the Mind of God: The Global Rise of Religious Violence* (Berkeley: University of California Press, 2000).

expressions of religious engagement such as question-and-answer sessions following sermons, call-and-response, and consciousness raising come to sustain political campaigns such as extended strikes of union workers, neighborhood defense in minority enclaves, and sanctuary offered to illegal immigrants. These oral expressions, data in the hands of today's social scientists, represent skills. They are significant skills, moreover, as their application helps realize a type of civil society.

1. St. Mark's United Methodist Church in Camanche, Iowa: The Reverend Gilbert Dawes, a former missionary in Latin America, preaches a sermon of exploitation and its accommodation: "Just as [Saint] Paul was blinded by the slave-based economy of his time—we accommodate exploitation, blinded by our capitalist system." As Reverend Dawes castigates Paul, members of the congregation, many of whom are striking workers from the local grain-processing plant, sit quietly, nodding their heads. But the twenty-minute Q&A session that follows gives them the chance to respond. The ensuing discussion develops both strikers and church: congregants derive a sense of spiritual legitimacy for their strike, while the church becomes a class-conscious church.[23]

2. Groveland United Church of Christ on Chicago's South Side: Sergeant Bishop, neighborhood relations officer with the Chicago Police Department, attends a church meeting at which he and the congregation demonstrate black religious culture as a tool for political activism. Dressed in uniform, Bishop discusses police efforts to close down three drug houses in the area. Yet he breaks down the public-private divide between himself and his audience otherwise signaled by his uniform. By embedding his update in a parable and relating to the congregation's call-and-response formula of participation (communicating support through laughter, applause, and the occasional "Amen" or "That's right"), like feeding two birds from one hand he affirms both himself as a Christian and the congregation as a group committed to social action.[24]

[23] Rick Fantasia, *Cultures of Solidarity: Consciousness, Action, and Contemporary American Workers* (Berkeley: University of California Press, 1988), 201–3.

[24] Mary Pattillo-McCoy, "Church Culture as a Strategy of Action in the Black Community," *American Sociological Review* 63 (1998): 774.

3. All Saints of Tucson, Arizona, near the U.S.-Mexico border: Consciousness raising, a process of producing the language that compels action, represents a distinct transformative power in the U.S. sanctuary movement of the 1980s. After meeting with victims of Central American poverty and violence, church people realize they cannot live with themselves unless they actively side with the refugees and against the anti-immigration policies of their own government. As one Tucson sanctuary worker explains, participating in border crossings into Mexico as part of a contemporary underground railroad gives her a morally defendable answer when one day her child asks, "Mommy, what were you doing during the sanctuary movement?"[25]

Increasingly, in our efforts to understand how civil society is formed we are looking at learned practices and capacities—the skills to be free. These skills are acquired, carried, and wielded by individuals embedded in associations but with consequences for wider society. Investigating these skills moves us closer to appreciating the individual's practical link with an otherwise abstract sphere.

Back to Statue Square

If religion is involved in civil society, then how does the experience of religious life shape the nature of civil society, and how it is experienced by others?[26] The example of a self-described Methodist Taoist Native American Quaker Russian Orthodox Buddhist Jew reflects one experience of religion in today's United States.[27] When people in a vibrant religious marketplace adopt such a fluid style of spirituality, those of us interested in civil society may be tempted to discount the contributions of the seemingly uncommitted. Instead, we should consider the possibility that "strong practice," or intentionality grounded in the individual, "may be achieved at the intersection of several communities instead of

[25] Susan Bibler Coutin, *The Culture of Protest: Religious Activism and the U.S. Sanctuary Movement* (Boulder, Colo.: Westview Press, 1993), 68.

[26] The sociologist of religion Robert Wuthnow asks this very question in his essay "A Reasonable Role for Religion? Moral Practices, Civic Participation, and Market Behavior," in *Democratic Civility*, ed. Robert W. Hefner (New Brunswick, N.J.: Transaction Publishers, 1998).

[27] Documented by others like Wade Clark Roof in his book *The Spiritual Marketplace*.

through submersion in any one community."[28] In *Converts to Civil Society*, I explore the participation of intentional, individual Hong Kong Christians in the civic life of that polity. With over half a million people or 10 percent of Hong Kong's population Christian, this significant minority invites investigation. In fact, upon close scrutiny the experience of Christianity in Hong Kong is like that of Statue Square itself: inviting entry and exit.

To document this dynamic of entry and exit requires assuming a similar way of life: abandoning the street corner, entering the square. Life within a city is both integrated and scattered, and so the metaphor of scholar as traffic surveyor positioned on a street corner is an apt and popular one. Apart from invoking the memory of urban sociology embodied in the iconic study *Street Corner Society*, in which Italian Americans did in fact congregate on the street corner and mark out the boundaries of their world, it attests to the common work engaged by the researcher in the field attending to the movement of various actors who meet at some common intersection.[29] And here the researcher resolutely stands until she appreciates the limitations of that street corner. Determining which intersection will yield a particular vantage point and when, if ever, to pursue actors as they move away from the intersection are, however, for the researcher and no one else to resolve.

During my original nine-month field investigation of Hong Kong on the eve of its return to Chinese sovereignty from winter through fall of 1997, I was directed by the chaplain at Chung Chi College, the Chinese University of Hong Kong (CUHK), to two local Christian NGOs. As an exchange student at CUHK conducting research for my doctoral dissertation in sociology at the University of California, San Diego, I wanted to understand how different Christian communities were anticipating political change. Did the scheduled handover to the People's Republic of China sound alarm bells among those with a vested interest in religious freedom? Did it inspire organized response in a political arena relatively open compared to that of its future sovereign? And did it highlight a distinct and separate identity for Hong Kong, one based on individual choice, not only in the commercial marketplace for which Hong Kong is famous but also in other spheres of life, such as religion and politics?

[28] Wuthnow, "A Reasonable Role for Religion?" 126.
[29] William Foote Whyte, *Street Corner Society: The Social Structure of an Italian Slum* (Chicago: University of Chicago Press, 1943).

Having already spent several months as a participant-observer of a thriving fundamentalist evangelical community into which I was drawn by a friend, I decided to explore a decidedly different context by offering my services as an English-language editor at these two ecumenical and politically liberal NGOs. During this time I maintained engagement in both fundamentalist and liberal communities to keep similarities and differences among Hong Kong Christians in perspective, as I sought to do throughout the course of study, but found myself increasingly repelled by the former and drawn toward the latter by my growing self-awareness.

While my own social position (as student at CUHK, renter in a Mong Kok household, and friend of almost a decade to Hong Kongers from Yuen Long to Cheung Chau, who I'd met during travels in China) afforded me exposure to several known Hong Kong religious institutions, this nudge in the direction of the Christian NGO and neither church nor school revealed a pivotal institution for understanding religion and civil society in one urban, Chinese world. Before I even knew their names, and well before they appeared together in the square, Karen, Queenie, Rachel, and Jefferson themselves gathered at the NGO. These diverse individuals were not members of the same church; nor were they classmates at the same school. They were not even members of the same organization. Instead, they came together through the NGO as a distinct institution, with its office space for meeting, telephones for communicating, financial resources for sustaining, and project goals for inspiring, but most importantly, its lessons in realizing Christian identity. Whereas alone they may have faced alienation, lacking affirmation from the mainstream or legitimization from any organization, in the Hong Kong NGO as a voluntary association they gained a stabilizing foothold in company with like others. And with time I, too, came to know Karen, Queenie, Rachel, and Jefferson through the NGO so that I recognized them as distinct faces in Statue Square and followed them as individuals out of it. The NGO as an institution of political, social, and religious life was how I met the more than fifty people whose experiences are documented in over eighty separate interviews that inform this book. Of the fifty-four people I interviewed, exactly half figure as significant, quotable voices. First, as individuals, these twenty-seven people vividly captured a common experience they themselves did not admit. Second, with follow-up visits they proved to maintain some connection to NGOs across time. And third, they made themselves available to me for updated interviews—sometimes for as many as five interviews across ten years. The bulk of the data for this study come from these interviews conducted between 1997, the time of Hong Kong's return to Chinese sovereignty, and 2008.

With the coming and going of so many people, NGO-centered research drew my attention to both the unity and the fluidity of Christian memberships. And then I realized that the NGO as a vessel that held a particular population was of valuable but limited use in understanding the process by which voluntary association and public commitment functioned in Hong Kong. While I chose the NGO as a starting point for political performance, the NGO was not the starting point for either religious performance or political awakening. In Hong Kong, people begin on a path of choice and commitment bridging religious and political life in the schools and churches. And though the NGO serves as space for religious life, neither does the NGO resemble a congregation in the sense of being the center of religious community. While it draws together its own members, it is less a container than a locus of multiple sites, networks, and individuals. Some members are more frequently pulled into this locus than to any other place, while others gravitate seldom. In my research, I dealt not only with the founders and paid employees with whom I interacted regularly in their offices; I also attended to the experiences of more transient members: people who take a course, for instance, but do not write for the NGO journals, let alone participate in an NGO-organized rally or prayer service. Whether they call themselves Christian or not, these Hong Kong people have known Christianity through an array of schools, fellowships, churches, organizations, literature, and courses whose theologies have hardly been uniform.

Interview data collected in 1997, 1998, 2000, 2001, 2007, and 2008 are, moreover, supplemented with participant observation within NGOs conducted in 1997 and 1998. I spent four-and-a-half months working for two NGOs, from May to September 1997, and then again served as volunteer editor in summer of 1998 from June through August. I learned early on in my fieldwork that spending time within the NGO offices would only provide a limited understanding of the members and their experiences. As it turned out, there were important encounters between NGO staff and their members, their international peers, their funders, and their rivals within the confines of their offices. But offices were certainly not the only site where ideas were shared, interests promoted, and identities realized. Christians commemorated and questioned historical events in diverse churches and fellowships, discussed issues in noisy restaurants and cramped apartments, organized marches by phone from home after a long day's labor, conducted demonstrations and debates in housing estates and on ferry piers, and staged international and local conferences at seminary facilities. Although I could not follow them every time they went, I followed them into each of these corners for communion. I stepped off the street corner and into the square. Return trips to Hong Kong in 1998, 2000, 2001, 2007, and 2008 were opportunities to reassess across eleven years how our lives changed as we married, completed studies, changed jobs, raised families, and even retired. Like civil society, Christian community in Hong Kong is a collective space of multiple entrance points and exits. And just as a great investment of time and energy went into orchestrating the Alternative Handover, years of decision making, studying, and testing directed these key figures to Statue Square.

Let us return to Statue Square, the site of the Alternative Handover, as the intersection of freely associating individuals. Through the efforts of a coalition of thirty NGOs, privately founded organizations standing decidedly apart from official, government bodies, Statue Square drew a crowd the night of Hong Kong's return to Chinese sovereignty. Moving backward from this starting point, we can use individual lives to map something of the ample space that exists between family and state in contemporary Hong Kong.

Take Karen, for example. We saw her in Statue Square handing out programs at the Alternative Handover, a deceptively humble role for a veteran activist. On the face of it, Karen as a Christian activist is committed to a particular calling. She spent her youth in a section of Hong Kong densely populated by refugees from mainland China. Joining a mainline Congregationalist church in her neighborhood started her on a path of development within the Protestant community. But this path led further and further away from church. As she explained to me the day after I began my internship with her NGO, "I have embarked on a different life journey, and although I am still a member [of my original church] on paper, I am not an active member. That church no longer meets my needs or matches my priorities."[30] After working for her former pastor at a multidenominational Protestant organization, Karen applied her knowledge in leadership roles at more than one Christian NGO. While still leading one of these, Karen assumed the job of convener for a

[30] Author's interview with Karen, May 21, 1997.

broad coalition created specifically to mobilize the Hong Kong public to demand universal suffrage, direct elections, and the shelving of sensitive legislation (Hong Kong's version of "No taxation without representation"). This coalition oversaw on July 1, 2003, the mobilization of well over half a million citizens, the largest demonstration in Hong Kong since the outpouring of support for Chinese democracy that ended in the Tiananmen Square crackdown June 4, 1989. NGO responsibilities have taken her all over Asia and into Europe, as well as North and Central America. In fact, through her broad exposure, Karen has been a mentor and guide to many, Christian and non-Christian alike.

Performer, composer, T-shirt designer, emcee, spokesperson, and mobilizer Queenie led the crowd in song the night Hong Kong returned to Chinese sovereignty. She is a creative person with resume-worthy particular skills in communications and art. Her career path winds through the worlds of radio and television, magazine and (public) stage. For livelihood as well as lifestyle, she has run telephone hotlines, NGOs, and an electoral district. During an interview at the Christian NGO she managed in 1998, she told me, "I am Catholic—*was* Catholic along with my entire family, but I left at fifteen. . . . Actually, I have not been a Christian from the first day. I tell you, they washed me and baptized me without my consent!"[31] As she has journeyed through jobs, she has traveled the paths of a Catholic, a Protestant, a Jew, and a Buddhist. Jesus is for Queenie a great leader, a good model, but not a Savior. And Karen the Christian activist has served as her personal mentor. While Queenie wants to take the treasures of different spiritual traditions, she cannot fully commit to a single one.

Rachel is rooted in the Catholic Church after enjoying a Catholic education and Catholic conversion at age fifteen, precisely the age Queenie left the church. She marked the Handover with her Catholic friends and a bottle of red wine, a token from a priest who was with her in spirit. But as an adult, Rachel repeatedly articulates one complaint, bounded and yet boundless: "I'm sick of the priests. When they preach, they never talk about the society, they never tell people what the real world is; they always tell you to pray to Mary, or [they] say something very remote."[32] She finds in volunteering rather than prayer a way to overcome a general sense of helplessness, as well as to sustain her

---

[31] Author's interview with Queenie, August 4, 1998.
[32] Author's interview with Rachel, August 19, 1997.

Catholic identity. "Okay. You do not go to church on Sunday," Rachel reflects aloud. "You do not go to Mass. Then you go to this commission as your service to the church."[33] Applying lessons from years in the corporate world, she directs and oversees the work of regular staff on a commission of the diocese to help Catholics understand society's injustices, help them apply faith in real life, and in so doing help reconnect the commission to its historic tone and purpose. Rachel's own organizational work and the commission's membership are linked with Karen's organization. Such overlap crosses a religious line, that between Catholic and Protestant, still fraught with distinction in today's Hong Kong.

With work and study committed to advocacy for labor, Jefferson has pinned his personal development on a particular cause. As a researcher and budding scholar, he educates himself and the public on labor issues in Hong Kong and China. But this interest takes Jefferson into territory most academics avoid: Marxist critical theory leads him into Christian social and professional circles; intellectualism takes him onto the streets, where he dons lipstick and raises a banner. Unlike Queenie and Rachel, Jefferson enjoyed an Anglican education, but one without any commitment to Christianity he would ever admit. He laughs at the idea that his involvement in social concerns is inspired by God. "But I really feel uncomfortable," he explains with all seriousness, "when I think of others' suffering."[34] This concern for the suffering worker trumps any hostility to the church as an institution of social control as Jefferson gains work experience in both faith-based and secular commissions on labor affairs. In fact, it was through the opportunity to work for these two types of commission that he came to help organize the Alternative Handover, to debate unemployment trends in public forums with local politicians, and to meet Fiona, a worker in the NGO led by Karen and the woman he eventually married.

By combining participant observation and interview, I follow people's community affiliations and development through time as communicated in words, something they carried within them to Statue Square and beyond. While connected to Christian schools, churches, and NGOs at some point in their lives, people like Karen, Queenie, Rachel, and Jefferson have forged individual relationships with their faith-based affiliations that are in no way identical. Precisely because their commitments

[33] Author's interview with Rachel, August 19, 1997.
[34] Author's interview with Jefferson, August 4, 1997.

are not fixed or static, they are comparable. All involve the negotiated terms that describe modern membership. What can be learned from Christian experience in Hong Kong is identical to what is required of civil society. And this is because Hong Kong Christian society, like civil society, functions as an open space, not a closed vessel. The diversity of Christian institutions and their inability to satisfy all needs exclusively are the conditions in Hong Kong necessary to instill skills of democratic competence in free-flowing individuals.

CONVERTS TO CIVIL SOCIETY

Commitments, whether they are callings, identity structures, or compelling causes, help individuals navigate life. What more potent concept exists that encompasses choice and commitment than conversion? Modern conversion is a process of transformation and development, whether transformation happens when an individual switches from one religious tradition to another or when the individual changes his or her identity within a single tradition.[35]

Conversion is singular in capturing the process of change documented in *Converts to Civil Society*. This book offers studies of the change possible when willing, voluntary individuals commit themselves to a way of life that sets them apart from others. Membership in the early church involved both making and breaking social bonds.[36] Repeated over time, across hundreds of years, conversion to Christianity established the individualism necessary for civil society. In *Converts to Civil Society*, the making and breaking of bonds occurs repeatedly within an individual's lifetime, leading that person into the realm of civil society.

Conversion is key to understanding how Hong Kong people committed to religion become committed to the public sphere. Conversion as entry to Christian communal life marks the pathway to mobility and the acquisition of skills, the most basic being individual agency itself. Because of the weight of scholarly and popular notions of individualism in Hong Kong society, as well as the weight of a family-centered conception of Chinese society, social scientists are burdened with the responsibility to explain the social possibility of agency in the Hong

[35] Bruce Lawrence, "Transformation," in *Critical Terms for Religious Studies*, ed. Mark C. Taylor (Chicago: University of Chicago Press, 1998), 336.

[36] As Seligman notes in his sociological essay on civil society, "Between Public and Private."

Kong context. In response to certain prevailing theories of Hong Kong culture, it is not enough to direct attention to evidence to the contrary, saying, "Look: here are people joining and acting together." One must account for the distinct dynamics possible in Hong Kong by grounding them deep in Hong Kong history as well as everyday practices.

Initial conversion to Christianity is an important step in the process of gaining membership and agency. But this book cannot privilege that account of conversion alone. Having entered into a faith community, converts do not end their transformation. In fact, those with exposure to the NGO realize new ideals of religious and political engagement, whether they come as Christian converts or not. Most who enter the NGO can tell of their outright break with the rituals and beliefs of their parents. Most who enter the NGO communicate an outright expression of conversion to Christianity. But a significant minority, people like Queenie and Jefferson, reject the restrictions of the institutional church. Together nonbelievers embark on the common journey with believers who struggle with the restrictions of the church, leading them through a faith-based organization into the public sphere. Taken together, these conditions suggest that we cannot appreciate the full scope of transformation if we limit the concept of conversion to a reinterpretation of general faith or even particular theology within faith.

But neither is the sole and significant conversion the turn to social concern or social justice understood in a social movement sense of either term, where people commit themselves full time to public action, even hell-raising. The crucial border under investigation in a study of civil society is that between private and public. Just as one need not be a Christian to transcend that border, one need not be an activist either. In fact, many Christians shy away from applying the term activist to themselves. Either they associate it with a level of commitment to public actions their own commitment does not achieve or encompass, or they associate it with radicalism they consider intemperate or inappropriate. In either case, Christianity does not easily align with activism. And yet individuals in Hong Kong become participants in the public sphere because of the legacy of Christianity in Hong Kong. Christianity supports civil society as a pathway to civil society, not by requiring entry but by inviting entry and exit. A matter of choice, Christianity promotes the development of the individual agent. Within Christian voluntary associations that depend on a negotiated relationship with their members, people develop collective identities at the same time they develop a heightened sense of themselves as individuals. From the perspective of democratic political life, voluntary associations (with NGOs being an important contemporary example) are a precondition to having a citizenry capable of being agents of liberty, not simply subjects of the state. That people convert to civil society is thus the answer to how faith and democracy are bound together in the contemporary Hong Kong experience.

CHAPTERS IN THIS BOOK

We begin acquiring the skills necessary to be free when we open ourselves up to membership. How did Hong Kong people gain their freedom to join? In chapter 2, "Conversion to Christianity," I demonstrate how, at a stage in their young lives when they sought both self-affirmation and collective activity, my informants found Hong Kong's church-run schools, Christian social services, and churches. Conversion often occurred against parents' expectations and express wishes. Yet the vast educational and cultural gap between child and parent during this period of Hong Kong's modernization was precisely the space required to exercise individual volition. The conversion account presents a rational, dispassionate history of an immature believer choosing the path to further learning within faith. It hints, moreover, at the negotiated relationship between believer and organized religion.

Rather than a comfortable place to escape among like-minded others, Christian voluntary association urges more choices for group affiliation and personal cultivation. In "Conversion to Civil Society," chapter 3, I follow individual converts on a path beyond the church to the NGO. Uncertainties associated with Hong Kong's return to Chinese sovereignty after 156 years of British colonial rule and after the June 4 crackdown on prodemocracy demonstrators push Christians to find alternatives to their existing faith communities. From the community of worship, where struggle is an introspective and confessional exercise, converts move to the NGO, where struggle is a collective and critical debate. By shifting membership, Christians fashion a new, public commitment to faith. This represents a second conversion, into the realm of civil society.

"The Work of Civil Society," chapter 4, documents the product of NGO labor, civil society. Working to found, sustain, and even replace the faith-based NGO, individual Hong Kong Christians promote the dynamic of voluntary membership necessary for civil society in at least one Chinese polity. NGOs, as understood not only by members but by staff and founders too, serve the individuals who people them. They function as a gathering point of individuals to sustain Christians along their often-solitary journey of budding religious commitment. Work, then, is not limited to its conventional meaning in the context of NGO middle management: office chores, intellectual output, or street organizing. Rather, in the Hong Kong Christian's quest to align religious, professional, and social selves, work through the NGO is the work of self-discovery. Such work ultimately develops in the Christian an expression of individualism that compels initiative for further group formation. In a diverse and dynamic religious marketplace, it is through individualism that Christians find society.

The experience of conversion is personal. As individual commitment to a changed life, whether Christian or otherwise, conversion is a project of individual development. How can a civil society based on individual choice attract, cultivate, or identify leadership for tomorrow? "Passing the Torch" represents a practical concern among converts to civil society. In chapter 5, I focus on two possible successors: the younger generation within the organizational pipeline, and the younger generation within the home. In the early history of the church, students had always been a ready source of committed workers. Now this pipeline appears less sound, so that individualism may adversely affect the life of organizations crucial in channeling Christian commitment into the public realm. And where youngsters in the home had once broken away from the traditions of the Chinese household, now the cultural gap between parent and child is considerably reduced. I address how parents understand the place of individualism, of choosing to be oneself, in their own children.

In chapter 6, as conclusion I take up a comparison already introduced in previous chapters: that between Hong Kong and China. "The Question of Convergence" reflects on the implications of the experience of Christianity in Hong Kong. Now an SAR of China, Hong Kong is an example for evaluating China as a whole. First, I summarize the process by which committed individuals are stretched so that the space of civil society is peopled with more and diverse individuals and groupings. In this way, Hong Kong is able to function democratically under the persistent cloak of a partial democracy. Second, I evaluate whether Hong Kong and China, despite the arrangement of one country, two systems, are converging on a trajectory of civil engagement. I investigate three pathways addressing the openness required of civil society, pathways evident in the Hong Kong case: (1) the pathway of a marketplace of ideas and individual struggle, (2) the pathway of voluntary association and individual agency, and (3) the pathway of Christian membership and individual conversion.

A unique feature of this book is the conclusion of each chapter with a focus on an individual. Each chapter weaves together the experiences and voices of individuals to reflect common, aggregate patterns among Christian participants in civil society. Yet the scope of my fieldwork enables an additional, alternative approach to analysis. Employing interviews conducted on the tenth anniversary of Hong Kong's return to Chinese sovereignty allows us to reconnect with the individuals whose lives and voices make this book distinct. By casting a spotlight on a particular person, I highlight the enduring process and sentiment of individual development I emphasize in this study. While this is a book about Hong Kong people, their experiences offer more general lessons for all of us as modern people who are seeking direction in our lives. The decisions we make to exit and enter associational life as individuals do not mean we surrender on a personal level. Nor do those choices mean we undermine solidarity on a societal level. Moreover, in living out our own lives, while facing these choices may produce feelings of disquiet and create the impression of our own uniqueness, such experiences are in fact shared and normal processes. Facing them alone adds to their sense of urgency in our lives, but in aggregate they also build hope for self and others. Attending to reflections on personal lives, I document the complex and fluid "form of life" that is the least known but most telling aspect of civil society. That people convert to civil society becomes the answer to how faith and democracy are bound together in the contemporary Hong Kong experience.

Conversion to Christianity

Jesus is Lord / *Yèhsōu sih Jyú* high above Victoria Park, Causeway Bay
(photograph by Lida V. Nedilsky, 2005)

Understanding conversion is the first step toward understanding Hong Kong civil society. In converting to Christianity, individuals choose to enter a world of voluntary association, with many subsequent choices. Especially in the aftermath of Hong Kong's modernization, hundreds of thousands of people have converted to Christianity in a spiritual sense; they have at some point in their lives accepted Jesus Christ as their personal savior (*gwàiyì Yèhsōu*). By making the single decision to believe (*kyutjì*), they have subjected themselves to transformation or experienced conversion in a social sense. Responding to accessible options and budding interests, individuals come together with others who share something in common. Then they keep exiting and entering existing doors within the wider community, sometimes across a lifetime. In so moving, converts define the experience of Christianity in Hong Kong.[1]

Joining a group begins with identification on the basis of some existing common attribute. According to Ms. San, head of youth development programs for a regional Christian nongovernmental organization, her parents allowed her to attend the Salvation Army's Sunday school because they believed that the church would make their child a good person. Looking back twenty-five years on her conversion, Ms. San demonstrates the imprint of her church on her self:

> Church (*gaauwúi*) literally means a place for teaching your children to become good people. That is why we went to church from a very young age, and eventually many of us became soldiers in the Salvation Army. We are called soldiers because they say, "We will fight a war with love." By demonstrating Christ's love we help the world, help the poor.[2]

Taken at face value, this story suggests that joining a church means following one's parents into faith and adopting the distinct character of the institution—in this case, the Salvation Army. Yet much lies behind the block quote. Ms. San's parents, although Christian converts, never attended the same church as their daughter. Likewise, not all of Ms. San's five siblings decided to become soldiers in the Salvation Army. And

---

[1] Georg Simmel predicted this impact when he wrote that voluntary association affects the nature of institutions as individuals imprint their own beliefs and desires upon their affiliation. Georg Simmel, "The Web of Group-Affiliations," in *Conflict & The Web of Group-Affiliations*, trans. Kurt H. Wolff and Reinhard Bendix (New York: Free Press, 1955), 130.

[2] Author's interview with Ms. San, July 23, 1998.

while conveying little agency or charisma in joining the church, Ms. San as an adult has built a professional and intellectual life around her personal faith.

Membership experienced in a society of choices invites self-assertiveness. At one time in her adult life, Ms. San quit her job as a social worker to focus on her faith. She says, "I think that as a Christian, it is important for me—I think it is good for every Christian, actually—to spend some time like a personal pursuit in the Christian faith."[3] After finishing a master's degree in ministry at Chung Chi College, she took a position as assistant chaplain at one of the universities, and later over-saw a Christian NGO headquartered in Hong Kong yet attending to the wider Asian region. Within a couple of years of assuming the job, Ms. San left this work, too. While the social concern aspect and youth focus satisfied many of her ideas about the Christian mission, she ended up burnt out by the heavy workload and hectic travel schedule.

While a personal story, Ms. San's account, when considered with the conversion accounts of other Christians involved in Hong Kong's faith-based NGOs, speaks to a wider experience of individualized faith within a subculture of Hong Kong. Backward looking and dispassionate, Ms. San's conversion account reflects the interplay of family, school, and church in shaping the development of a child. Since development takes place separate from the nuclear family, allowing associational networks to extend far beyond the family from an early age, such a transforma-tion in contemporary Hong Kong signals an important break from the forms of religious life that have dominated traditional Chinese expe-rience.[4] Individual commitment and increasing self-assertiveness define the Hong Kong experience with faith. Here, Christianity is pivotal to individualism because Christianity is pivotal to the individual.

---

[3] Author's interview with Ms. San, July 23, 1998.

[4] See C. K. Yang, *Religion in Chinese Society* (Berkeley: University of California Press, 1961); David Jordan, *Gods, Ghosts and Ancestors* (Berkeley: University of California Press, 1972); Arthur Wolf, ed., *Religion and Ritual in Chinese Society* (Stanford: Stanford University Press, 1974); and Robert P. Weller, *The Unities and Diversities of Chinese Religion* (Seattle: University of Washington Press, 1987). For a Hong Kong case, see John T. Myers, "Traditional Chinese Religious Practices in an Urban-Industrial Setting: The Example of Kwun Tong," in *Social Life and Devel-opment in Hong Kong*, ed. Ambrose Y. C. King and Rance P. L. Lee (Hong Kong: Chinese University Press, 1981).

The Conversion Account

For social scientists, conversion refers to a dramatic change in thought and its demonstration in action. The individual who converts experiences transformation, switching worlds by assuming a new way to interpret and experience life.[5] Such reorientation in how an individual perceives reality may come about through nonreligious institutions and military training, as two examples. Yet religious conversion acted out through ritual, manifested in rites, communicated through distinct and often vivid language, and sustained within a community of closely associated members can transform any man, woman, or child.[6]

Since conversion connotes a change in perception and understanding, conversion accounts trumpet this change. Telling one's story of change, like deciding in favor of conversion itself, exercises selfhood.[7] Converts structure their accounts around a turning point dividing the past with the present and future, marking the intensity of the moment when life was transformed.[8] For instance, in describing their conversions, people might recall how life was bleak or empty, unhealthy or deprived, misguided or ignorant before religious authority signaled an alternative. Stories of gaining through conversion self-esteem or life purpose, sound body or domestic peace, economic stability or spiritual truth simultaneously communicate the power of the faith and the gratitude of the faithful.

[5] Peter L. Berger and Thomas Luckmann, *The Social Construction of Reality* (Garden City, N.Y.: Anchor Books, 1967), 157.

[6] Whether the dramatic change conversion represents is actually possible is far from certain. Thomas Luckmann, describing the modern religious experience in general, notes that religious membership today is less about conversion (transformation) than consumption (appropriation). The individual places less emphasis on conforming to guidelines than on finding suitable or tolerable guidelines that match self with faith community. Thomas Luckmann, *The Invisible Religion* (New York: Macmillan, 1967). As Christianity permeates American political, social, and psychological spheres of life, argues Peter L. Berger, Christianity cannot stand as distinct and so offer the convert an alternative to the general social reality. Peter L. Berger, *The Noise of Solemn Assemblies* (Garden City, N.Y.: Doubleday, 1961).

[7] David A. Snow and Richard Machalek, in "The Sociology of Conversion," *Annual Review of Sociology* 10 (1984): 177, cite W. B. Bankston, C. J. Forsyth, and H. H. Floyd, "Toward a General Model of Radical Conversion: An Interactionist Perspective on the Transformation of Self-Identity," *Qualitative Sociology* 4 (1981): 285.

[8] Berger and Luckmann, *Social Construction of Reality*, 160.

Because conversion accounts are guided by others in the religious community, they should be treated as information telling more about converts' current orientation than about their preconversion past.[9] Once the individual has made the step to switch worlds, even objective, personal facts can be imbued with new meaning. An ethnographic study of converts to indigenous Christianity in Africa dramatically demonstrates such a reformulation. Church doctrine so carefully framed the personal conversion accounts of members in the Apostolic Church of John Maranke in south-central Africa that the answers to interview questions required spiritual interpretation to avoid appearing nonsensical.[10] For instance, interviewees often responded to seemingly straightforward questions about age, name, and occupation by including biblical passages. Some even asked the interviewer how well they had done on their test of doctrinal literacy.[11] Striving for consistency in their new lives, the apostles of John Maranke used doctrine as the ordering framework for their perceptions.[12]

Yet conversion accounts fundamentally look backward, commenting on a previous point in people's religious biographies. For example, the experience of withdrawal, whether forced or voluntary, colors conversion accounts of apostates formerly affiliated with the Unification Church in the United Kingdom.[13] Time has passed since joining the church; commitment has been tested within the church. Social circumstances have turned dramatically away from religious association. Expectedly, individuals speak from a reference as ex-members who still face pressure to tell the story of conversion in a particular way. Now in answer to the question "At what point in your own life or in the life of the religious movement did you enter the religion?" apostates insist that membership had been a mistake. Backsliding and negativity, in addition

[9] Snow and Machalek, "The Sociology of Conversion," 177.
[10] Bennetta Jules-Rosette, *African Apostles: Ritual and Conversion in the Church of John Maranke* (Ithaca: Cornell University Press, 1975), 67–69.
[11] Jules-Rosette, *African Apostles*, 53–54.
[12] Jules-Rosette, *African Apostles*, 72. Jules-Rosette herself, who experienced conversion in the field, established a wedge between past and present by recasting events in her life in terms of biblical images that predicted them.
[13] James Beckford, "Talking of Apostasy, or Telling Tales and 'Telling' Tales," in *Accounts and Action*, ed. G. Nigel Gilbert and Peter Abell (Hampshire, U.K.: Gower, 1983).

to devotion and maturity, shape believers' accounts across an expanded horizon of time.[14]

On the one hand, religious engagement introduces members to a new way of thinking and speaking about everyday life. On the other hand, spiritual disengagement that can appear as a sudden split attests to the reality that religious commitment may not be permanent. Less noticeable shifts in spiritual orientation lie between these extremes. Conversion accounts of Hong Kong Christians involved in NGO work suggest voluntary membership in Christian community introduces new ways of thinking and talking. Yet with conversion as an experience of the child, and with individual development occurring through a variety of Christian communities of learning, notions of growth and maturity also color the tone of these backward-looking and reflective conversion accounts. Hong Kong Christians understand conversion as a beginning, hardly an end. The gradual process of spiritual development, in particular the fluctuations and shifts in group membership within Christianity, thus accounts for variability and affects the reasoned way individuals articulate belief.

But before turning to these accounts, we must appreciate the context for conversion, including how it came to be Christian membership and Christian individual development that defined Hong Kong's experience with voluntary association. The beginning of the convert's story goes back further than the conversion itself.

CONTEXT FOR CONVERSION

Christianity's presence in Hong Kong has been documented since the British first claimed authority there in February 1841. At that time, as Ernest Eitel writes in *Europe in China: The History of Hong Kong from the Beginning to the Year 1882*, foreign missionaries berated colonial administrators for rampant gambling in the territory.[15] They found few Chinese in Hong Kong interested in Christianity, and missionaries were not overly concerned about the riffraff and fugitives judged to be populating the outpost, except for their part in spreading vice. Instead, missionaries set their sights on converting Chinese in China proper. For decades the majority of Europeans who endured the trip to evangelize

[14] Beckford, "Talking of Apostasy," 85.
[15] Ernest John Eitel, *Europe in China: The History of Hong Kong from the Beginning to the Year 1882* (Hong Kong: Oxford University Press, 1895/1983).

made bases in Hong Kong but did their work in rural and urban China, accessing the country as did the merchants, through its waterways. But in villages and cities alike, kin and neighbors derided Chinese converts to Christianity as rice Christians, traitors to family and tradition for a handful of grain.[16] Conflict between missionaries and Chinese in the late nineteenth and early twentieth centuries did not deter religious emissaries in their campaigns to gain converts.[17] When in 1949 the Chinese communists gained victory in China's civil war, however, clergy and lay Christians soon turned to Hong Kong as more than a temporary haven.[18]

Hong Kong's colonial rulers raised the visibility of Christianity in a number of ways so that it enjoyed an advantaged platform from which to proselytize.[19] They did this by associating leaders of the Anglican and Catholic churches with the local power elite, instituting Christian holidays as nonstatutory holidays, and incorporating Christian ritual into political and legal ceremonies. In addition, they empowered church authorities to distribute several strategic social goods. One of these was education, and, in turn, others were offices in the civil service and professions.[20] Today churches still run approximately 45 percent of primary

[16] This connotation stuck under the Chinese communists. See John Pomphret, *Chinese Lessons: Five Classmates and the Story of the New China* (New York: Henry Holt, 2006), 194–200.

[17] See Paul Cohen, *China and Christianity: The Missionary Movement and the Growth of Chinese Antiforeignism, 1860–1870* (Cambridge, Mass.: Harvard University Press, 1963); and Joseph Esherick, *The Origins of the Boxer Uprising* (Berkeley: University of California Press, 1987).

[18] Chinese Communist Party policy officially forbade the return of missionaries once they left on furlough, so that by 1954 foreign missions had withdrawn their staff from China.

[19] See G. B. Endacott, *A History of Hong Kong* (London: Oxford University Press, 1958); and Deborah Brown, *Turmoil in Hong Kong on the Eve of Communist Rule: The Fate of the Territory and Its Anglican Church* (San Francisco: Mellen Research University Press, 1993).

[20] As early as the 1870s, the colonial government invited any school with more than twenty students to partner on the basis of payment by results. Traditional Chinese education, resembling a private tutorial, adjusted to urban Hong Kong by becoming neighborhood based. Yet teachers in these schools, skilled in calligraphy and the Confucian classics, prepared young people to serve a bygone public. In contrast, institutions of Christian learning, including the Morrison Education Society, the London Missionary Society, the Roman Catholic Church, and the Baptist Board of Foreign Missions, linked colonial subjects and administration. By 1903 government grants only funded English and westernized Chinese schools, recognized collaborators in meeting the colony's needs. See Catherine Jones, *Promoting Prosperity:*

schools and are associated with three of Hong Kong's eight universities.[21] The colonial government relied heavily on a voluntary sector to fill its own administrative weaknesses, education being a primary example. Another was social service. In the postwar years, when Hong Kong absorbed vast waves of Chinese refugees and migrants, faith-based voluntary agencies including Catholic Relief Services, World Council of Churches Refugee Service, Lutheran World Federation, Methodist Committee for Overseas Relief, Caritas, and CARE provided health and social service.[22] To support the work of educating, healing, and aiding Hong Kong's growing population, the government awarded land in a territory where very few were permitted its legal claim.

In comparison to Christianity, traditional Chinese religions were limited in what they could offer and accomplish. For example, not until the 1960s did the Hong Kong government approach Buddhist leaders at the Hong Kong Buddhist Association to participate in public service and claim private property.[23] Consequently, in a Chinese-dominant society, Buddhism, Taoism, and Confucianism presented few options for participation between individual, private worship and collective, monastic life. In the case of Confucianism, its similarity with Christianity as a path to both individual development and public service was striking.[24] Perhaps for this reason, mainland Neo-Confucianists who sought to sustain their unique vision of reform by relocating to Hong Kong in the 1940s were destined to fail.

Although Christian churches knew a long history of advantage in the religious marketplace, they secured only a small share of membership among Hong Kong's people. Christianity remains a minority religious experience, representing approximately 10 percent of the population, despite public service activities that exposed Hong Kong's non-Christian

The Hong Kong Way of Social Policy (Hong Kong: Chinese University Press, 1990), 145, 146.

[21] Baptist University, Lingnan University, and Chung Chi College at the Chinese University of Hong Kong have roots in Protestant educational enterprise.

[22] Jones, *Promoting Prosperity*, 169, citing P. R. Webb, "Voluntary Social Welfare Services," in *Chung Chi College, 25th Anniversary Symposium, 1951–1976: A Quarter Century of Hong Kong* (Hong Kong: Chinese University Press, 1977).

[23] Author's interview with Hong Kong Buddhist Association representative, August 9, 1998.

[24] See Jon L. Saari, *Legacies of Childhood: Growing up Chinese in a Time of Crisis, 1890–1920* (Cambridge, Mass.: Council on East Asian Studies, Harvard University Press, 1990).

population to Christian faith, buildings that provided shelter, and schools that set the next generation on a more fruitful path than the previous generation could tread. In fact, all organized and doctrine-based religions in Hong Kong represent a minority experience. Most Hong Kong people express no religious affiliation. The proportion of Hong Kong people unaffiliated with religion, moreover, appears to be rising, increasing from 58.3 percent in 1988 to 60.2 percent in 1995.[25] Contrast this to the case of another religiously pluralistic society, the United States, where nearly 90 percent of Americans claim an institutionally based religious identity.[26]

Among Hong Kong's middle class, Christianity has its roots in precisely those nineteenth-century missionary strategies meant to convey status.[27] Conversion was most often associated with the opportunity to gain stature in the British colony, especially through the link between Christian missions, English-language education, and the civil service. Among the poor, in contrast, the derogatory title "rice Christian" was doled out to any who accepted Christ in exchange for charity. Taken together, conversion to Christianity in Hong Kong suggests pragmatic, even calculating, terms of membership rather than a faithful turn to organized religion, raising suspicions and inciting distinctions among Christians.

Yet, figuring as they do in what individual Christians tell about the context of their conversion, Christian relief efforts and schooling influenced conversion. Urbanization and selective education both figure

[25] May M. Cheng and Wong Siu-Lun, "Religious Convictions and Sentiments," in *Indicators of Social Development in Hong Kong, 1995*, ed. Lau Siu-Kai, Lee Ming-Kwan, Wan Po-San, and Wong Siu-Lun (Hong Kong: Chinese University Press, 1997), 302. The Census and Statistics Department of the Government of the Hong Kong Special Administrative Region, like the same department under Government House of the colonial era, does not collect data on religious affiliation. Researchers estimating the size of any religion's population in Hong Kong employ figures published by the U.S. State Department, which in turn cites Hong Kong's Home Affairs Bureau without source(s) for its data: 2 million Buddhists and Taoists, 350,000 Protestants, 450,000 Catholics, 250,000 Muslims, 40,000 Hindus, 10,000 Sikhs, 4,600 Jehovah's Witnesses, and 4,000 Jews. Cheng and Wong's survey-based study poses the question of self-identification but investigates neither changes across nor changes within religious affiliation.
[26] Wade Clark Roof, *The Spiritual Marketplace: Baby Boomers and the Remaking of American Religion* (Princeton: Princeton University Press, 1999), 36.
[27] Carl T. Smith, *Chinese Christians: Elites, Middlemen, and the Church in Hong Kong* (Hong Kong: Oxford University Press, 1985).

prominently in the dispassionate and backward-looking accounts of conversion. This environment provided first an entry into association other than family, next the opportunity for personal development within a group, and ultimately alternative religious communities within Christianity. While conversion appears to be a pragmatic exercise in individual development, it eventually illustrates longstanding and changing commitment to a set of principles. Stories of Christian NGO participants during the decades of their youth and development weave throughout the following depiction of life in Hong Kong.

When immigrants came from the Chinese countryside in the 1950s, they hastily constructed squatter areas of wooden shanties that covered the Hong Kong hillsides thick as mushrooms. New arrivals made do with what they had, whether housing materials or job prospects, to establish greater security in their lives. As Professor Bok, a middle-aged academic and member of the Church of Christ, China, recounts his childhood in this urban environment,

> Entire families worked together for the garment industry or manufacturing plastic toys, work that saved those living in poverty. So it was with my family. Today we use plastic bags, but back then we earned a living for a time folding old magazine pages into bags. We went to the shop to get the unsold, heavy magazines early in the morning—seven or eight o'clock—and returned with the folded pages the same day to get the money.[28]

Hungry, working families crowded into squatter settlements vulnerable to natural and manmade disasters. At least one belt of camps, containing some 300,000 squatters, enveloped Northern Kowloon.[29] On Christmas Day of 1953, fire leveled the squatter settlement at Shek Kip Mei, igniting government action in response. By the 1960s, emergency housing known as resettlement areas, meant to thwart urban disasters like residential fires and landslides, was common. Crowding assumed a distinctively vertical and orderly character that is familiar today. Early standards for multiunit housing were extremely basic and spare; each adult was allocated 24 square feet of usable floor area, with family units measuring 120 square feet. Residents negotiated their way through communal sanitary facilities, and cooking was relegated to the apartment

---

[28] Author's interview with Professor Bok, April 26, 2000.
[29] D. J. Dwyer, "Introduction," in *Asian Urbanization*, ed. D. J. Dwyer (Hong Kong: Hong Kong University Press, 1971), 4.

complex's balconies and hallways.[30] Such close quarters were not attractive to young people seeking a place to study or socialize. As explained by a Catholic couple, Mr. and Mrs. Chu, who are approximately the same age as Professor Bok, life in the housing estates encouraged young people to find an alternative space for themselves outside, because "they wanted to study there but the cramped environment wouldn't allow them. They needed a safe environment. Anyway, they would normally leave their homes."[31] Despite the difficulty of identifying and securing a place that was safe, young people spent as much time as possible outside the home.

The unhealthy atmosphere of the resettlement area where Ms. San and her family lived made church membership especially beneficial. While others recall an urban Hong Kong that, although poor, was collective and supportive,[32] Ms. San characterizes the situation of the 1960s as disorganized. Support did not come from within the community; deviant behavior was more typical. She says, "We were living in a resettlement area that was very shabby. Lots of sexual harassment and rapes occurred because the whole flat was made up of small households that shared common toilets."[33] But a Cantonese-speaking missionary invited Ms. San's father to work whenever her church needed a carpenter. And the neighborhood church offered the children instruction and supervision. At a time in Hong Kong's history when general education was nonexistent, and pressure existed to employ children in whatever cottage industry was available, Mr. San's children learned to read as they discovered the Bible.

> My father was never educated formally; he only learned on his own. That is why he was happy to become a Christian. Later my mother became a Christian. So when we were still very young, they decided to let us go; not to their own church, which was a bit far from where we lived, but to a nearby church, the Salvation Army.

---

[30] Jones, *Promoting Prosperity*, 185; and Rance P. L. Lee, "High-Density Effects in Urban Areas: What Do We Know and What Should We Do?" in *Social Life and Development in Hong Kong*, ed. Ambrose Y. C. King and Rance P. L. Lee (Hong Kong: Chinese University Press, 1981), 16.

[31] Author's interview with the Chu family, April 25, 2000.

[32] Oi Ying, "Growing Space" [*Sìhngjéungdīk Hùnggàan*] in *Estate Reminiscence* [*Ngūkchyùn Naahnmòhng*], ed. Victor Luk (Hong Kong: Breakthrough, 1995), 182.

[33] Author's interview with Ms. San, July 23, 1998.

> Through church we got extracurricular activities regularly: every Saturday, fellowship, every Sunday, Sunday school. If you could recite a difficult verse they gave you prizes. And some instructors or counselors there were happy to be your tutor. You could bring your homework to do at the church. It was a way of evangelizing, of course.[34]

In the context of rapid urbanization and economic development, challenges emerged to social stability and family cohesion. Some decided that Christian institutions taught the moral and intellectual survival strategies needed to weather these ordeals.

Reflecting on their youth, Mr. and Mrs. Chu recall that the Catholic Church imparted lessons on how to be good people. When asked what kind of people were good people, husband and wife collaborate in explaining their meaning:

> Mr. Chu: In our Hong Kong, when we were young, there were many troubled youth—in the habit of fighting, using drugs, gambling, and drinking. If we didn't have those habits—
> Mrs. Chu: [Interrupting her husband] We called such people good people.
> Mr. Chu: —then we would be good people. Isn't that right? Especially we young people, in the 1960s, we all wished to leave our circumstances and have a good future. So, at that time we said we believed in Jesus. We seldom said, "What the Bible says, up to that passage, you should do thus." What we said was, "If you really believe in Jesus, Jesus will lead you on the way to a brilliant future." That's the way it was: growing up without a penny, and with those bad people acting that way. Those, then, were good people.[35]

Growing up at this time meant witnessing Hong Kong's development as a city, with all its trials and hopes.

Between 1960 and 1980, Hong Kong's economy expanded dramatically, with average annual GNP per capita growth of 7 percent. In 1976 alone, the city, fueled largely on light manufacturing for export, achieved 18.8 percent growth in its GNP.[36] Along with its surge in productivity and wealth (where real wages doubled), its population also expanded. Within just six years following the end of World War II, Hong

---

[34] Author's interview with Ms. San, July 23, 1998.
[35] Author's interview with the Chu family, April 25, 2000.
[36] Peter L. Berger, *The Capitalist Revolution: Fifty Propositions about Prosperity, Equality and Liberty* (New York: Basic Books, 1986), 36.

Kong's population rebounded from its Japanese-occupation-period low of 500,000 to exceed 2 million.[37] Within another twenty-five years, by 1978, the population more than doubled to reach 4.6 million. On average, its urban density contained 26,000 people per square kilometer. But particular districts, notably Mong Kok, exceeded 150,000 people per square kilometer.[38] Today the population has again almost doubled its 1978 total; more than 7 million inhabitants now vie for limited space. By the time the colonial administration assumed the social burden of public housing (as opposed to emergency resettlement estates) in the 1970s, square footage per individual increased to thirty-five feet, and government-funded construction accommodated nearly half of Hong Kong's total population.[39] Despite Hong Kong's economic development, people like Mr. and Mrs. Chu and their teenage son, who live in public housing, have just a modest kitchen, bath, and balcony as the only distinct spaces within their home; they eat, sleep, watch TV, and study in a single room.

In part, the crowded living conditions of resettlement areas and public housing, combined with the absence of parents, who were manning factories, served as an early impetus in the 1960s and 1970s for youth to venture into a church as welcome sanctuary. The church structure invited young people to find a private place for themselves in a built environment that confounded, if not overtly discouraged, such attempts. Mainline Protestant churches, including Anglican, Baptist, Lutheran, Methodist, and Presbyterian, as well as the Catholic Church, were in a particularly good position to offer such shelter. Benefiting from early government sales of land, they still today retain buildings that are among the most visible structures in Hong Kong.[40] Houses of worship

[37] John T. Myers, "Residents' Images of a Hong Kong Resettlement Estate: A View from the 'Chicken Coop,'" in *Social Life and Development in Hong Kong*, ed. Ambrose Y. C. King and Rance P. L. Lee (Hong Kong: Chinese University Press, 1981), 24.

[38] Lee, "High-Density Effects," 6.

[39] Lee, "High-Density Effects," 16.

[40] Newer churches, especially indigenous evangelical and imported fundamentalist churches, lack resources to obtain land holdings. To accommodate worshipers, most acquire space in office or apartment buildings, negotiate shared use of church facilities, or rent venues like the Hong Kong Jockey Club. A notable exception is the Hong Kong China Temple of the Church of Jesus Christ of Latter Day Saints in Kowloon Tong, built in 1996, with new administration headquarters in Wan Chai, erected in 2005.

often have adjacent schools and ample room for private space. Such spaces provided by the churches, whether courtyards or auditoriums, reading rooms or offices, contrast sharply with the traffic-filled streets and sidewalks meant for public use. According to Rachel, her personal affiliation with the church was enhanced by its sheltering effect. By the time she was a child growing up in the 1970s with four other siblings, Rachel was getting up at 7:00 every morning to attend Mass, not to fold magazine pages into bags. Recalling a time when everyone lived in government housing estates and no one had enough space, she says, "At least two summer holidays I spent my time in the church. There they provided study rooms for you, and then you could meet your friends there. I enjoyed a very interesting life."[41]

As highlighted in examples of conversion, through schooling many young people of both sexes established a connection to this alternative community. This school-age time thus colors the meaning of conversion; converts can look back upon themselves as immature children capable only of a child's perspective, as young persons seeking a space to social-ize, as adolescents growing independent of parental authority, and as novices learning how to do new things and be new people. Much as church-run schools and their approach to teaching have come to repre-sent the ordinary, conversion to Christianity within the schools is all too common today for converts to associate it with Hong Kong's colonial past. It is, however, a legacy of colonialism and distinct from the culture passed along in the home.

FAMILY RESISTANCE AND CONSENT

Christian converts remove themselves from family not only in terms of social activities but also with regard to a personal future bound in some way to a relationship with God. In many cases, this includes basing edu-cational and career decisions not on a family's wish for material welfare but on God's wish to be known as Savior. Christianity challenges the utilitarian and family-centered existence characteristic of Hong Kong society in the 1970s and 1980s, when most of the people interviewed for this study were in high school.

As commonly experienced among Christian converts in other parts of Asia, past and present, individual believers in Hong Kong often face

---

[41] Author's interview with Rachel, August 19, 1997.

family resistance.[42] Reverend Hei, a female pastor on one of Hong Kong's outlying islands, expresses her spiritual conversion in a language of such intimacy as to move any listener. But her account also presents the central problem of conversion in a Chinese family, the question of parental authority:

> I studied at a Christian school. At assembly they told stories of Jesus. I felt very close. I felt that we were old friends. Ever since I was in the womb, my Lord chose me.[43]

As she tells it, before she knew her parents, she already had a father in the Lord. His influence was so profound that Reverend Hei couched it as elemental. In contrast, she recalls the earthly conflict with her family over divided loyalty:

> At first my parents objected because I was always going to church. It wasn't far from my house, so I didn't come home all day. They scolded me. Perhaps they feared they would lose their daughter: gone all day, all day at church, everything is the church.[44]

By entering faith as individuals, converts do not lean upon parents as their spiritual guides. While converts may use parental example and experience as reference, most often they use that example as a foil. That converts' parents are not themselves Christians might explain for this tendency. As Joseph, a young Pentecostal working for Hong Kong's Democratic Party, attested, a convert often finds himself or herself the lone Christian in a family. As such, they occupy a special and thus awkward place within the social group at the center of folk religious practice in Chinese societies. Their refusal to continue traditions such as honoring ancestors (*baaisàhn*), burning incense (*jonghèung*), and performing ritual *kautàuh*, makes it difficult for family to deal with them. This leads Joseph to conclude, "Until there are more family members who become Christians, a lot of Hong Kong people will have a hard time."[45] In these cases the line between competing sources of authority can be an obvious

---

[42] On Japan, see Irwin Scheiner, *Christian Converts and Social Protest in Meiji Japan* (Berkeley: University of California Press, 1970); and Mark R. Mullins, *Christianity Made in Japan: A Study of Indigenous Movements* (Honolulu: University of Hawai'i Press, 1998).

[43] Author's interview with Reverend Hei, April 20, 2000.

[44] Author's interview with Reverend Hei, April 20, 2000.

[45] Author's interview with Joseph, April 8, 2000.

one. Religious authorities in school encourage departure from the usual path established in the home.

Actual accounts suggest that entering into faith while in school often means securing some form of consent from parents, as the young seek consent in other situations. For Reverend Yam, who grew up in the neighboring Portuguese colony of Macau, his parents' unfamiliarity with schooling created tension between themselves and their son. His parents harbored suspicions about the faith-based nature of his school, one administered by the Church of Christ, China. Christianity to them was a Western faith, and Jesus had a foreign face. At the same time, they valued his educational experience—not only because it imparted knowledge but also because it taught their son to be a good family member and to respect others. Despite holding these conflicting perceptions, Reverend Yam's father consented to his son's baptism in one of China's indigenous churches.

> At that time I was just fourteen years old, and not what you call mature enough; I had to respect my parents and get their permission. That was my understanding. And I appreciated my parents very much, because, although they are traditional Chinese, and not well educated, but, especially my father told me, "Now you are a secondary school student. When you decide to do something, you have to take responsibility. If you think that the decision is right, then you decide yourself."[46]

Reverend Yam is the head of one Hong Kong NGO, a university graduate, and a trained theologian. In sharp contrast to his own academic accomplishments, Reverend Yam's father received only a primary school education. Permitting the young person to decide for himself may have less to do with age than the fact that the child has already received more education than either of the parents achieved in their lifetimes.

In fact, people whose parents were immigrants from China—until the 1970s, the majority of Hong Kong residents—almost certainly came from families that lacked formal schooling. Most migrants from the mainland were neither gentry nor capitalists from sophisticated cities like Shanghai. Instead, they were people who had grown up in villages and experienced political, economic, and social upheaval. Like the place they had left behind, their new home needed institutional support for educating the masses. Even into Hong Kong's development as an

---

[46] Author's interview with Reverend Yam, April 20, 2000.

export-led industrial economy, there was no general schooling in place. Finally, responding to European pressure in the late 1970s to ensure child labor was not involved in the manufacture of cheap textiles, the British colonial government introduced a nine-year compulsory and free education program.[47] As recently as the early 1980s, a startlingly high proportion of Hong Kong residents lacked even primary education (see table 2.1).

TABLE 2.1

PROPORTION OF POPULATION WITH LESS THAN PRIMARY EDUCATION AND WITH SECONDARY EDUCATION OR ABOVE (1961–1981)

	1961	1966	1971	1976	1981
Percent of population with less than primary education	42.0%	39.3%	31.9%	25.6%	22.1%
Percent of population with secondary education or above	16.3%	19.3%	23.6%	31.4%	41.2%

Source of data: Lau Siu-Kai and Kuan Hsin-Chi, *The Ethos of the Hong Kong Chinese* (Hong Kong: Chinese University Press, 1988), 339.

Not only university education but also high school level or secondary education existed for a privileged few. Today, entry into college-preparatory high school is based on examinations, and university entrance is more competitive than in Japan. In this economically sophisticated city, only 8 percent of eligible students were able to secure admission to local university education in 1989.[48] Having children in school offset the usual parent-child relationship associated with Confucian culture, where parental authority prevailed in an almost nonnegotiable fashion. In times of dramatic change, however, parental authority could be limited.[49] It should be added that by arriving in Hong Kong before mandatory schooling

[47] Gerard Postiglione, "The Decolonization of Hong Kong Education," in *The Hong Kong Reader: Passage to Chinese Sovereignty*, ed. Ming K. Chan and Gerard A. Postiglione (New York: M. E. Sharpe, 1996), 100.

[48] Postiglione, "Decolonization," 113. But in 1989 the government resolved by the year 1996 to increase tertiary admissions by 100 percent, adding the Hong Kong University of Science and Technology, Hong Kong Baptist University, City University, Lingnan University, and the Hong Kong Polytechnic University to existing tertiary education, the University of Hong Kong and the Chinese University of Hong Kong.

[49] Historian Saari (*Legacies of Childhood*) demonstrates this in his study of reform-era China at the turn of the twentieth century.

was instituted, most parents of converts I interviewed lost a chance to establish relationships with Christianity on terms similar to their children's.

Gaining Christian membership does not end conflict with parents. Honoring ancestors becomes another issue needing negotiation, with the young convert testing the tolerance both of family and church. While older, more established churches today permit traditional practices like ancestor worship in the home and at the cemetery during the annual grave-sweeping festival, fundamentalist sects especially popular among young people demand that members strictly observe rules against the worship of idols. Noah, a thirty-something staff member at an international, student-centered, Christian NGO, originally converted into a Pentecostal church. He currently considers himself a member of the Anglican Church and is aware of the difference his church membership has made in relations with his parents.

> Because my parents are not Christian they wanted me to wait until I exhibited an ability to be independent (*duhklahp nàhnglihk*) before I decided to convert at age sixteen. There was some opposition, especially because my parents thought conversion inharmonious with worshipping ancestors. When I was in the Four Square Gospel Church, ancestor worship was prohibited. Now [that I attend an Anglican church] I can do it, but I cannot do any of the traditional postures, like *kautàuh*. No one in the family is supposed to. So my parents felt baptism, this action has a lot of symbolic meaning. [In their eyes] it would break me away from traditional practice.[50]

While Noah's parents agreed to let him decide matters once he had reached the appropriate level of maturity, their sensibilities were noticeably tested by their son's baptism.

Noah's new identity was a disappointing development for his parents but one they would have to tolerate, similar to the way some parents react upon learning that their child possesses an alternative sexual orientation or has no interest in attending college. Noah continues:

> Perhaps they did not have the heart to accept that their son would turn out this way. In contrast to my generation, I guess their traditional concept was strong. I had already changed, gone to a different faith. So they had insecurity about losing that tradition. I guess that this factor was great.[51]

---

[50] Author's interview with Noah, April 26, 2000.
[51] Author's interview with Noah, April 26, 2000.

For Noah's parents, Christianity disrupted their home lives, confounded expectations, and undermined the lessons they themselves sought to impart to their son.

An accidental Catholic, James shares much in common with Noah and his situation. Distinguishing between Christianity and Catholicism in the manner common in Hong Kong, James says, "If I had been in a Christian school I probably would have gone to Protestant churches."[52] As a student in Catholic secondary school, James became a Catholic convert and then a religious studies major at Chung Chi College, a Protestant affiliate of the Chinese University of Hong Kong. In his conversion account, he explains that religious authorities helped him resolve his customs at home with the religion he chose for himself; they assured him his fealty in performing ritual obligations. Answering a question about Christians in his family, James says,

> No, no, no, no. No one in my entire family is either Protestant or Catholic. It is just a typical Chinese family. They worship ancestors. I am the first who believes in the Catholic faith. Actually, I still perform the ancestor worship ceremony, because in my church the priest doesn't see ancestor worship as offending any religious doctrines. It is treated as a show of respect to parents. So I do not have any difficulty. I do not even have any struggle when I burn incense for the ancestors.[53]

If not for the tolerance of his religious guides, James would likely have suffered from conflicting demands. Instead, he found affirmation not only at his church but also at Chung Chi College, the Protestant institution where he looked for guidelines on how to be a good Catholic.

Although once strictly a male domain, today ancestor worship challenges female progeny to demonstrate their willingness or resistance to carry out the rites. One of James's distant female relatives, possibly a Baptist (James is not sure), has rejected all activities associated with ancestor worship, including the consumption of chickens given as religious offerings. While it makes her family visibly unhappy, she insists on following strictly her own religious doctrines and behavioral guidelines, especially now that she is a minister. James adds that his cousin's actions do not serve as a guide for his own. "That is her way of doing things," he explains, "but I am not following her way. So I think that will make

---

[52] Author's interview with James, April 4, 2000.
[53] Author's interview with James, April 4, 2000.

my parents accept my religious faith."[54] As the only Christians in their families, James and Noah have had to negotiate their new religious identities with parents who harbor reservations but offer consent. To relieve some of their personal concerns, the two young men apply the tools that speak to their maturity and learning; they analyze the local culture and objectify their parents' practices as traditional, popular religion. Religious learning goes beyond literacy or morality to include theology. The endorsement or tolerance of custom by religious guides, including priests and professors, makes it possible for James and Noah to perform rites like ancestor worship that affirm familial ties.

Parents in Hong Kong have a say in the social choices their children make, and children seek out affirmation of their decisions. The subtext of these accounts, however, implies that parental opposition does not impede the child's decision to respond to the ubiquitous presence of Christianity and fulfill a personal calling. Not once did parental opposition prevent Christians interviewed for this study, whether Catholic or Protestant, from affiliating with a community that they entered on their own terms.

Breaking and Forging

One of the distinguishing features of Christianity in Hong Kong believers' frame of experience is transformation, a departure from previous ways of being and doing. While some experience Christianity as a family unit (this is especially true among Catholics), far more often young people enter into faith on their own terms. As they forge relations with other people as members of a single faith community, they also break from previous commitments.

Reverend Gwong is a minister anticipating retirement from her church. With memories going back half a century, she recalls a different time in Hong Kong's history. Yet, like other converts, she describes the chasm between her father's belief system and the one she chose to follow. She says,

> He did not believe in Jesus, of course. And he did not like the idea of me converting to Christianity, because in those days he is a Chinese scholar. Chinese intellectuals do not believe in anything. They think Christianity is too simple. If you compare the Ten Commandments with the commandments of Confucius, it's nothing! They despise Christianity. And then I

---

[54] Author's interview with James, April 4, 2000.

think they have a reason. Because the teaching of the Bible, it's wrongly taught—it's nothing to do with the Bible. It's oversimplified: if you believe, you're saved; if you don't believe, you go down to hell. Just ridiculous![55]

At the time of her initial interest in Christianity in the 1940s, Reverend Gwong was living under the care of her school, run by a British missionary society. Practically orphaned by the Second World War, which scattered her family, she had the chance to observe adults living in what she understood as unique circumstances. They were missionaries, and they had left their homes to live in a climate that did not suit them, to eat food that was not agreeable to them. For a girl who had known separation from family, it seemed these missionaries led happy lives despite having infrequent occasion to return to their own families in Britain. Their positive disposition while living in humble circumstances distinguished them from other foreigners and ordinary Chinese, who pursued material gain yet never achieved peace of mind. This intrigued her, and she set out to discover for herself what made them special. She began to ask questions:

> I was young, only a student, and lived with two of the teachers. They weren't Christian either. They told me, "Those are the missionaries," and explained to me missionaries were Christians. So I said, "What do you mean, they are Christians?" "They believe in Christ, God." And I said, "Who is this God?"[56]

Reverend Gwong's account lays out the circumstances of her conversion quite clearly and objectively. She was young, inquisitive, and not too shy to ask questions.

The next step for Reverend Gwong was to educate herself with the help of a Bible. But again she interjects her current standpoint. She reveals a critical stance stemming from her personal experience with religion and, more specifically, religious education. She juxtaposes two points of reference:

> Now, we had Bible lessons, but I must say at that time I was very—I mean, since becoming a teacher myself I have made changes in the religious education because I think it is a *failure*. It is so useless *telling* people the Bible stories. What does it have to do with me, whether David killed Goliath? That is not my business!

[55] Author's interview with Reverend Gwong, April 14, 2000.
[56] Author's interview with Reverend Gwong, April 14, 2000.

So I said to myself, if they believed in Christ and they had a better life, this Christ must be something. I wanted to know what it was. Because the Old Testament was too complicated, I bought the four gospels in order to find Jesus. And I think, as the Bible says: where you search, there you will find. Exactly! That's what happened.[57]

Reverend Gwong chose to break with her family's aversion to Christianity, forging her own relationship to Christianity through text.

Perhaps Felicia's critical faculties postponed her formal conversion; perhaps her Buddhist grandmother's objections delayed Felicia and her siblings (including a sister who is now a Jehovah's Witness) from converting. Her introduction to Catholicism in primary school came at a time when she lacked the capacity to fully understand the meaning of conversion. In secondary school she tried to learn some Catholic dogmas but ended up deciding against baptism.

My case is quite rare in that I had to think through my commitment. Even among my college classmates, those who were Catholic mostly came from a Catholic family background. Maybe they also had their unique history.

But our family is traditional; it practices ancestor worship. And my grandma was a Buddhist. She did not like us joining the church. Although my grandmother's objection did not affect me much in deciding to postpone baptism, still, we thought that while she was alive she would not have liked us being baptized—because I thought about being baptized when I was young. At that time my understanding of faith was a bit different. Later I came to think that being baptized afterwards is better. Yes, that is also why I chose not to get baptized.[58]

Only later in life, after she joined a Catholic student group on her university campus, did Felicia gain the understanding necessary to convert and so commit herself to a prolonged, personal project.

While many young Christians contend with being the odd believer in the house, others stand apart from family despite having parents who also profess belief in Christ. This has much to do with the personal nature of conversion, whether we speak of evangelicals in particular or Hong Kong Christians in general. Among Baptists and Evangelical Christians, infant baptism is not accepted as the credible starting point for a believer's relationship with Jesus. In fact, most of Hong Kong's independent fellowships reject infant baptism. To be a Christian is to

[57] Author's interview with Reverend Gwong, April 14, 2000.
[58] Author's interview with Felicia, August 24, 1998.

decide for one's self as a sentient being. Young Doctor Loi, a highly specialized medical doctor with practical experience in psychiatry and a self-described Protestant Christian, draws a sharp line of distinction between his own Christian faith and that of his parents. He says,

> Because my parents were Christians I received infant baptism in the Congregational church. But that might not be related to my so-called faith, in my heart, because at that time I was far from knowing what a Christian is. And although my parents were Christians they seldom went to church, so as a child I had very little contact with the church.
>
> I grew up in a Christian family, but not until high school was I converted. I do not consider myself a Christian before that conversion. Otherwise I would not call that incident [induction through fellowship] a conversion. At the time of conversion, I talked it over a bit with my parents, but not that much. That incident was not so important to them. They thought I had always been a Christian.[59]

Doctor Loi's parents are better educated than many Hong Kong people. His father graduated from high school in Guangzhou (Canton), China, and his mother received the training necessary to become a nurse. Such learning as they achieved was an exceptional feat among their age cohort. For Doctor Loi it explained not only his parents' acceptance of his exploration of faith but also their tolerance of other religions. They had each converted to Christianity in their youth, moreover, despite the fact that their own parents (Doctor Loi's grandparents) had themselves been converts.

Apart from underscoring the personal nature of conversion, the drawing of lines of distinction is a reflection on the type of Christian the convert has become in adult life. As indicated in many of the accounts already presented, Hong Kong Christians are not only focused on individual development but they also implicitly and explicitly engage in judging the status of other Christians. Some discount their parents' religious life because of the circumstances of the older generation's membership. For countless Chinese refugees, baptism was the price paid for charity. Having fled the mainland after various attempts at land reform or bouts of natural disaster, refugees in Hong Kong accepted staples from the hands of religious men and women whose mission it was to assist them. Local families, too, received rice and other foodstuffs in the 1950s, when, disrupted by war a decade before, Hong Kong's economy

[59] Author's interview with Doctor Loi, April 20, 2000.

was still considered Third World. For taking such charity, and accepting the church, this earlier generation of converts became known in Cantonese as milk powder believers (*náaihfán seuntòuh*). Because they appeared complicit in a material-spiritual quid pro quo, their conversion was judged by other Christians not as a sign of deep commitment, but as a gesture of surrender, even a form of payback. Carrying this negative connotation, the term "milk powder believer" in Hong Kong (as opposed to rice Christian, on the mainland) refers to a traitor to Christianity rather than to Chinese tradition.

Luke, who works for an organization catering to the spiritual and social development of evangelical students on Hong Kong's university campuses, communicated such an impression of his parents:

> My parents were born after World War II. At that time the Catholic Church provided charitable works, so everyone called himself or herself Catholic. If they went to church, then they could get rice, they could get milk: *náaihfán seuntòuh*. Back then no one was a practicing Catholic. They just got baptized; that's it. I grew up in what was on the surface a Catholic family, but we didn't practice any rituals. Then when I was in secondary school, about sixteen or seventeen years old, I became a Christian.[60]

Luke not only distinguishes between himself as a Christian and his parents as Catholics, but he also distinguishes between himself as a voluntary, committed Christian entering freely into belief and practice and his parents as involuntary, uncommitted milk powder believers.

Future choices concerning personal development are guided by considerations that effectively replace the convert's parents with the pulpit. This turn represents a striking break culturally with Chinese, Confucian intellectual tradition. Although also about self-improvement for the sake of wider social harmony, in Hong Kong traditional Chinese intellectualism has lacked the intermediary institutions between family and state crucial for socializing and sustaining followers in a semblance of community. Instead, Christian churches and organizations, schools and informal associations practically monopolize this space. These perform the private role of imparting important values, even the Confucian value of filial piety. Likewise, in its multiple forms and expressions, Hong Kong Christianity supports the individual believer in the quest for deeper self-knowledge.

---

[60] Author's interview with Luke, April 24, 2000.

Developing within Faith

With the interpretive categories of conversion emphasizing personal growth and maturation, development within faith rather than health, prosperity, or submission becomes the ordering framework for the conversion account. As Ms. San, through her encounters with the Salvation Army, observed, church leaders use schools as avenues to establish relationships with young people in Hong Kong, and to evangelize among them. Whether in the capacity of priests and nuns or as instructors and mentors, part of their work is to identify not only possible converts but also others open to an even deeper religious commitment.

Theological study can be an attractive hook to entice the Christian novice to enhance connection to faith. From the perspective of the church, extending such training produces model laity, missionaries, or potential clergy. An example of a convert with a calling, Reverend Gwong has been a dedicated teacher at a girls' school, a member of a missionary society, and a popular speaker at key functions within the wider Hong Kong religious community. One day, while Reverend Gwong was in the early years of her teaching career, a missionary who had been her teacher approached her with an offer to train in Europe, as she recounts:

> During the first few years, one of my colleagues encouraged me to study theology. She thought I was interested in theology, which was true. Not that I wanted to be a minister. I never thought of it, really.
>
> She said she would get me a scholarship to go abroad. But I had only taught for about five years, and I did not want to leave that school. So I turned her down once. And then the second time she offered it, I could not resist. I thought I might just take a chance. If it is not God's will, so to speak, he will stop it some way: I won't get the passport or something like that. Just leave it to him.[61]

The passport did come and Reverend Gwong embarked upon her own experience living abroad, not unlike the missionaries at her school, who first piqued her interest in the Christian faith. And despite the sense that being a minister would not be "her cup of tea," in 1966 Reverend Gwong became the first woman ordained in Hong Kong. Years later, as a missionary herself, she traveled extensively through Europe, Asia, and Africa.

[61] Author's interview with Reverend Gwong, April 24, 2000.

Young converts also delve deeper into their faith when training in theology for intellectual and social purposes. Such is the case with Professor Bok. His mother, as a girl from the countryside, grew up without any education. His father received only three years of schooling. Professor Bok, however, completed twenty years of formal education. As a youth, he was encouraged by his pastor to view his future as a vital person, able to effect change in himself and others. In retrospect, Professor Bok finds amusement in the thought that mere boys were instilled with a sense of influence and responsibility: "To give us a mission while we were still very young and had no idea—I mean, even before we knew ourselves, we were told we have to renew the world!"[62]

Professor Bok's pastor, Reverend Hap, cultivated agency and vision within the context of Christian community. More importantly, he disseminated these lessons at a school designed to support the spiritual quest of lay believers, a school for every Christian, a lay school of theology. Offered in the summer, along with requirements for practical involvement in the parish, curriculum included courses on church history and the Bible as well as theology. Professor Bok's pastor, not his father, encouraged general education in a general way: the boy was to study theology as a Christian, for his own personal benefit. But his pastor also emphasized education as a respectable occupation.

> Education is another dimension that inspired more training for my own benefit, to prepare myself for an educational role. So I talked with my pastor, and finally we agreed, or I was led in a sense, guided to do theology. And I think that was good for me.[63]

Professor Bok took this suggestion to the limit, becoming a professor of theology at a top Hong Kong university. Church culture promulgated the project of edification (*gaauwúi*), and Professor Bok accepted the undertaking of self-improvement.

Within the wider conception of self-improvement is the idea of self-cultivation: learning to be a better version of oneself. While studying at a Bible college, seminary, public university, or NGO, converts realize other paths within Christianity and see the boundaries of their faith expand. James mentioned that his plan to pursue a degree in religious studies followed his conversion to Catholicism. He had only just begun

[62] Author's interview with Professor Bok, April 26, 2000.
[63] Author's interview with Professor Bok, April 26, 2000.

participating in church and wanted to comprehend better what it meant to be a Catholic. "I was very curious about my religious faith," he says. "What do I believe? What is the purpose of having religious faith? I was just trying to search for something."[64] While studying in a seminary was one option for gaining deeper spiritual understanding, teachers there cultivated interest in joining the clergy. In a seminary, moreover, priests who instructed him might question James's maturity in taking on such a course of study immediately after high school. Their objections would be added to those of the wider community, as James explains, "Because your secondary school classmates and teachers, or your neighbors, or your relatives have different voices, different judgments. They will think you are wasting four years in the university studying religious studies, which has no market value."[65] From James's own perspective, he was set to accomplish two goals at once: to gain religious knowledge and to earn a degree.

In the space between conversion and his conversion account, James learned to cast a critical eye on his past, with the result that his conversion account reflects the immaturity of his early connection to faith:

> Why the Catholic Church attracted me was because of the priests. I was just fifteen or sixteen years old, and went to a very traditional Catholic church: a big church with traditional Catholic Mass. The priests seemed very holy, at least in my eyes. Also, they taught me English and ethics. They were a role model for me to imitate during my younger days.[66]

Looking backward, James explicitly imposes the logic of a child. As his teachers and friends, the priests appealed to him for a closer look at faith. Now capable of casting a critical eye, James reinterprets his entry into faith; admiration for the priests yields to admiration for the power exuded by the priests:

> Because they were very kind to me, and loving, I even wanted to be a priest when I grew up. That kind of feeling has already left. I think I've found that the reason for admiring them, or wanting to become one of them, was probably because I wanted to be a person with power. I admired them when they were presiding over the Mass, and thought them very authoritative. Everybody respected them as they became the representatives of God

---

[64] Author's interview with James, April 4, 2000.
[65] Author's interview with James, April 4, 2000.
[66] Author's interview with James, April 4, 2000.

through that ceremony. And in their daily life, it seemed they were very holy, unlike us, who are very human.[67]

Today James communicates a reasoned assessment of religious membership that speaks more to his present than to his past. First, James reflects on and qualifies religious authority by emphasizing the temporal distance between himself and his conversion to Catholicism. Second, he conducts a self-analysis that can only be achieved when the framework of the conversion account enables and encourages reflection. Such objectivity highlights how James uses personal development to understand his own conversion.

Not surprisingly, many achieve a sense of maturity as they develop broader and more complex perspectives on faith. Noah originally joined the Four Square Gospel Church, a Pentecostal church. After graduating from a conservative seminary, however, he decided to work for an ecumenical organization, the YMCA. To achieve the necessary harmony to do his job, connecting the YMCA with other Christians in collaboration, Noah had to adjust his religious perspective. Ultimately, this work experience opened a door for Noah's faith: he could learn about his faith outside the confines of his church. As he put it, "I could find space to reflect on my own church's understanding (*gìngyihm*). I could then gradually see that my earlier faith had been a bit narrow."[68]

Soon Noah began participating in an Anglican church. And then he entered the Chinese University of Hong Kong for further studies, seeing it as an excellent way intellectually to try out other possibilities. That was the first time he came in contact with the NGO for which he currently works. His switch from Pentecostalism to Anglicanism involved gradual preparation psychologically. His change in spiritual outlook was a matter of degree. But encountering this Christian NGO was revolutionary. In his mind it was a second conversion; the alternative views he learned were totally new:

> The first issue that raised my interest [in the NGO] was the sex worker issue because it is very deep, especially from the evangelical ethical standpoint: How do you view family? How do you view sex? How do you view work? Actually, I felt I could not continue as an evangelical anymore.
>
> Anglicans cannot accept the sex worker, either. My personal transformation was not an Anglican transformation. I can admire Anglicans,

[67] Author's interview with James, April 4, 2000.
[68] Author's interview with Noah, April 26, 2000.

but in some respects they are very conservative. Theologically, the Anglican Church more than others offers a space to discuss different problems. While it may not agree with you, you can have a different opinion. If it can accept my difference of position, then I am very happy.[69]

In effect, Noah entered the web of Christian community and learning and experienced development within it.

Taking pains to be abundantly clear, Doctor Loi explains that although he received infant baptism at the behest of his Congregationalist parents, he was a Christian only when he had decided for himself what he believed. Moreover, his Christianity rejected exact or particular doctrines or practices pertaining to denominational affiliation. Rather, during secondary school, within a community of classmates, he became a Protestant Christian ascribing to a general set of beliefs within an interdenominational fellowship. He comments,

> Being a Protestant Christian has a very general meaning. That means I recognize that there is a God, a personal God, who loves me, who created the universe, who sent his only Son, Jesus Christ, to us, to die for us on the cross, and to save us from our sins, from our original sins. And by that I can have eternal life after my death. And it is all that I believe. And also, the Bible is an inspired document from God. And it is trustworthy.[70]

It just happened that the group that invited him, and with which he participated in fellowship, was a Protestant group. At this time in his religious development, the idea that he may have ended up Catholic does not faze Doctor Loi. Like other Christians, Doctor Loi carefully qualifies his attitudes at the time of his conversion when he was fifteen or sixteen.

> At my conversion, I didn't know what the Catholic Church was, what the Protestant Church was. I happened to be invited by a group of Protestants, and therefore converted in the Protestant fellowship. During that so-called junior period, I thought that Protestantism was right, and Catholicism was wrong.
>
> Especially after going to the seminary—I have to mention that I enrolled in a part-time bachelor of arts in religious studies course at the Hong Kong Baptist Theological Seminary in 1993—I learned a lot, especially about the relationship between the Catholic and the Protestant churches. In fact, at the time of religious reformation, Protestantism was considered a heresy in

[69] Author's interview with Noah, April 26, 2000.
[70] Author's interview with Doctor Loi, April 20, 2000.

relation to the Catholic Church. And now my idea of faith (*seunyéuhng*) is that at least at the level of doctrine they are very similar.[71]

Today a mature believer, Doctor Loi assesses earlier views through the lens of one who has sought and received extra education in faith. His account outlines the layers of his experience, each layer superimposed by a later understanding of membership and faith. First, his parents see to his baptism as an infant. But infant baptism does not make him a Christian. Second, he converts within a fellowship, making him a Protestant Christian, pure and simple. Third, he enrolls in a seminary, where he gains a sense that it is not theological purity that separates forms of Christian faith, but largely politics. That he became a Protestant Christian in primary school was a matter of circumstance. His realization that chance made him Protestant can only come from his later understandings gained through religious studies.

Noah, the Anglican member and NGO convert, can hold to his own positions both within his church and within his NGO; but Doctor Loi, through his particular journey, has been taking to further limits the individual believer's right to his own perspective. In 2001 he discovered limitless theological options, even antidoctrine Christian theology sustained within a religious community. He continues,

> Because the churches in Hong Kong are erected by conservative evangelists from the West, they are all conservative. I can say so definitely because for years I had been searching for a liberal church, but could not find one until now. True, mainline churches, for example the Anglican Church, are more open towards the questioning Christians. But the rituals are so systematic, orderly. And the doctrines are there: the Apostolic Creed, the Nicene Creed, that the Bible is all trustworthy if not explicitly inerrant.[72]

The Internet affords access to a liberal church exceeding Doctor Loi's expectations for openness. In fact, from the comfort and convenience of his personal computer, Doctor Loi has literally signed on to the most open church he could find or imagine, the Boston-based Unitarian Universalist Association (UUA).[73]

> I have found some churches on the Internet. And one that is very, very important to me is the Unitarian Universalist Association. Now, the two

---

[71] Author's interview with Doctor Loi, April 20, 2000.
[72] Author's interview with Doctor Loi, June 4, 2001.
[73] Author's interview with Doctor Loi, June 4, 2001.

words are theological words: Unitarian refers to those who believe that God is one God; Universalist refers to those who believe that everybody on earth, from the past to the future, is saved.

These two words may lead us to think that the church believes in one God, and believes that everybody will be saved. But now this UUA church has evolved so that it has no doctrine, has no creed. And what it values is the individual's search for religion; his search for the meaning of life. That is the ultimate model of a liberal church![74]

Without his extra studies at the seminary, Doctor Loi confides, he would not have had the confidence to take this plunge and become a member of the UUA. He would not have had the capacity to know for certain whether the theology espoused by this group was legitimate or heretical. His learning enabled him confident entry into an online community.

Confidence gained through new community does not resolve conflict between self and existing community. To enjoy the intimate and social aspects of church life, Doctor Loi maintains membership in his evangelical church. But in this church he has earned public reprimand for sharing the idea over which he has long struggled: that the Bible, rather than being the word of God, is an inspired document. The pastor has denied him the rite of communion.

SPOTLIGHT on Benedict

A Protestant Convert Converts to Catholicism

The extent to which a convert's change in perception can be achieved and communicated raises questions. What are the religious group's mechanisms for sustaining the individual believer's identity as one within the community of faithful? And how important is it to secure the individual within the group?[75] Living as a commune in a suburban setting, south-central Africa's Apostles of John Maranke, for example, not only established rules for everyday activities but employed monitors to enforce these rules. Their conversion accounts show the depth to which each believer was bound to the community and its structure: learning to be an Apostle occurred daily, throughout the day. But for Hong Kong's converts to Christianity, conversion accounts demonstrate the openness

---

[74] Author's interview with Doctor Loi, June 4, 2001.
[75] Berger and Luckmann, *Social Construction of Reality*, 158.

of the relationship to faith in an urban setting and the demand for self-monitoring one's commitment to a particular community.

Finding a fit is a constant consideration for Benedict, as his life choices through 2007, when last I interviewed him, demonstrate. When he joined the NGO, he was seeking work through which he could be true to himself as a Christian. But once 1997 passed, and the expected political disruption gave way to real economic disruption, he realized an organizing role with an NGO did not fit his true self. Not content to find just another job, he drew instead on his earlier identity as a social worker. This career reorientation did not solve Benedict's problem; neither did his conversion to Catholicism in 2003 after being first an evangelical and then a liberal Protestant. Rather, his new conversion helped him accept suffering, as when his wife's decision to become a Catholic jeopardized her job with a Protestant service center she had managed for thirteen years.

> In the first few years after leaving the NGO to earn a Ph.D., my Christianity was not sustained, no. But then I experienced a rather drastic change. My supervisor, although born Catholic, had not been practicing his faith for at least twenty years. Around 2003 he reconverted. I learned a lot from him. He introduced me to a whole new world, to a whole new series of literature I hadn't heard of in the Protestant tradition. And that made me and my wife seriously rethink how we understand our faith. We came to appreciate the reality of the Eucharist. In the Catholic Church we do not just take the wine and bread as commemoration of Christ; what we are offered in the Mass is in fact the blood and body of Christ. This raised a serious question for both of us: How can we participate in the Mass and have union with Christ through his body and blood unless we are converted? So in 2003 I started taking classes with my wife, preparing for conversion. With conversion our understanding of the world, of our burdens and sufferings in life, changed. We can have the honor of following the example of Christ and Mary, to serve as co-redeemers. We have to carry our cross. The Catholic tradition stresses that suffering and burdens are meaningful—they help this world to change, bring salvation. I'm not saying that my wife and I are suffering this way, but we face many sufferings since our conversion. And we have to learn from them.[76]

Being in an urban marketplace of Christian institutions, three-time converts like Benedict testify to Christianity's ubiquity. In fact, a conversion viewed ten, twenty, thirty, or more years down the road no longer

---

[76] Author's interview with Benedict, June 27, 2007.

appears as *the* turning point. Instead, the conversion begins a long journey toward an individual's intellectual and spiritual development.

Benedict, in converting to Protestant evangelical Christianity, did not stop there. He converted again when he sought an orientation within Protestantism that satisfied his requirement for social concern and reconciled his commitment to Christianity. And then in 2003, with his dissertation supervisor acting as both intellectual and spiritual guide, he converted once more by accepting the distinction of Catholicism. By willingly entering the door of a Christian religious institution, the convert, Benedict being but one example, steps onto a path leading to multiple associations. Voluntary group affiliation with a fellowship or church brings both self-assertiveness and conflict. Once entered upon such a quest, the novice finds the journey resembles a lifelong endeavor forever complicated by new possibilities.

—3—

Conversion to Civil Society

Handmade sign from Hong Kong's annual June 4 demonstration, Hennessy Road, Wan Chai (photograph by Lida V. Nedilsky, 2001)

By becoming Christian in Hong Kong, converts accept a distinct life-style. They pull away from both the influence and the company of nonbelieving family members and the general society. Whether in a school fellowship, a parish, or an independent church, they build a world based on voluntary commitment peopled by others like them, engaged in like rituals. But what is the quality of this commitment to faith and community? Having set the precedent of leaving one way of life for another, do converts face any limits to choosing, and choosing again? Whether in the United States or in Hong Kong, in a diverse religious marketplace people leave one religious community for another; searching for a personal fit with religion, they go questing.[1] In fact, Hong Kong Christian converts go on choosing as a form of life. They continue to look for a religious community and culture that suits them individually. Repeatedly employing their newfound mobility, they conscientiously relocate themselves in churches and jobs and courses and public gatherings as expressions of their religious commitment.

Fellowships and churches that draw in the convert enable further choices when they introduce the lesson of commitment. Christian religious institutions teach how to dedicate a lifetime to Jesus Christ, put religious faith into practice, and gauge individual progress toward such abstract ends. While reference to commitment and its expression may feature in countless sermons and Bible study sessions, the practical lesson of how to judge individual progress toward commitment is a more subtle one. Researchers and converts alike seldom note its presence or recognize its value. Yet if we listen, we can detect across individual lives the particular practice of self-reflection with which Hong Kong Christians assess their own commitment.

Consider the following comments from James, a Catholic convert and participant in two Protestant Christian NGOs. During an interview conducted roughly three years after Hong Kong's return to Chinese sovereignty, he describes Hong Kong's predicament in becoming part of China: uncertainty as to whether the society should play it safe and align more with mainland Chinese norms, or whether it should take risks and maintain what is distinct, even oppositional. Within the same breath, James turns to his own identity crisis, saying,

---

[1] Wade Clark Roof, *The Spiritual Marketplace: Baby Boomers and the Remaking of American Religion* (Princeton: Princeton University Press, 1999).

I am at a crossroads to see what I should do. But my struggle (*jàngjaat*) is similar to that of Hong Kong society as a whole. I ask myself, "Should I stay in such a stable working environment the rest of my life? Or abandon stable income and get a more challenging job, more sensitive to social issues?" I could have a very comfortable life. Anybody would want to have it. But I do not think that is my deeper desire or goal in life.[2]

James introduced this concept of struggle before, when he explained what it meant for him to be a Catholic convert. As a Catholic he need not struggle over whether to fulfill his parents' wishes to respect his ancestors by burning incense; the Catholic Church accommodates family demands in this case and allows its members to perform the ritual. James distinguishes by degree one use of the term and another when he reflects on his commitment to put into practice the demanding doctrines of his faith, saying,

I think it is a matter of different degree of struggle. For ancestor worship is a very trivial thing; it is not affecting me a lot. But for the current issues that I am struggling with, I think it is more important; it affects my whole life commitment. That is more fundamental. And that goes back to my religious faith.[3]

Unconvinced that the sensible thing is always the right thing to do, James revisits Hong Kong's peculiar dilemma and his own place in resolving it. Not content with the status quo of partial democracy, he must commit to full democracy in Hong Kong; with the example of Jesus Christ available to him, he must fight the good fight. He introduces a second Chinese language term to describe struggle:

China's democratization movement is a spiritual movement since it widens my understanding of faith. People have different interpretations of what happened in Tiananmen Square. But what is most important is that a group of people could stand up and struggle (*jàngchéui*) for what they believed was true. I will interpret it as a kind of Jesus movement. Jesus stood up and fought for what he believed was true.[4]

Converts like James develop a Christian ritual voice of discontent. They communicate inner transformation by using two distinct terms, *jàngjaat* and *jàngchéui*. As with their conversion accounts, they learn and repeat

[2] Author's interview with James, April 4, 2000.
[3] Author's interview with James, April 4, 2000.
[4] Author's interview with James, April 4, 2000.

struggle, reinforce and alter it. Fueled by disappointment, however, they render these accounts passionately, even painfully.

Pursuant to finding a good religious fit associated with questing, Hong Kong Christians develop struggle as a practical skill and apply it within and beyond the church. For when they as individuals register dissatisfaction with the offerings of the immediate religious community, they take themselves and their devices for judging commitment elsewhere. Moving from the community of the church, which seeks conformity to behavioral standards, converts generalize struggle beyond an exercise of testimony addressing personal weakness within the context of religious community, *jàngjaat* in Cantonese. Within the NGO they rework and rename it *jàngchéui* to underscore commitment to Christ on earth and righteousness in the face of political compromise. Anchored within the individual believer, struggle thus shifts from a strictly internal process of religious commitment inside the church to a process of political activism in an alternative religious affiliation. Carried across Christian institutions in a diverse religious marketplace, struggle actually blurs the line between private and public, two spheres scholars of modern society once assumed to be clearly separate.[5]

Struggle reflects how individual believers, through everyday words and deeds, make religion public. Christians channel what was personal and particular to their social world, or private, into something for general, public impact as they monitor Hong Kong's political future under the People's Republic of China.[6] In expressing struggle from the margins of the political arena, these Christians evidence the existence of civil society from which citizens can participate in the discussion of political, social, economic, and cultural affairs. Taking into the public sphere of contestation and debate their introspective and interrogative experience of struggle, converts shape Hong Kong's democratic future.

Modern Religious Struggle

Hong Kong Christians practice struggle as a project of self-discipline. How do they link struggle to Christian religious life? Where do they go

---

[5] Jose Casanova, *Public Religions in the Modern World* (Chicago: University of Chicago Press, 1994), 7.

[6] Thomas Luckmann, *The Invisible Religion* (New York: Macmillan, 1967); Adam B. Seligman, "Between Public and Private: Towards a Sociology of Civil Society," in *Democratic Civility*, ed. Robert W. Hefner (New Brunswick, N.J.: Transaction Publishers, 1998).

as individual believers compelled by struggle? The minority of religious who seek salvation through individual agency enact a process of self-realization associated with modern life. They struggle to achieve consistency in upholding the standards of the faith, as Max Weber remarked upon the ascetic:

> [The ascetic] by virtue of his transcendental self-maceration and struggles, and especially by virtue of his ascetically rationalized conduct within the world, is to be forever involved in all the burdens of created things, confronting insoluble tensions between violence and generosity, between empirical reality and love.[7]

Intent on embodying the ideals of faith, believers confront temptations and challenges throughout their lives that require self-reflection as a gauge of progress. Weber's ascetic regularly encountered tension between normative standards and social reality on two levels: struggle experienced in relation to the personal, internally, and to the external. At the same time a distinct religious community communicated and exercised standards, the surrounding world of less than ideal behavior served as foil. Struggle as introspection dominated the believer's overall religious experience. It enabled the ascetic to progress spiritually. Yet in order to reduce the tension with the world in general, the inner worldly ascetic needed to alter the surrounding world to make it more compatible with the ideals of the religious faith. Personal integration into the faith thus translated into a worldly agenda of wider social change.[8]

In this scenario, the believer actively, voluntarily internalizes control. Striving for piety, the person initiates introspection and so becomes an agent of change. But the perspective disregards how individuals perform struggle in public view and how church leadership and laity involve

---

[7] Max Weber, *The Sociology of Religion*, trans. Ephraim Fischoff (Boston: Beacon Press, 1963), 171.

[8] Among those relating Weber's work on religion to action in the public sphere, see John A. Hannigan, "Social Movement Theory and the Sociology of Religion: Towards a New Synthesis," *Sociological Analysis* 52, no. 4 (1991): 311–31, which cites N. Birnbaum and Gertrud Lenzer, *Sociology and Religion* (Englewood Cliffs, N.J.: Prentice-Hall, 1969), 15. Also, see Mayer Zald and John D. McCarthy, "Religious Groups as Crucibles of Social Movements," in *Sacred Companies: Organizational Aspects of Religion and Religious Aspects of Organizations*, ed. N. J. Demerath III, Peter Dobkin Hall, Terry Schmitt, and Rhys H. Williams (Oxford: Oxford University Press, 1998).

themselves in this exercise of control via self-reflection.[9] Yet across the history of organized religion, especially medieval Catholicism, power imposes rather than simply encourages self-reflexivity.[10] As Michel Foucault writes, individuals engage in confession, a ritual of words "in which the expression alone produces intrinsic modifications in the person who articulates it: it exonerates, redeems, purifies, unburdens, liberates, promises salvation."[11] Confession reaffirms the tie between individual and religion as the church exercises its power of forgiveness. Following guidelines and responding to prompting, the confessor expresses publicly his personal actions, feelings, and thoughts to a spiritual authority who, in turn, offers judgment and blessing. Along with his preoccupation with prohibited acts, the confessor communicates a strong element of struggle as introspection. Admittedly, it is a disciplining introspection periodically administered, carefully monitored, occasionally fabricated.

The modern state expands this practice of self-disclosure. Together with priests, new authorities such as therapists, doctors, and law enforcers help monitor people's attitudes and behavior. The Chinese Communist Party, from its days of experimentation at Yan'an to the present, offers an excellent contemporary example to rival the reach of the

---

[9] Weber's discussion of asceticism describes the individual's experience. By contrast, his treatment of sects (Max Weber, "The Protestant Sects and the Spirit of Capitalism," in *From Max Weber: Essays in Sociology*, ed. and trans. Hans Gerth and C. Wright Mills [New York: Oxford University Press, 1946]) touches on the dynamics of group scrutiny, especially prior to membership. Yet neither account offers a description of organized group dynamics functioning to pressure members to consistently uphold the behavioral standards of the faith. Sacvan Bercovitch's *The American Jeremiad* (Madison: University of Wisconsin Press, 1978) provides evidence of such pressure in Puritan America's rhetorical culture, specifically the jeremiad, while Susan Friend Harding's *The Book of Jerry Falwell: Fundamentalist Language and Politics* (Princeton: Princeton University Press, 2000) updates the lesson on the classic Puritan jeremiad through study of sermons by the Moral Majority.

[10] While all the time underscoring the potency of this power play, Foucault suggested the internalization of the self-disciplining process. He referred to both the "arts of existence" and the "techniques of the self" as the voluntary actions whereby humans pursued behavioral ideals and consistency, guidelines by which to achieve a change in their "singular being." Yet, while having roots going back to Greek culture, such individual exercises, Foucault argued, lost much of their weight once the ideals behind them were appropriated by early Christianity. Michel Foucault, *The History of Sexuality*, vol. 2, *The Use of Pleasure* (New York: Random House, 1985), 10–11.

[11] Michel Foucault, *The History of Sexuality*, vol. 1, *An Introduction* (New York: Random House, 1978), 62.

medieval Catholic Church.[12] To foster the individual's conformity to the communist party state, it maintains a vast system of surveillance, struggle, and confession. People's Armed Police, neighborhood commit-tees, peers organized into small groups (in Mandarin, *xiǎozǔ*), family members, individuals themselves, and most recently Internet police and closed-circuit TV cameras check and correct the political commitment of China's citizenry, whether party officials, intellectuals, workers, peas-ants, soldiers, or capitalists.

Hong Kong's own experience of struggle, though contemporaneous with the often violent struggle sessions and self-criticisms on the Chi-nese mainland, stands apart from practices instituted there.[13] Following Hong Kong Christians as novices, with the fervor of ascetics, and as NGO members, with the disciplining introspection of confessors, we can trace a discrete ritual of introspection. Performed primarily to unite the believer with God rather than with the nation, this religious practice only gradually encompasses the nonreligious spheres of believers' lives. In the context of Hong Kong's political transition to Chinese sovereignty, yielding conflicts with both church and state, we see how the individual who converts to Christianity becomes a convert to civil society.

CONVERSION AND THE DEMAND TO STRUGGLE

Whether couched in terms of self-transformation, self-constitution, or the reflexive project of the self, individual efforts around identity today are products of individual choice.[14] Under the conditions of economic

---

[12] See Mark Selden, *The Yenan Way in Revolutionary China* (Cambridge, Mass.: Harvard University Press, 1971); Lida V. Nedilsky, "Loneliness and the Re-socialization of Intellectuals in the First Decade of Post-liberation China" (mas-ter's thesis, University of California, Berkeley, 1994); Orville Schell, "The Re-emer-gence of the Realm of the Private in China," in *The Broken Mirror: China After Tiananmen*, ed. George Hicks (Essex: Longman, 1990); Michael Dutton, *Polic-ing Chinese Politics* (Durham, N.C.: Duke University Press, 2005). Even in Hong Kong, absolution is a personal as well as a collective compulsion, as evidenced by requests every June 4 to reverse the counterrevolutionary and thus criminal verdict on Tiananmen Square demonstrators (*pihngfáan luhksei*).

[13] For a rare account of one mainland intellectual's struggle, including its reli-gious qualities, see Geremie Barmé, "Confession, Redemption, and Death: Liu Xiaobo and the Protest Movement of 1989," in *The Broken Mirror: China After Tiananmen*, ed. George Hicks (Essex: Longman, 1990).

[14] See, respectively, Robert N. Bellah, *Beyond Belief: Essays on Religion in a Post-traditional World* (New York: Harper & Row, 1972); Talal Asad, *Geneologies*

and political development as well as integration, individuals in Hong Kong, Asia, and elsewhere throughout the world face weakened claims on their affiliations and a widened array of options for personal development. Individuals strive to construct and manage a coherent account of who they are, something they can no longer take for granted.

New religious identity especially demands such reflection, combining as it does the modern imperative of choice with the modern mission of improvement. Accounts of conversion, as established in the previous chapter, can almost be "defined in terms of their peculiarly self-reflexive nature in so far as they draw attention to the claimed significance of . . . transition in self-identity, consciousness, value-commitments, etc."[15] In Hong Kong, the experience of introspective struggle revolves around challenges common to many Christian converts there. These challenges occur daily because the majority of Hong Kong people are not themselves Christian. Among Hong Kong converts to Christianity, accounts of struggle also serve to indicate commitment and gauge progress on the way to personal transformation.

In becoming Christian in Hong Kong, believers select an association that offers a new framework through which to interpret and experience life.[16] This framework also requires them to be culturally distinct from the non-Christian society at large. Challenges abound in such a context. Peculiar time commitments and ritual demands of Christian community strain relationships with non-Christian family and friends. Worldly claims like materialism, consumerism, and pursuit of economic interest require management. In combination, the context in which Christians exist and the status most hold as neophytes compel Christians to monitor individual progress in living up to prescribed standards. Whether Pentecostals or Catholics, new believers juggle aspirations to live up to the principles of Christianity and commitments to serve family and society.

---

of Religion: Discipline and Reasons of Power in Christianity and Islam (Baltimore: Johns Hopkins University Press, 1993); and Anthony Giddens, Modernity and Self-Identity: Self and Society in the Late Modern Age (Stanford: Stanford University Press, 1991).

[15] James Beckford, "Talking of Apostasy, or Telling Tales and 'Telling' Tales," in Accounts and Action, ed. G. Nigel Gilbert and Peter Abell (Hampshire, U.K.: Gower, 1983), 83.

[16] Peter L. Berger and Thomas Luckmann, The Social Construction of Reality (Garden City, N.Y.: Anchor Books, 1967), 157.

Invited by his church to lead a mission effort in mainland China, Dennis, a young Protestant fundamentalist, articulates this Weberian struggle over religious and social commitment. Although unaffiliated with Hong Kong's NGOs, Dennis nonetheless produces the language of struggle popular among converts striving to demonstrate their faith. While keen to fulfill expectations and act as faithful disciple of Jesus Christ, he wavers on the eve of his church's deadline for a decision.

> When I was studying the Bible, I saw God's mission. He wants everyone to be saved. I know China needs someone to meet the people's spiritual needs, but I do not know if it is God's plan for me to go to China right now. Questioning if this is God's real plan for me is a struggle in my heart, just like a spiritual war. Am I willing to give up everything to follow God's plan? This is my struggle.[17]

Questioning his own calling, this young believer fights to decide his future on a demanding and possibly dangerous path. He believes that personal inhibitions should not stand in the way of God's will, and that the Bible communicates to him God's will. Yet Dennis vacillates. Even if the ultimate decision to act rests solely with himself and God, he openly interrogates himself and reveals to me his psychological dilemma.

Reverend Gwong, too, employs the concept of struggle when she shares her account of realizing God's plan for her to work as a missionary and in the ministry. An invitation from a missionary society to leave her job at an all-girls' school in Hong Kong for a post in London prompted the young teacher decades ago to reconsider her place and her purpose as a committed Christian.

LVN: What do you mean by struggle?

Gwong: Pardon?

LVN: You say struggle. What does that involve?

Gwong: Struggle inside, because I couldn't decide whether or not to go. Not knowing what lies ahead, you wonder, "Is this the step to take?"

LVN: And the decision is made how? By rationally weighing the benefits and costs?

---

[17] Author's interview with Dennis, September 7, 1997. The struggle to decide compares to the process of Jesus surrendering himself to his destiny as martyr. In the garden of Gethsemane the night before his capture, Jesus called upon God when he could not act with certainty. In choosing to surrender, he became the Savior; he left his fate to God's will.

Gwong: I made two long lists. My reasons for accepting included that being a product of the missionary society I wanted to do something in return; and they thought I could do it, so that was another very good reason. But I had a long list of reasons why I should object, including my love for the school, and my love for the students. Having made those two lists, I sent them to the people I admired, the people I respected, asking them to comment. The result was that I should go ahead. In looking back it was really a big step. I always think it was a bit like when Jesus asked Peter to step out from the boat, into the water. You really take that leap of faith; and you find you can actually stand on water![18]

In similar fashion, James, whose remarks begin this chapter, testifies to his personal struggle over the implications of Catholic teachings. His religion teaches him to avoid the stability that ordinary people seek, and that the government espouses through its slogan of stability and prosperity (*wándihng fàahnwìhng*). As he discloses,

I ask myself, "Should I stay in such a stable working environment for the rest of my life?" My religious faith presents me with a challenge to be in a less stable environment. Well, that is my understanding. But in the past three years I have been living a very stable life. Stability can do more harm than good. Yes, that is my experience. A stable lifestyle will make you think less about society, and become less sensitive to other things.[19]

As a conscientious Catholic, James appears ready to reject a complacent lifestyle in order to remain sympathetic to the sufferings of the poor. Yet, as unemployment in Hong Kong rises, he continues in his well-paying, middle-class job.

While the private, interrogative model of self-reflection is common, introspection takes other forms as well. Paul, another Catholic, describes a decentralized form of sharing and decision making: discernment. As a member of a Christian Life Community (CLC), he practices Ignatian spirituality.[20] When contemplating the possibility of volunteering for a

[18] Author's interview with Reverend Gwong, April 14, 2000.
[19] Author's interview with James, April 4, 2000.
[20] The central concern in Ignatian spirituality, as Jesuits explain, is finding God in all things. Practitioners of Ignatian spirituality contemplate everyday life in order to identify, or discern, and then respond to God's demands. They ask themselves, What have I done for Christ? What am I doing for Christ? What will I do for Christ? This exercise of questioning and responding through action is the primary purpose and

Catholic NGO whose reputation could jeopardize his professional aspirations, he prayed with other Catholics for guidance.

> Most of our members have done the thirty-day retreat of St. Ignatius of
> Loyola, the founder of the Jesuits. He had spiritual exercises for people to
> reflect on what they did in their daily life, and to repent. We must discern
> in our daily lives and trust in the Lord. We have to pray, and also we have
> to share with our spiritual guide.
>
> I discerned when I joined the Diocese Commission, and I continue
> discerning in my CLC group. I learned from a priest that the Diocese Com-
> mission had been labeled a protest group against the government, or even
> against China, for its support of China's 1989 prodemocracy movement.
> And so I was afraid that my future, my work prospects would be affected
> by my involvement.[21]

Neither relegated to a private questioning within the mind or heart
of the individual nor limited to the domain of confession between individual and religious authority, struggle takes place both on the individual, intellectual level and within the community of believers. In the
case of present-day Catholicism, as with Protestantism, clergy no longer
interpret God's will exclusively through their mediation. Increasingly,
individuals assess and groups reveal God's will in the context of prayer
and discussion. Pastoral power, if it maintains any significance to the
individual, relocates to a sphere of lay leaders and equals.

The exercise of self-reflexivity starts out as a process at once personal and communal. From this starting point the convert directs it outward; the experience of self-reflexivity with struggle moves further away
from an exercise overseen by authoritative judges to one participated in
jointly among friends. These features continue to play off one another as
struggle eventually transcends church boundaries to include the sphere
of government and society. This is the first of several iterations the experience of struggle as introspection and struggle as self-discipline undergoes within the Hong Kong context to move toward a reconversion: a
personal conversion to civil society.

---

characteristic instrument of CLC, modeled on the life communities of Jesuit priests.
See "Ignatian Spirituality," Jesuits' website, http://www.jesuit.org/Spirituality.
    [21] Author's interview with Paul, April 11, 2000.

GAUGING STANDARDS OF FAITH

Sometimes individual believers struggle to relate their Christian faith to the rather complacent church community. Since the time of Hong Kong's industrialization and economic development, fault lines have appeared between individual Christians and the institutional church that grew to serve the poor. Testimonies of Hong Kong Christians engaged in social concern express a strong sense of disappointment. Churches' emphasis can be too much on personal development, so that the spiritual form of social service needs a boost. Or their emphasis can be too much on the administration of social services, so that social concern needs a boost. One example comes from two future pastors at a Pentecostal Bible college near the new town of Tai Wai, who communicate dissatisfaction with a church-centered approach to fulfilling God's will. Certainly for them, spreading the gospel is a central concern because, in the words of Krista, "within the gospel Jesus said there is love, there is eternal life, there is fullness in life."[22] But involvement in society is neglected by churches and believers alike because, as Simon puts it, "for us Hong Kong Christians participating in society is not primary."[23]

Krista and Simon feel themselves to be in a distinct minority. It is easy to focus on personal growth, Bible study, and church attendance, yet, as they reflect, it does not enable them to fulfill the true wish of Jesus to connect with society, to touch others. Seeking a clearer understanding of social issues and social change so they can help facilitate needed social transformation in Hong Kong, Krista and Simon have enrolled in courses at one NGO and experimented with new methods of pastoral care. By conducting work within society, they hope to identify some aspects for social change. But looking beyond their church's example sparks dissonance. They feel conflict over what roles they imagine for themselves. (Krista, for instance, once aspired to be a Christian barrister advocating on behalf of the poor.) Yet, as their church evidences change, Krista and Simon gain confidence that their particular vision of Christian work will be compatible with their Pentecostal faith. Simon offers an example:

> Now we are conducting more activities outside the church to approach society. For instance, for the April 4 public holiday [Easter] we held an

---

[22] Author's interview with Krista, April 12, 2000.
[23] Author's interview with Simon, April 12, 2000.

open day in an auditorium, performing dramas and songs about Jesus. We had many people there. Families could stay to eat food. It was a very good family day. For the elderly we had additional activities outside the church. But the purpose was to let them see the love of Jesus. It seems our church is growing more open to the public and the society.[24]

A more stubborn disappointment lurks: the sense that in Hong Kong, churches' willingness to connect with society presents a deeper problem. As Simon relayed a couple of years later, this struggle about the priorities of the churches seems harder to resolve in an evangelically oriented religious milieu. On one hand, even if evangelism is a fundamental step in becoming a Christian and being saved, evangelizing through social engagement places too much emphasis on empty, self-serving, numeric goals. On the other hand, evangelizing through administration of schools and hospitals emphasizes the maintenance of the kingdom of social services. This paradigm of evangelizing appeals to such an extent, Simon explains, that even small churches aspire to build their own schools and hospitals, investing whatever they have in such projects. And when the question becomes how best to maintain the daily operations of the social service agency or how to provide more hospitals or to build better schools, then the church has forgotten its basic reason for being.

> Focused on that project they grow completely ignorant of what is happening in society. But if you do not know what is happening outside, then how can you tell church members to be more concerned or to be more understanding? If you do not know what is going on, then how can you push members to help others?
>
> I struggle because it is *my* problem. Is it that *my* interpretation is this way? Or is it that the majority of interpretations are this way? Actually, in a modern society one ought to take responsibility to answer what kind of Christian one ought to be.[25]

The believer, with Simon being just one articulate example, begins to question whether this conflict over priority is simply a personal problem of the individual or a structural problem of the churches. While self-reflection and personal struggle might underscore personal weakness, the critical gaze looks beyond the individual's assessment of personal

---

[24] Author's interview with Simon, April 12, 2000.
[25] Author's interview with Simon, April 12, 2000.

conviction or individual resolve. It turns on the community of believers as well.

Seen from this perspective, individual struggle comes to mean not failure on the part of the believer to realize the standards of faith, but instead disjuncture between the individual believer concerned with proper Christian behavior and those members within the church who apparently lack such concern. Where communal sharing might be considered the first iteration of struggle, a second iteration yields a more encompassing self-reflexivity among Hong Kong Christians. Struggle emerges as individual Christians notice a considerable gap between biblical teachings on justice and lack of activism for justice within the church.

Political change, anticipated since the 1984 signing of the Joint Declaration between Britain and the People's Republic of China, illuminates how even the faithful get mired in earthly concerns. A good example is the story of Harriet, an NGO worker who converted to Protestantism shortly after returning from graduate studies in Britain. Harriet initially settled into a large Baptist church in Kowloon but later found her pastor's sermons unnerving. Whereas she felt concerned about democracy after Hong Kong's return to China in 1997, her pastor appeared quick to compromise. In late summer 1997, Harriet commented,

> Well before the Handover—I think it was in 1996—my pastor said, "Democracy is not a perfect model of politics. But it is a comparatively better one." But when the days came near to the Handover, he said, "Democracy is not a good model. It is not that good at all, because you can tell from many westernized countries."
>
> And before the Handover he would say, "Should we obey the government? We should decide from how it treats the people." But recently he asked us to be more obedient of the government. I think it's horrible. How can a person change his mind so soon, in only one or two years?[26]

Formerly convinced of her pastor's rectitude, Harriet quickly shifted into utter disappointment at his seeming lack of integrity in the midst of political uncertainty.

Not simply a problem of individual clergy incapable of serving as a moral compass in a fast-changing society, the clergy as a group and church as a community fail to inspire individual believers. Noah presents a complicated account of expectation, frustration, and reconciliation:

---

[26] Author's interview with Harriet, August 13, 1997.

In 1988 I had already found the Anglican Church, but I only decided to continue in it in 1989, especially after the Tiananmen Square Incident. On the morning after June 4 I was very unhappy, so I went to the Pentecostal church of my youth. On that day, prefacing his sermon the minister said, "Everyone knows what happened last night. I know that I should have some response to this issue. But I cannot say anything because I do not know how to respond. What I can do is read my message prepared several days ago."

At that moment I felt very disappointed. I could not accept that the church was unable to respond to so significant an event. I guess it confirmed to me that the majority of Hong Kong's evangelical churches have problems in their interpretation of belief (seunyéuhng). Because they are too individualistic, too church centered, their world, their life is very small—limited within the sacred walls.[27]

For Christians coping with a future shrouded in doubt and political pragmatism, the failure of clergy members to address complex concerns about political life in Hong Kong exposes the institutional failure of the church. As Catholic convert Rachel vents,

I'm sick of the priests. When they preach, they never talk about society, they never tell people what the real world is; they always tell you to pray to Mary, or they say something very remote. I think that if Jesus Christ is so far away from us why should I follow him? Does he only exist in the church? I mean, in that church?[28]

In a time of political change and uncertainty, many believers find it intolerable that their church deems political reflection taboo. They ask themselves, what can and should one do as a Christian?

Struggling for an Alternative

Having learned within the church community to show commitment to faith, Christians seek the church's instruction when political and social crises challenge the moral standards of the faith community. But when the churches fail to offer the expected guidance, members look elsewhere for answers. In the case of Hong Kong Christians, disappointment leads them to conclude that the struggle for fulfilling moral standards of Christianity is a struggle with the church, not with the self. To resolve this conflict between church affiliation and individual identity, believers

[27] Author's interview with Noah, April 26, 2000.
[28] Author's interview with Rachel, August 19, 1997.

develop through the NGO an alternative way of experiencing Christianity, as evidenced by their responses to the prodemocracy movement centered in Beijing and subsequent government crackdown in China's Tiananmen Square on June 4, 1989.

The weeks leading up to the Tiananmen Square crackdown, referred to by Chinese people simply as June 4 (*luhksei*), captured the imagination of Hong Kong's citizenry. In Beijing and other major Chinese cities, students demanded change to the closed and corrupt political system in the time-honored fashion of young patriots before them. In Hong Kong over one million people took to the streets both before and after the crackdown as an expression of their solidarity with the Tiananmen Square demonstrators.[29] Their fundraising efforts provided demonstrators in Beijing with tents, cash, and other resources to sustain their occupation of Tiananmen Square, even after many students grew restive and sought a return to their campuses.[30] The prodemocracy movement, as many Christians experienced it, offered hope that the Chinese and Hong Kong people would realize their dream of political empowerment together. This common aspiration was embodied in the Goddess of Democracy, a statue unveiled May 30, 1989, in Tiananmen Square, reproductions of which appeared everywhere in Hong Kong thereafter. Featured in all sizes, the goddess occupied prominent places in Hong Kong peoples' homes, on university campus walls, and on conference tables. It was as familiar and powerful an icon of June 4 for Hong Kong people as was the solitary man barring the way of a tank on the Avenue of Eternal Peace for Americans.

But Beijing's prodemocracy movement ended in the forced evacuation of the square by the People's Liberation Army and harsh enforcement of martial law. With blood spilled in the capital of Hong Kong's future sovereign, Hong Kong's own democratization process now gained an urgency and immediacy before unknown. Whatever verdict the authorities passed on democracy in China was of direct significance to people in the British colony. Gauging the impact of June 4 on Hong Kong, one

[29] Wong Pik-Wan, "The Pro-Chinese Democracy Movement in Hong Kong," in *The Dynamics of Social Movement in Hong Kong*, ed. Stephen Chiu Wing-Kai and Lui Tai-Lok (Hong Kong: Hong Kong University Press, 2000), 66.

[30] See Philip Cunningham, *Tiananmen Moon* (Lanham, Md.: Rowman & Littlefield, 2009), 219; and Jimmy Ngai Siu-Yan, "Tiananmen Days," in *New Ghosts, Old Dreams: Chinese Rebel Voices*, ed. Geremie Barmé and Linda Jaivin (New York: Times Books, 1992).

local social scientist remarked on the sharp rise in emigration, "When Hong Kong people who desire democracy and freedom seek them in the U.S., Canada and Australia, the prospects for democracy and freedom in the territory cannot be bright."[31]

Although it prompted the emigration of Hong Kong businessmen and professionals, the violent suppression of demonstrators and sympathetic citizens in Beijing actually fuelled further commitment to democracy in Hong Kong. Among those who stayed were Christians whose personal religious commitment heightened their sensitivity toward the issue of political development. In response to June 4, these Hong Kong Christians turned to their clergy to start the healing process, to pass judgment, and to act out their conscience. But many church leaders failed to satisfy the moral and spiritual concerns of their flocks. The prodemocracy movement in Beijing gave rise to popular calls for democracy, freedom, and justice in Hong Kong during the 1990s just when Hong Kong anticipated political reunion with China. As Mrs. Mou, a Catholic and a housewife, explained her inspiration to participate in shaping Hong Kong's own political future, "It is about struggling for democracy (*jàngchéui màhnjyú*), struggling for freedom (*jàngchéui jihyàuh*), struggling for the rule of law in society (*jàngchéui séhwúi faatjih*). It is different from actions like visiting the elderly."[32] In striving for righteousness, a sense of justice, she fed her critical awareness. As her own voice for action was met with stony silence, Mrs. Mou's criticism turned to the clergy and other faithful who were indifferent to political and social issues:

> And towards the church, the Catholic community, and the priests, also, I have experienced disappointment. I feel they do not care about society. Yes, even the priests. They say that they care; but if you want the church to help, to teach about the social movements in Hong Kong, for example, oftentimes they are not okay with that.[33]

Such political apathy frustrated not only Catholics but members in the evangelical Christian community, too.

---

[31] Joseph Y. S. Cheng, "Prospects for Democracy in Hong Kong," in *The Broken Mirror: China After Tiananmen*, ed. George Hicks (Essex: Longman, 1990), 293.

[32] Author's interview with Mrs. Mou, April 13, 2000.

[33] Author's interview with Mrs. Mou, April 13, 2000.

In the case of Benedict, a politically concerned man with social work experience, membership in an evangelical church failed to bring the social solidarity he sought. When fellow church members refused to engage him in discussing political and social concerns, Benedict thought something must be wrong with him. Maybe the man he was and the man he was expected to be as a Christian did not match:

> At first I did not realize I had had to sacrifice my past history to be a Christian. I tried to mold myself into a new way of life, a new way of being. But something deep in my heart said to me, "No, you cannot live like this anymore." So I fled once, then fled for a second time, because I could not blend my lives from before I was a Christian with my life after I became a Christian. That was really a painful struggle for me.[34]

Benedict's journey eventually led him into an alternative community of Christians, an NGO.

In response to Hong Kong's political, spiritual, and social uncertainties, renegade church leaders and educated Christians founded their own faith-based NGOs in the decade before Hong Kong's return to Chinese sovereignty. As with church-run public schools and social service agencies in Hong Kong, these NGOs filled a place within the organizing structure of the city to deal with problems the government was itself unable or unwilling to address. Inspired by efforts to generate a Hong Kong theology specific to the challenges of life in this global city, these new NGOs addressed political change. Today they conduct courses, produce literature and educational materials, organize gatherings and discussions, and offer jobs to educated people with middle-class ambitions but religious demands. Within such a distinct space, Benedict resolved, if only for a time, the divide between his past and present selves.

> To do something—not to act as a witness so that someone may come to believe in this faith, but to be true to yourself, to secure your own integrity. Because you cannot witness all that suffering without being moved and without trying to do something, and still say you are a follower of Christ.[35]

Benedict developed a new understanding of what it meant to be a Christian.

---

[34] Author's interview with Benedict, August 15, 1997.
[35] Author's interview with Benedict, August 15, 1997.

Wilson, another evangelical Christian employed at the same NGO, saw the Chinese prodemocracy movement of 1989 as a good example of well-intentioned souls striving for justice only to be brought down unjustly. Along with many others, he asked what he should do as a Christian in response to the June 4 tragedy. Although Wilson's evangelical church provided a forum for discussion shortly after the military crackdown, it focused on evangelization when the real issue at hand was social justice. Wilson commented more passionately on his break with his church than on his break with his pre-Christian life:

> And the sermon, oh! I was getting tired of it. Getting *sick*! Because of my church's viewpoint on June 4, on the democratic movement, I changed to another church. The passion then, the churches' focus in Hong Kong, was so much on the students there in Tiananmen Square. But I do not know whether the churches got the point.
>
> There were many prayer meetings, and many of them were for justice, for the safety of the students, and, from an evangelical point of view, for conversion. That means, "Please let them know Jesus Christ!" "Let China become a Christian country!" Such requests may have been on the lower order of the prayer item, but actually they were the priority, and last, but not least, was evangelism for the students.[36]

Recognizing among its members an intense concern for the well-being of the students in Tiananmen Square, his church organized prayer meetings, too. With the church's understanding of well-being married to the Christian concept of salvation through conversion, however, the common ground among its members gave way. One small group approached the pastor to discuss this point. As Wilson recounts,

> We told him, "We do not see much concern from the church. We only see that you are concerned about evangelism. Everything is evangelism." He explained to us, "Okay. There is not much we can do. We do not have many resources. Our efforts should concentrate on evangelism."[37]

The fact that his church lacked a sophisticated understanding of social sentiment pushed this self-reflexive believer to the very edge of his chosen community. Even with attention to issues of justice, moreover, the evangelical interpretation of justice was problematic. With no hope of resolution within his church, Wilson eventually fought to distance

[36] Author's interview with Wilson, August 6, 1998.
[37] Author's interview with Wilson, August 6, 1998.

himself from his evangelical past. He rejected the fundamental under-pinnings of his original belief system. Instead, Wilson went on to study theology. He became a liberal Christian and met people with concerns similar to his own through his work at a faith-based NGO. Yet the language of the evangelical lingers alongside a new vocabulary of faith:

> When [evangelicals] say justice or righteousness, they stress the personal dimension; God is just, and man is unjust, and we have become righteous because of the salvation of Jesus. Justice or righteousness has become a personal issue: not a social one or a collective one. So the first thing is to believe in Christ, to become a Christian.
>
> It may be logical, but that does not mean it is true, or that it represents the whole picture. And I was at the stage that I changed my evangelical thinking. I struggled for a more open-minded or so-called liberal Christianity.[38]

These examples reveal a more subtle impact of Tiananmen Square on Hong Kong than the motivation of demonstrators or émigrés documented by local scholars. The examples show the idea of struggle emerging from a formidable disjuncture between the church's teachings and the believer's perception of what should be the priority within the faith. Conscientious believers, both in the context of the 1989 prodemocracy movement and today's partial democratization of Hong Kong, condemn the church's failure to act on issues of social justice so pressing in their lives. But not all believers experiencing this level of struggle leave their churches. Some believers search for an alternative form of Christianity. Liberal-minded Catholics, for instance, draw upon the Latin American model of base communities, worshipping at home with a sympathetic priest. Some stay with their church in order to influence others and teach a more socially oriented form of Christianity. And some seek an outlet outside the institutional church. Against this background, the most entrepreneurial and educated people from among the churches established Christian NGOs in the 1980s. There they harnessed the highly personalized experience of struggle (*jàngjaat*) for the purpose of social action or public struggle (*jàngchéui*), propelling Christians in their movement into the space of civil society.

---

[38] Author's interview with Wilson, August 6, 1998.

Voicing Out for Social Change

Christians seeking to demonstrate their commitment have created a moral platform from which to engage in the popular struggle for democracy and justice in Hong Kong. By contributing their own voices to those of the disempowered, they offer a distinct critique of the established political, social, and economic order. They also actively participate in the annual June 4 commemorative demonstration through Central, Hong Kong and candlelight vigil in Victoria Park. Their actions merge dissenting voices in a single public protest against both the communist authorities in Beijing and the Hong Kong government.

From these movements emerges a minority voice that underscores the political and social commitment of Christian activists. We return to James, who remarks, "Student movements have changed people's lives, changed their life commitment. The most significant thing I have experienced is June 4. Some interpret June 4 as a religious movement."[39] For him, the movement for democracy that ended in bloodshed was a kind of Jesus movement, the reason why he still joins June 4 commemoration activities every year. James's interpretation of the original prodemocracy movement suggests a blurring between the boundaries of individual and shared interpretation. It also blurs the distinction between a social movement and a religious one. By linking Jesus Christ's efforts to those of the protesters in Beijing, James transcends the boundary between sacred and profane and develops a spiritual interpretation of a political event. His continued participation in the annual commemoration of June 4 thus represents his commitment to the Christian faith. It also entrenches his struggle with his church, because his actions express the view that, in the example of Jesus Christ, Hong Kong's churches should provide a platform for people to engage in political and social debates.

What James's account does not do is replicate or credit China's distinct experience of protest. Curiously, no one I interviewed in Hong Kong singled out any student leader or intellectual in the Tiananmen Square prodemocracy movement as relevant in his or her interpretation of the event. But then Christians set up their own faith-based alternative to the Hong Kong Alliance in Support of Patriotic Democratic Movements in China, the local organization channeling funds, equipment, and rhetoric to boost student efforts in Beijing. Individual Christians

[39] Author's interview with James, April 4, 2000.

emphasized the personal nature of religious struggle and the religious import of China's general struggle for democracy as they formed the Hong Kong Christian Patriotic Democratic Movement. Much as Hong Kong Christians realized (both comprehended *and* achieved) a cultural gap between themselves and their parents, they realized a cultural gap between themselves and their mainland Chinese counterparts. Turning to the operation of the faith-based NGOs, we achieve a better understanding of the particular cultural imprint of Christianity on Hong Kong people and the reinstitutionalization of individual struggle there.

Among faith-based NGOs, the private introspection fostered within a communal setting undergoes a third iteration. Through the action of voicing out (*chēutsèng*), individuals' struggle for religious commitment and justice becomes public in both the communal and the political sense. Several aspects of the NGO experience contribute to this transformation. First, the NGO communities validate and reinforce the personal struggles of their members. As the NGO worker Benedict states, "I started to see a ray of hope because there seemed to be an alternative way of being a Christian: one that might allow me to be the person I am, not negate my past twenty-something years of experience."[40] For Krista, with her complexity as a Pentecostal willing to try more than one way to open people's hearts to the loving power of Jesus, the NGO offers more occasional support:

> Frankly, I believe in the influence of the Holy Spirit more than in the influence of human beings. If we depend only on human works, then these efforts will not amount to anything. I use revival rather than argument with the government. But sometimes Christians need to witness what is right: to face society, face the people. We need to know how to help them. This means not only sharing the gospel but also helping them in other ways, too.[41]

This reinforcement of diversity takes place when individuals concerned about Hong Kong's future come together as voluntary members of Christian NGOs. There they discuss a wide range of social and political issues with their peers, publicize their viewpoints, and realize they are neither alone nor uniform in their actions.

---

[40] Author's interview with Benedict, August 15, 1997.
[41] Author's interview with Krista, June 6, 2001.

Second, when they participate in Christian NGOs they acquire a new identity as socially concerned Christians. They are not simply Sunday Christians but true (*janjingdīk*) Christians. As Faith, one independent evangelical who has continued to participate actively in her church, described the NGO where she works,

> In Hong Kong's churches, there is no one to discuss with you Hong Kong society. There is no education for you apart from learning how to love God, how to love your family. As a pupil, as a Christian, one does not know how to face social problems. The reverend, he says, "You come to church to worship God. Do not talk about social issues in church."
>
> My bosses [in the NGO] and I feel that as Christians who have attended church for many years, we understand that being a Christian, being a Hong Kong person, it is impossible *not* to be concerned about those things that are out there. The government's every policy will influence you! So once June 4 happened, organizations came out and people came to know that you cannot just be a Sunday Christian. I quit work [as a kindergarten teacher] and came out to educate more Christians to be concerned about their own society.[42]

Faith's remarks point to a third transformative aspect of the NGO: the strength of mobilization among Christians themselves as they institutionalized their shared struggle. The NGO prompts further self-reflection through internal activities designed to raise political and social consciousness and expand intellectual horizons. As if an extension of their university education, exposure introduces members of NGOs to issues they did not recognize on their own. For example, through courses in feminist theology, both men and women acquire greater consciousness about the pervasive influence of patriarchy within both church and society. In a discussion group on Taiwan's presidential elections and the history of the Presbyterian Church there, they learn that no church represents the interests of society but that each church's agenda responds to particular interests and opportunities. The NGO enlightens individual Christians' struggles and guides Christians in determining what constitutes a legitimate basis for such struggles.

Fourth, the NGO facilitates more struggles to enable Christians to promote their alternative views among fellow believers and citizens. When they stage events to raise public social awareness, Christians voice out the grievances of the marginal sectors of society. When they

[42] Author's interview with Faith, April 11, 2000.

come face to face (or, in the virtual community of the Internet, screen to screen) with detractors, they collectively underscore that sense of struggle. With Hong Kong feeling in 1998 the effects of the Asian economic downturn—whose markets from Thailand to Indonesia crashed on July 2, 1997, the day after Hong Kong's return to Chinese sovereignty—members of the Diocese Commission drew attention to the plight of Filipina helpers in the city. They urged local families, especially Catholics, who share a common faith with people from the Philippines and commonly employ Filipina domestics to clean their homes, cook their meals, and tend to their children, not to ignore employment contracts by firing domestic helpers or slashing their salaries during the recession. Outside the Catholic church in one of Hong Kong's most popular new towns, Diocese Commission members set up an information table to engage the faithful as they exited after Sunday Mass. Rachel recalled one man's challenge to the group's activity: " 'What gives you the right to discuss these matters on the steps of the church? This is a place of worship. I don't want to hear it on my Sunday.' Such a response to our efforts happens all the time."[43]

In fact, voicing out an alternative and critical view outside the space of the NGO itself means staging a situation in which members as a group are almost certain to struggle together. Through the act of voicing out, Christians highlight the moral failures of others. While they may resign themselves to the likelihood of encountering not just indifference but antagonism, Diocese Commission representatives can still be hurt by such a negative response to their critical perspective. The hurtful impression made by this particular confrontation compelled several members, including Rachel and Paul, to recall the incident many months after. But such a test of the group's commitment highlights what individual members share in common as a group.

Voicing out with critical and reflexive thinking in a group context leads to powerful results. On the one hand, the NGO reaps the benefits of the Christian practice of self-reflection. In a fashion similar to that of confession, with prompting from their friends, people articulate frustrations and concerns. Basically, the NGO channels energy generated by the individual's struggle to contest matters it singles out as important. As Joseph, a Christian working for the Democratic Party of Hong Kong, indicates, his work in politics sharpens his gaze on society (although he

---

[43] Author's interview with Rachel, July 18, 1998.

often feels disappointed by his party's myopia). Joseph has to consider policies to help Hong Kong people living in substandard conditions. By changing the structures within society, the poor can find their circumstances improved. By raising awareness about economic, social, and political injustices, the NGO has a special part to play in fixing Hong Kong's problems. As Joseph says,

> Because in Hong Kong churches seldom criticize the government, individual Christians must offer opinions on policies. Perhaps churches don't know what's going on. And if they do know, they won't voice out. So I feel that the NGO has a good method: it will go to voice out, it will criticize.
>
> With the type of work I do [for the Democratic Party], I must also criticize the government's policies. But I help the legislature do it. What I'm saying is that while the work I do enables me, in addition to policy I personally have to be criticizing, too.[44]

While some Christians consistently generate social concern outside the NGO and fuel the NGO fire in this way, other individual believers seeking a resolution with their faith through NGO membership come to seriously challenge themselves. They grow aware of and strive to achieve new ideals of Christianity. Rather than leaving Christianity behind for some alternative, they gain a new voice. With it they challenge other Christians to consider the way Jesus would have them live. Likewise, they challenge non-Christians to support the causes they, as Christians, hold dear. In Wilson's case, this is not activism but honesty:

> I'm not an outspoken person. I will not stand up for everything. Or an issue comes up and I won't be the first to stand up and speak. I am not the person. But on the whole, I agree with what [this NGO] is doing, and the organization's direction as a countercurrent: speaking for the underprivileged people.
>
> It's a minority's voice. But the Bible's prophetic writings are also the minority's [voice]. They tell not of the good news, but of the bad news—and not the journalistic bad news, but from the prophetic viewpoint that we are not in a peaceful way. In Jeremiah there appears "Shalom, shalom, shalom." Actually, there is no shalom. Some false prophet said, "shalom, shalom, shalom," peace, peace, peace. But actually there is no peace. And [this organization] does not want to be a false prophet, to please people saying, "Oh, there is peace!" It will say, "There are problems! There are issues!" Yes.[45]

[44] Author's interview with Joseph, April 8, 2000.
[45] Author's interview with Wilson, August 6, 1998.

In this final iteration, a sense of righteousness imbues struggle. The NGO, by offering the mission of social concern, creates the basis for a variety of activities that legitimate personal struggle in a political context. In that case, believers should not suppress or conquer struggle. Instead they should embrace it as a common experience to be expected and harnessed within a significant minority seeking to behave as true Christians. Hong Kong's NGOs themselves experience struggle. In an annual report to foreign supporters summing up the events of 1997, one Christian NGO described the disappointments of the political transition, including the Provisional Legislative Council's passage of a resolution imposing stricter guidelines on demonstrations, and arrests of demonstrators during Hong Kong's hosting of the World Bank and IMF Conference. What was to be done in response? The NGO, as expressed in its testimonial, concluded the following:

> Encountering such threats to freedom of speech and suppression of the people's movement, the media [has] responded with self-censorship, some NGOs have changed their position strategically to avoid direct confrontation with the government, and the church has become more and more silent. Under such circumstances, [we have been] in a struggle to find our way out. We finally decided to continue to voice out our position against the unfairness and injustice in society, and to stick to what we believe to be true.[46]

Ultimately, struggle expresses commitment itself. Believers communicate it through the public—both shared and political—activity of voicing out.

CONVERSION TO CIVIL SOCIETY

Hong Kong people who convert to Christianity set themselves on the path to a second conversion: conversion to civil society. Enabled with the skill to gauge personal commitment, they continue to gauge and judge. They do not limit struggle to the political contest to redefine, reform, even overturn some general order. Instead, they refer to struggle as the ongoing process of personal conflict within the Christian faith and the indecision that accompanies it (jàngjaat). Their quest to effect change in society through group action (jàngchéui) stems from this internal struggle of the self. While the unique historical context of Hong Kong reverting to Chinese sovereignty after a century and a half under

---

[46] Center for Reflection, annual report, 1997.

British colonial rule inspires self-reflexivity, more than political events prompt it. Christians practice and nurture and ultimately institutionalize struggle in multiple religious communities, including the faith-based NGO.

Self-reflexivity is a disciplining practice long cultivated within church communities as a means of gauging individual moral understanding, righteousness, and commitment. Once cultivated within the particular power dynamics of the church, however, self-reflexivity has over the centuries become generalized. Among individual converts to Christianity in Hong Kong, self-reflexivity and struggle begin in the churches as a gauge of individual progress in religious development. But then they undergo several iterations. Initially, the notion of self-reflexivity develops into a public action when it is shared by members of the same group. Next, the focus of self-reflexivity is redirected to the very source of moral teachings, namely the church community. When self-reflexive Christians are disaffected by the disjuncture between Christian faith and everyday practice in the churches, they turn to faith-based NGOs and search for alternative means of expressing their faith in public. This highly personalized struggle is channeled into wider political and social action. Seen from this perspective, group struggle makes Christians realize their pastors are not necessarily their leaders and the church is not necessarily the model to emulate. Instead, changing circumstances require a refashioning of religious culture, one that frees participants from all kinds of institutional constraints and adds a new dimension to their personal struggle. The public sphere turns out to be a legitimate terrain in the struggle for Christian justice. There a discursive battle takes place, manifesting individuals' genuine commitment to be true Christians.

What can be overlooked simply as an exercise in self-discipline, of personal consciousness development, and of institutionalized social control within certain Christian churches is in fact a testament of faith propelling Christians into the realm of civil society. Here lies a paradox. This fashioning of a vocal and active citizenry first takes place in the church with a lesson in commitment to Christ. It should not be so surprising that it is within the church that we find the exercise of self-reflexivity and judgment. Those people working with Christians, those studying Christians, and even Christians themselves recognize that the establishment of behavioral standards and the mechanisms meant to achieve them fulfill a social control function. Take, for example, non-Christian NGO staffers in Hong Kong who wonder aloud at the overwhelming concern with Christian standards. As Fiona, one such staff member affiliated with a Christian NGO, stated after representing her organization at a church meeting,

> After the meeting, the organizer told me that most church members will find the topic of justice too abstract unless you talk about Christian values. They will say: "If your belief is just justice, it is so vague. Where can I find it in the Bible? Give me concrete rules or concrete words about what I should do or how I should react." They are so concerned about their Christian identity and their Christian community. If you want them to do some good for society—for example, you want them to go to demonstrations or donate money, or work for the welfare of certain groups—they have to do it with Christian values.[47]

Non-Christian employees of NGOs, such as Fiona, see the demand for Christian commitment as an obstacle to Christian involvement in civil society. Scholars, too, criticize evangelicals in particular for a preoccupation with achieving behavioral standards that seems to preclude political participation and general, innerworldly concern.[48] Most importantly, NGO Christians themselves fail to see what commitment has meant in their own lives, having distanced themselves from the past as if nothing good could come of it. Yet, religiously cultivated introspection turns out to be a practice fundamental to participation in debate. The struggle that is grounded within committed believers has evangelical roots. Without their initial pull into the church and break from family, tradition, and other guides to behavior, converts to Christianity would not communicate struggle that liberalizes and converts them a second time.

SPOTLIGHT on Wilson

The Liberated Evangelical Still Struggles

In Hong Kong, religious community cultivates a practice of personal assessment that individual believers in turn apply toward a public, vocal contest. Unlike members of the religious right in the United States,[49]

---

[47] Author's interview with Fiona, August 4, 1997.

[48] One example is Robert D. Putnam, *Bowling Alone: The Collapse and Revival of American Community* (New York: Simon & Schuster, 2000). For an alternative, see Robert Wuthnow, *Christianity in the Twenty-First Century* (Oxford: Oxford University Press, 1993).

[49] See Robert Liebman and Robert Wuthnow, *The New Christian Right: Mobilization and Legitimation* (New York: Aldine Publishing, 1983); Christian Smith, *Christian America? What Evangelicals Really Want* (Berkeley: University of

individual Christians interviewed in this book establish a critical space between themselves and their churches. Current scholarship on evangelicals in the United States, while providing evidence of independent self-expression and diversity of opinion,[50] or documenting practices of deliberation,[51] has moved us a long way from the assumption that evangelicals in America speak with one voice or simply echo the voices of their chosen leaders. Nevertheless, new scholarship has yet to produce accounts of individual struggle with the self in relation to the chosen faith as opposed to someone else's chosen faith, expression of faith, or lack of faith. In fact, Jon A. Shields, in his book *The Democratic Virtues of the Christian Right*, distinguishes between what he describes as the deliberative norms of civility, dialogue, moral reasoning, and nontheological appeals and the deliberative norm of skepticism. While religious leaders may teach the first four, they do not go so far as teach skepticism, because, Shields posits, "advocating such skepticism would undermine the very moral passions that sustain the Christian Right."[52] In Hong Kong, in contrast, conversion points believers outward as it directs them inward. The NGO partially fills and feeds this space of reflection. It becomes an alternative community through which Christians address fellow evangelicals, fellow Catholics, and fellow Hong Kong citizens on issues affecting them all. Voicing out their struggles of commitment as members of an NGO is a step toward widened engagement. After several iterations, struggle itself becomes communal and critical, a voice of debate. Thus, an introspective religious practice gains public relevance.

But the acceptance of a new form of struggle does not reduce the tendency or replace the need for introspective, faith-inspired struggle. As a 2007 interview with Wilson attests, even the seasoned convert to Christianity does not stop struggling with internal conflicts and searching for ways to reconcile them within his chosen religion. Wilson is not an outspoken person, but he has agreed with his NGO's direction, speaking for the underprivileged. He asks rhetorically, "If you cannot affirm one person's sexuality, or disability, or status as a sex worker, how can you affirm his own person in a Christian sense? Why, if God

California Press, 2000); Jon A. Shields, *The Democratic Virtues of the Christian Right* (Princeton: Princeton University Press, 2009).

[50] Smith, *Christian America?*
[51] Shields, *Democratic Virtues.*
[52] Shields, *Democratic Virtues*, 19.

accepts you, for in Romans it says, 'You are accepted,' are certain people not fully accepted? What does it mean to be accepted?"[53] Whereas an evangelical perspective repeatedly failed to provide a way out of this dilemma, Wilson found in the NGO an open environment to think. He left his first two churches because of various disappointments and now attends a third church.

> In the last ten years there have been changes in my life: becoming a property owner of a negative equity, gaining a new, cultural perspective on society and on my Christian faith—one that is more liberating, more socially concerned and active—and enjoying life more.

Denying that the church's burden of social concern ironically brings greater liberation, he continues,

> No, this responsibility comes not from church but from my work. I found it very disappointing at my church, so I left. Although I did not change church membership, I joined another for services. At my evangelical, middle-class church people were very inward looking, concerned with their own children, families. Anyway, I think the first five years [after the Handover] were quite stressful for me with the economic burden, my children being young, and my career requiring much of me, to struggle in my mind. But after that it seemed settled. I began to develop my hobbies. You know I like tea, photography, and movies. Years ago I could not afford to do these things. Now I can.

Then, responding to whether this less stressful life is not the result of stability and prosperity (*wándihng fàahnwìhng*), a government slogan he criticizes, Wilson concludes,

> Yes! Yes! If you, like the government, say Hong Kong should be like that then it is a spell, a mantra. And the mantra makes you ignore people's suffering. We have stability and prosperity at the expense of many underprivileged people! Maybe my stability and prosperity is also at the expense of some people.[54]

After eight years with the NGO, he intends to resign from his full-time position to return to Christian publishing.

The conditions for a civil society, as Wilson's narrative attests, do not go away. After ten years, the language of struggle with the self, struggle

---

[53] Author's interview with Wilson, June 21, 2007.
[54] Author's interview with Wilson, June 21, 2007.

with Hong Kong's system of economy, and struggle with its system of governance directs Wilson's reflections on life. He feels required to voice out, not as a vessel of God,[55] but in order to resolve all these conflicts. As with Christians in their quest to be true, Wilson exercises his skill of self-reflexive struggle readily and unremarkably to populate Hong Kong's public sphere.

[55] Again, Shields's fieldwork helps mark the contrast between evangelicals in the United States and those in Hong Kong. He documents how pro-life students, for example, trained to engage others around the issue of abortion on American university campuses, subdue their individual responsibility and agency. Instead, they submit to the will and grace of God, even in debate, as Crystal communicates: "I trusted that if I opened my mouth, God would fill it just with what was needed. He is faithful and can glorify Himself, even through the weakest vessels." Likewise, as Elaine stated, "In many ways it is a relief because we do not really have to do anything but be willing, and the Lord is faithful to do the rest. When I opened myself up to be a vessel, the Lord gave me words, direction, and wisdom." Shields, *Democratic Virtues*, 75.

— 4 —

The Work of Civil Society

NGO worker engaging the media and passersby following rally at Star Ferry Pier, Tsim Sha Tsui (photograph by Lida V. Nedilsky, 1998)

As individuals, Hong Kong Christians move physically and socially from school to fellowship to church and beyond; looking for the right way to show their personal faithfulness to Christianity, they establish a general experience of religious life in Hong Kong. Taken in aggregate, these individuals demonstrate that religious membership is fluid, shifting, and developmental. Yes, there are those countless among Hong Kong's Christians for whom total disengagement is part of their fluidity. They join a fellowship or church only to drop out entirely, losing interest in or finding no time for collective, religious life. For others inspired by commitment to a chosen rather than an inherited religion, those who are the focus of this book, fluidity might mean breaking with one collective only to seek a new mode of expression to satisfy the need for deeper religious understanding and personal alignment.

Where do they turn for help? Finding guidance in one's quest for spiritual development requires, as Wade Clark Roof states simply, "some degree of scouting around, and very much depends on how a person goes about trying to find it."[1] In Hong Kong, individual Christians receive direction from friends by word of mouth, use institutional resources like pastors or professors, and thus make their way through a diverse array of small groups, seminaries, university courses, lecture series, bookstores, and gospel camps as well as revival meetings and crusades. They also make their way through jobs, working for Christian publishers, parishes, and social services, among others. In so doing, they encounter and affirm contemporary innovations in spiritual cultivation supplied by religious entrepreneurs themselves demanding alternative forms of religious engagement. One innovation in particular stands out among those on offer today: the nongovernmental organization. For those individuals who choose to work for and/or participate in programs organized by the NGO, the NGO extends and alters that religious commitment. Through the NGO experience, Christians develop their religious selves by joining, discerning, growing, and even leaving to start their own organizations. In other words, through the group they find themselves.

Unlike entering upon the square, as described in chapter 1, whether a person accesses the NGO is not open to chance. Whereas the square lies at the crossroads of heavily used urban systems of infrastructure, carefully located to facilitate such movement, the NGO sits on the city's

---

[1] Wade Clark Roof, *The Spiritual Marketplace: Baby Boomers and the Remaking of American Religion* (Princeton: Princeton University Press, 1999), 119.

margins; its design and location do not so much discourage as limit chance encounters. When not positioned on church property, with yard and gate at street level, the Christian NGO in Hong Kong tends to be located in an office building, off the main streets, in low-rent and high-density areas such as Mong Kok and nearby Yau Ma Tei. It exists side by side with other purveyors typically found in these cheaper and older neighborhoods, whether suppliers of products like bathroom fixtures, rice porridge, or plastic combs, or of services like auto repair, prostitution, or recycling.

Anyone seeking out the NGO location must navigate a maze of stairways and elevator shafts to find its headquarters. One often has to ring to get into the NGO office. Security concerns arise in buildings where strangers come and go, and thefts of petty cash are common. Once in, one finds the office typically combines individual work spaces and a modest conference area. Employees occupy desks with computers, Internet, fax machines, and phones that readily connect them to partners in Hong Kong, throughout Asia, and beyond to Europe and North America. Conference space doubles up as reading and display room, with book racks marketing the product lines that are the specialty of the NGO, titles like *Uncertain Times, Liberating the Church from Fear,* and *Ushering in Tomorrow.* Tables bear the day's newspapers (*Ming Pao, Sing Tao Daily,* and the English-language *South China Morning Post*) as well as NGO brochures announcing workshops on self-defense or lectures on gender studies, planned collective action like the June 4 candlelight vigil, and annual reports in both Chinese and English. Cupboards and even bathtubs stow the surplus of paper, excess of the information age. Walls and shelves exhibit objects that communicate issues dear to the organization: a poster for the Fourth World Conference on Women in Beijing, 1995; a banner depicting Latin America's movement for liberation; or a modest-sized, white statue of the Goddess of Democracy. Finally, desktops yield personal photographs of (real) children or (imaginary) pets. Teacups, a thermos of hot water, and loose tea leaves add to the impression that this is a place for quiet, pensive labor.

Because it does not fall easily across anyone's path, the NGO as a destination must make itself known. Its managers must seek out those who are seeking, those more deliberate—even if irregular—patrons of religious development. To do so, the NGO relies not on a physical infrastructure but on a social infrastructure, a network of institutions and people by which priests and professors, students, seminarians, and social workers recommend and are routed into the NGO for the particular kind of work the NGO offers. Rather than focus on the stated mission and vision of each NGO, this chapter attends to the latent function of the NGO: its role in populating civil society. And rather than provide a segmented story for people who occupy different roles in the NGO structure, common experiences and vantage points emerge from what might appear as distinct interest groups and so underscore their similarities rather than their differences. Accounts of founders, staff, volunteers, and clients thus demonstrate how involvement in Christian NGOs came to be an attractive option and thereby worked to populate civil society in Hong Kong.

A New Form of Religious Expression

The concept of nongovernmental organization is a recent invention. The term originally came *en vogue* in the 1940s postwar period of geopolitical realignment and international governance. When the United Nations and offshoots like UNESCO became established, nonstate actors as a category emerged as identifiable partners in agendas of economic development, education, and public health. By the 1970s, NGOs enjoyed recognition by the UN and World Bank to do their work. By the late 1980s, the term further developed as an ideological marker, distinguishing the voluntary association of the free world from the mass organization of the Communist Bloc when in countries like Poland, East Germany, Czechoslovakia, and the Soviet Union that block showed serious cracks. In certain polities people enjoyed the freedom not only to mobilize themselves in membership for a particular interest but also to raise resources to sustain and promote that interest, while in others the state defined both membership and interest, either denying or validating group legitimacy and thus corporatizing it through official recognition and patronage. Whereas some organizations functioned freely outside the government's purview, others were mere extensions of the government.[2]

---

[2] This distinction still preoccupies scholars of organizational form in China. See Mayfair Yang, "Between State and Society: The Construction of Corporateness in a Chinese Socialist Factory, *Australian Journal of Chinese Affairs* 22 (1989); Gordan White, Jude Howell, and Shang Xiaoyuan, *In Search of Civil Society: Market Reform and Social Change in Contemporary China* (New York: Oxford University Press, 1996); and Jonathan Unger, ed., *Associations and the Chinese State: Contested Spaces* (Armonk, N.Y.: M. E. Sharpe, 2008).

In many parts of the world where such independence from the state could not be taken for granted, the term nongovernmental organization came also to stand in the stead of terms like nonprofit or charitable organization. In some instances employing the term NGO underscored the importance of independence as a value, while in others it highlighted public service. For the NGO, as with the charitable organization, the line was drawn between service and profit motive as the central interest of the organization. While mobilization of members around common interest could include financial services, such as rotating systems of credit and other microcredit arrangements, as a nonprofit organization orchestrating the economic development of others the NGO was not itself meant to seek wealth accumulation. Employing the term NGO, moreover, underscored the agency's independence from government in providing such services at a period of political development when government expansion in not only the socialist and communist worlds but also the capitalist world—the ebbs and flows of welfare state formation—meant centralized provision and oversight of medical services, unemployment benefits, housing, and education. Consequently, the NGO, like the charitable organization, stood apart not only from the state but also from the private business sector.

An NGO could conceivably be religious, but qualified with the tag "faith based." This religious qualifier has even informed the analysis of NGOs in general, calling attention to their importation of various religious devices such as beliefs and rituals employed to arouse emotion and affirm common identity or devotion around the cause of social justice.[3] And in a world where state power is called into question, ebbing and flowing on a global scale, some scholars point to religion as a natural and historic competitor in the transnational arena of socialization, employment, and allegiance.[4]

Since Christian faith and missionary zeal stimulated the formation of the earliest NGOs (labeled thus in retrospect), it would arguably be more appropriate to qualify NGOs in terms of those that are secular. More than two-thirds of NGOs engaged in international development

---

[3] Lauren Langman, "From Virtual Public Spheres to Global Justice: A Critical Theory of Internetworked Social Movements," *Sociological Theory* 23, no. 1 (2005): 66.

[4] Susanne Hoeber Rudolph and James Piscatori, eds., *Transnational Religions and Fading States* (Boulder, Colo.: Westview Press, 1996).

with founding dates prior to 1900 and surviving into the 1990s mention specific religious affiliations in their titles.[5] Oldest among these is the Moravian Mission of Switzerland, founded in 1734. Others, like the British and Foreign Anti-Slavery Society, founded in 1839, were created by individuals of faith (in this case, Quaker) or—like the Carnegie Foundation and Rockefeller Foundation of American philanthropy, founded in 1911 and 1913, respectively—were set up by individuals with strong Christian sectarian leanings. Religious ideas helped frame their purpose and actions, even if organizational titles did not always mark this affiliation explicitly. But neither was affiliation with colonialism necessarily marked in the titles of these organizations, even though colonial powers left the work of social service like healthcare and education to charitable, more specifically missionary, groups.

The faith-based NGO represents more than an innovation of social organization and voluntary initiative. It represents an innovation of religious life and religious expression, developed by entrepreneurs responding to the demands of the religious marketplace. In the tradition of innovative, collective, historical developments within Christianity, including the Catholic order, Protestant sect, covenant, base community, and, more recently, seeker church, the faith-based NGO through its very existence admits to an emergent and underserved segment among those striving for religion to fit, or align with, their self. Seemingly the NGO exists to meet the material and spiritual needs of the underserved or those who fall between the cracks. In Hong Kong, for instance, specialized Christian NGOs serve factory workers, schoolchildren, and migrant women. But those who form the NGO and maintain it through service (whether compensated by salary or not) themselves search for meaning and hope through religion.

NGO work is as much or even more so a matter of individual improvement as of societal improvement. Those who generate and serve the NGO are themselves Hong Kong people and converts to Christianity. In joining the NGO they can live out their lives as Christians, as God calls upon them to do. As demonstrated in the previous chapter,

---

[5] Colette Chabbott, "Development INGOs," in *Constructing World Culture*, ed. John Boli and George M. Thomas (Stanford: Stanford University Press, 1999), 228. On the secularization of faith-based charitable organizations, see Mayer Zald and Patricia Denton, "From Evangelicalism to General Service: The Transformation of the YMCA," *Administrative Science Quarterly* 8 (1963).

NGOs meet the faithful's demand for the skills and knowledge to assess their own religious growth and maturity. Frustrated and disappointed by their churches and fellow congregants, Hong Kong Christians as life-long learners look for an alternative source of authority within Christianity to resolve the dissonance between ideals and reality, a burden they know as modern individuals. Meeting and further fuelling this demand, entrepreneurs among them offer sophisticated educational tools for their fellow Hong Kong Christians seeking to educate themselves about their newly acquired religion. No wonder the paid work of a Christian NGO involves the production of books, theological coursework, grade-specific educational kits, forums, retreats, press conferences, prayer vigils, and public demonstrations.

While in the United States new entrepreneurs organize seminars on Native American spirituality or goddess worship, Christian NGOs in Hong Kong tackle topics such as citizenship, patriarchy, and immigration, as well as gambling, cults, and homosexuality. Whereas in the United States new entrepreneurs capitalize on individualizing trends such as self-help and human potential, these Hong Kong Christian NGOs demand of their participants a new kind of commitment to self, society, and God. They teach commitment as true believers voicing out their struggles and the struggles of Hong Kong in transition.

Shouldering the task of educating Christians about their faith, these NGOs also carry a latent function, existing as they do as voluntary associations within the wider network of religious institutions. Founded by local pastors and laity, funded by religious sponsors, drawing on individuals seeking resolution of religious questions and doubts, the Christian NGOs retain the individual convert within voluntary, religious affiliation rather than releasing the individual to a solitary and disorienting spiritual search for answers. More critical to our understanding of Christianity's link to civil society in Hong Kong than representation of the typical day in the NGO office or the orchestration of an occasional public rally is this work of collective yet personal education by the NGO that daily works to retain religion's hold on the individual.

Hong Kong's Faith-Based NGOs

When missionaries to China traveled along with merchants and colonial administrators in the mid-nineteenth century, they set up churches and seminaries, schools and hospitals. In time, Hong Kong possessed local equivalents to or branches of Christian voluntary organizations found in Europe and North America. By the mid-twentieth century, moreover, local people rooted in Hong Kong life responded to local needs, establishing charities and fellowships, professional associations and youth organizations. Eventually, by the turn of the twenty-first century, existing and new associations performing nonprofit, public-minded service work were calling themselves nongovernmental organizations. They addressed emerging concerns around environmental degradation, urban redevelopment, immigrant labor, sexual rights, and direct elections. Among these, some integrated networks of NGOs began purposefully distinguishing themselves according to current United Nations terminology as civil society organizations. Interchangeable use of these terms underscores the guiding assumptions of many working in NGOs; their efforts to generate fellowship and education, to equip people with information and the skills to express that information, and to create situations of role play and empathy all fit into the ideal of civil society. In addition, this union of concepts suggests the recent appreciation in political clout both of nonprofit organizations and of those advocating in public forums as nonstate actors.

TABLE 4.1
SELECT NGOs AND CHRISTIAN NGOs IN HONG KONG (WITH YEAR FOUNDED)

Primary Concern	Self-Described NGO	Self-Described Christian NGO
Conservation and sustainable development	The Conservancy Association (1968) Hong Kong Sustainable Development Forum (1998) Hong Kong People's Conference for Sustainable Development (2003) Society Environment Economy (2004)	Amity Foundation (1985)
Economic development	Oxfam Hong Kong (1976) Hong Kong People's Alliance on WTO (2004)	Christian Council of Asia (1957) World Vision, Hong Kong (1962)
Emergency relief	Engineers without Borders, Hong Kong (2008)	Hong Kong Red Cross (1950) Caritas Hong Kong (1953)
Environment	Green Power (1988) Society for the Protection of the Harbor (1995) Green Peace China (1997) Clear the Air (1997)	Christians for Eco-Concerns of the Hong Kong Christian Council (2002)

TABLE 4.1 (*cont.*)

Housing	Neighborhood Action-Advice Council (1968)	Hong Kong Housing Society (1948) Society for Community Organization (1972)
Human rights	Hong Kong Journalists Association (1968) Asian Human Rights Commission (1986) Hong Kong Human Rights Monitor (1995) Civil Human Rights Front (2002)	Documentation for Action Groups in Asia (1973) Diocese Commission* (1977) Concern for Hong Kong* (1987) Center for Reflection* (1988) Women Aware* (1988)
Labor	Hong Kong Confederation of Trade Unions (1990)	Hong Kong Christian Industrial Committee (1968) Hong Kong Catholic Commission for Labor Affairs (1991)
Migrant workers	UNIFIL-HK (1985)	Christian Action (1985) Bethune House (1986) Asian Migrant Center (1990)
Political development	Hong Kong Alliance in Support of Patriotic Democratic Movements in China (1989) Civil Human Rights Front (2002)	Hong Kong Christian Patriotic Democratic Movement (1989)
Religion	World Buddhist Sangha Council (1966)	Hong Kong Christian Council (1954) Diocese Commission* (1977) Concern for Hong Kong* (1987) Center for Reflection* (1988) Women Aware* (1988)
Sexuality/sex work/sexual health	Hong Kong AIDS Foundation (1991) Queer Sisters (1995) *Ziteng* (1996) HORIZONS (2001)	Blessed Minority Christian Fellowship (1992) Society of Truth and Light (1997)
Social service	Hong Kong Council of Social Services (1947) Hong Kong Social Workers Association (1949)	Saint James's Settlement (1949) Hong Kong Christian Service (1952) Samaritan Befrienders (1960) Wai Ji Christian Service (1979)
Youth	The Scout Association of Hong Kong (1914) Boys' & Girls' Clubs Association of Hong Kong (1936) Hok Yau Club (1949)	Hong Kong YMCA (1901) Hong Kong YWCA (1920) Student Christian Movement of Hong Kong (1949) Fellowship of Evangelical Students (1957) Breakthrough (1973)

* Pseudonyms are used for these organizations to preserve the anonymity of the sources, as was also done for individuals.

In the late 1980s, after the Joint Declaration announced to the world Britain's resolve in restoring Hong Kong to Chinese sovereignty, the four faith-based NGOs highlighted in this book—NGOs assigned the pseudonyms the Diocese Commission, Concern for Hong Kong, Women Aware, and Center for Reflection—emerged to help Christians cope with an uncertain future. As NGOs they represent liberal innovations to faith-based organizations established in the 1950s context of Christian service. Of the four, only one predated the Joint Declaration; the other three were founded through religious, professional, and friendship circles in a climate of doubt and vague anticipation. But all four NGOs were firmly in place once student demonstrators occupied Tiananmen Square in late spring 1989 in a bid for greater participation in governance. The Beijing leadership's ultimate mobilization against its citizens in the early hours of June 4 confirmed not only NGO suspicions about China's rulers but also their own sense of relevance. Furthermore, these four witnessed the subsequent formation and growing visibility of decidedly conservative Christian NGOs in their own likeness but with sharply competing social agendas for post-1997 Hong Kong. International, Chinese, and local politics combined to shape the development of these Christian NGOs and fueled their work of populating Hong Kong civil society.

The oldest among the four NGOs is the Diocese Commission, whose emphasis rests on organizing Catholics around issues of peace and social justice. In 1977, more than ten years after the drafting of the "Pastoral Constitution on the Church in the Modern World," a proclamation of Vatican Council II, the Diocese Commission was created in Hong Kong as part of a worldwide concerted effort to promote justice and Christian concern for the poor and afflicted. With a full-time secretariat, a regular, salaried staff of seven or eight, and anywhere between nine and eighteen volunteers, this NGO manages four working groups to deal with issues singled out as priorities for Hong Kong: human rights, social affairs, consciousness education, and China affairs.

The Diocese Commission's mission revolves around translating the Catholic Church's social teachings into actions aimed at developing all human beings and establishing their equality. In pursuing this objective, the commission makes recommendations to the bishop on matters related to justice and peace. At the same time, it works to foster recognition and raise parishioners' consciousness of the basic equality of all human beings and of principles of justice and peace. More concretely, it produces analyses of local social issues (such as social security or right of abode) through research and publications, putting together educational tools (such as kits, booklets, seminars) for democratic and human rights awareness, and advocating policy changes through meetings with government officials. Finally, both in principle and in practice, it aims to collaborate with people of other traditions and beliefs. An authorized representative of the diocese, accountable to the diocese and strictly funded by the diocese,[6] the Diocese Commission is where Felicia works as executive secretary, in close collaboration with Rachel, who chairs the commission in a voluntary capacity. Also involved in the Diocese Commission are Paul, Mr. and Mrs. Chu, and Mrs. Mou.

Second among the four NGOs is Concern for Hong Kong, which aims to engage evangelicals in monitoring the status of Hong Kong's rule of law. This group emerged in a more grassroots fashion after an independent fellowship of Christian university students deemed it valuable to maintain their social and spiritual ties to one another once they graduated and went their separate ways. Established in 1987, this NGO emphasizes financial independence in bringing Christians together around issues of public concern. To be a member, one must contribute to the organization both service and monetary support. Forty-two people, many of whom were born in the late 1960s, actively participate. Their resources are enough to hire no more than two full-time staff members and rent office space shared with a couple of other faith-based organizations. Members are roughly split between men and women; most are, by profession, teachers.

This group focuses primarily on developments in Hong Kong's rule of law, local media, and education. Issues like the legal boundaries between one country and two systems (right of abode), proposed limitations on freedoms (anticult law), and accountability and democratization (June 4/Tiananmen Square Incident) occupy their energies. As with the other NGOs, activities include producing educational materials and books, researching issues, and speaking at churches to spread the word of social concern. Unlike the other NGOs studied here (but representing a common phenomenon among parachurch organizations), this NGO is not a registered society. Seeking no money from foreign donors or public coffers but instead relying solely on membership dues, it is not required to provide official audits of its activities and funds. But, like

[6] Based on annual reports, 1996–1998.

most Hong Kong groups, it internally discloses documentation of activities and funds, in this case through its newsletter. This NGO often finds
itself running in the red. Although it has contemplated opening itself up
to the outside to secure additional funding, it has not done so to date
because of the original premise and principles of the group's founders,
including Mr. Fu.[7] Faith is currently the only full-time staff member.

Among the remaining two NGOs, Women Aware distinguishes itself
by focusing on the mobilization of women around issues of equality in
the faith. Formally established in January 1988, after prominent women
in the Christian community, including Karen, came together around their
gender-specific needs, it today has some 150 members. A staff of two or
three works to meet the NGO's aims, while a seven-person executive
committee elected by members monitors the staff's activities. According
to its stated mission, Women Aware exists primarily to realize sexual
equality in Hong Kong Christian and wider society according to God's
will. This task includes promoting awareness of women in the churches
and of women as a church, as well as coordinating local women and
their sisters overseas in activities that heighten their awareness of each
other. Concrete activities tend to involve coalition building, workshops,
courses, study groups, publications, the founding of the Feminist Theology Resource Centre, delivering sermons (since among its members
are female ministers), networking with Christian frontline groups, and
monitoring as well as lobbying the Hong Kong government for policy
changes. In the past, important projects have included participation in
the United Nations Fourth World Conference on Women in Beijing,
1995, as well as local efforts around feminist theology, land ownership
rights for indigenous women, and, more recently and controversially,
the rights of gays in church and society.

Funding for this NGO comes primarily, but not exclusively, from the
combination of member and other local donations, with overseas donations in an approximately 1:6 ratio. Additional moneys come from bank
interest and the sale of publications. Overseas funders include the Presbyterian Church, American Baptist Mission, Evangelisches Missionwerk
(EVM), Centrum Voor Zending, the United Church of Canada, Svenska
Kyrkans Mission, Board of Global Ministries of the United Methodist
Church, and the United Church Board of World Ministries. Individual
projects can also be associated with a particular funder, such as the

---

[7] Based on report for the first half of the 1990s.

United Church of Canada's funding of the *Women & Faith* series publication, and EVM's donation of special funds for the translation of one particular book.[8] Registered under the Societies Ordinance, this NGO is officially recognized as a nonprofit organization and is exempt from the Hong Kong profits tax. Staff members have included Karen, Queenie, Harriet, and Fiona, with members among them Professor Tung, James, Benedict, Felicia, Jefferson, and Ms. San.

Finally, Center for Reflection was established primarily to spark intellectual debate among lay leaders and clergy. The founding of this NGO by Reverend Hap and others of like mind in the fall of 1988 was, in part, due to a divergence of opinion within a preexisting NGO about Hong Kong Christians' future relations with China and with China's official churches. Breakaway members worried that favoring reconciliation and cooperation with the mainland authorities compromised the church's prophetic role. This organization consistently draws between 300 and 350 members, including local pastors, political figures, and seminarians. It has a full-time staff of four to six people, with a nine-person management committee. In the past, it has also drawn special volunteers around key issues such as civic education and social concern and regularly takes on theology students as interns. With a mission to promote fellowship and reflection, the Center functions as a forum for sharing views, as a medium for putting faith into practice, as a think tank for informing Christians inside and outside Hong Kong, as an educator for establishing a theology responsive to the people and circumstances of Hong Kong, and as a sign of Christianity's continued quest for human rights, democracy, and justice. Like the other NGOs, it pursues these ends through courses, seminars, internships, publications, written responses, and outreach to churches and Sunday schools.

Funding for this last NGO comes from members, local churches, course fees, publications, and bank interest, as well as from foreign donations, in a roughly 3:2 ratio. Foreign funders include the Association of Protestant Churches and Missions in Germany, Basel Mission, Christian Aid, Church of Scotland, Church of Sweden Mission, Evangelical Lutheran Church of Bavaria, Evangelical Mission in Southwest Germany, United Reformed Church UK, United Church of Canada, International Ministries of American Baptist Church, Methodist Church UK, the National Council of Churches, and the World Council of Churches. It

---

[8] Based on annual reports, 1996–1998.

is an approved charitable organization and so is exempt from payment of the Hong Kong profits tax.[9] Its staff, board, and membership base include Reverend Hap, Karen, Benedict, Wilson, Reverend Gwong, Doctor Loi, Felicia, Simon, Krista, Professor Bok, and Professor Tung.

All four of these NGOs seek to reform what they know as the institutional church, or Christianity, by making it more active and less inward looking, more vocal and less cautious, more inclusive and less narrow, less aloof, less privileged, and less intolerant (although each may vary in the degree and emphasis). Not only frustration with the limitations of existing Christian organizations and culture but a spirit of opportunity for self development and group development prompted the founding of these NGOs. As he explains in his autobiographical *My Ministry*, Reverend Hap founded Center for Reflection as a personal challenge of faith. He conceived of the Center in collaboration with a friend and fellow minister because their greatest hope was to expand faithful service. And as Karen writes in the preface to her collection of essays marking the fifteenth anniversary of the Center's conception, which she headed as director from 2003 to 2009, this NGO gives Christians the courage to be the dissenting church needed to defend the value of human dignity.

Work and Alignment

In Hong Kong's highly evangelistic, vital religious marketplace, believers actively organize. Small group meetings, for example, draw in new members and sustain the interest of existing ones. These gatherings stimulate reflection on both individual faith and the institutional church, prompting analysis as well as decision making. Jefferson is a nonbeliever who has been pulled into such small group meetings.

> Most of my friends come from various churches, and I've joined their meetings. The dominant practice of the church in Hong Kong is to concentrate on individual liberation from so-called sin and from personal alienation, so I criticize it. It's just masking the real [structural] origin of social problems, and calling people to save themselves from those problems in a very individualistic way. Because what it teaches conflicts with my values, I feel very uncomfortable at these meetings.[10]

[9] Based on annual reports, 1995–2000.
[10] Author's interview with Jefferson and Fiona, August 4, 1997.

Why does Jefferson attend such sessions? Attending is a matter of his personal choice. He says, "I'm always invited by my friends. They're good guys hoping that one day they'll learn I've become a Christian."[11] Chimes in Fiona, his girlfriend at the time, "He wants to know!"[12]

Jefferson and Fiona want to understand the source of their friends' impassioned activity. Each has experienced Christian education: Jefferson at the Anglican St. Timothy's Primary School and Fiona at Catholic Sacred Heart Canossian College. At the Christian NGOs where they have worked, they have asked their employers about Christianity, attended services occasionally, accepted invitations from friends to participate in gatherings, and considered whether the Christians they know from the NGOs share in their discomfort and disappointment. These religious guides are converts to Christianity themselves. Jefferson and Fiona wonder, what does it mean to confront a church with which they disagree? Why are they still Christians? Fiona and Jefferson can guess how their Christian friends, including NGO founders and staff, deal with dissonance. They suspect that their friends compartmentalize, withdraw, and reorder their religiosity.

> Fiona: No, they don't listen to these things [about individual sin].
> Jefferson: Because they don't think that the problem lies with Christianity, but with the practice of the church, the dominant church, the patriarchal church.
> Fiona: They don't go to church. Karen [Fiona's boss] doesn't go to church.
> LVN: And Reverend Hap takes the church wherever he goes![13]

Institutional reform and innovation such as the founding of NGOs tend to be pushed by religious entrepreneurs, people like Reverend Hap or Karen. But new entrepreneurs in the religious marketplace need not be ordained ministers or trained theologians. In fact, allowing a space for lay leadership makes the NGO an appealing religious institution. Moreover, assuming that pastors and theologians as professionals start up NGOs in response to others' needs and demands misdirects attention from their own personal needs for alignment between work and self. In the iconic figure of the clergy, observers tend to see a selfless actor decidedly different from those he or she serves, rather than an individual

[11] Author's interview with Jefferson and Fiona, August 4, 1997.
[12] Author's interview with Jefferson and Fiona, August 4, 1997.
[13] Author's interview with Jefferson and Fiona, August 4, 1997.

seeking to connect with like-minded others. Listening to founding members describe their motivations reveals that other story.

Take Mr. Fu, for instance. He reminds us that NGOs exist for their members, including founders and staff. As he explained in a 1998 interview, forming Concern for Hong Kong was a matter of personal problem solving. As a university student completing a B.A. in history at the Chinese University of Hong Kong in 1986, he had benefited from Christian fellowship as well as intellectual growth on campus. What would life be like once he shifted from the world of learning to the world of work, from being a student to being an adult? Mr. Fu felt he needed to anticipate that transition, and so he turned to his friends, who asked,

> What we searched for, or what we struggled over, while in the university—would it all go away once we joined society? Once we joined the workforce, maybe we would use a lot of strength and time to get a better job, get a promotion, and later on maybe we would have a family and children. Would that be it for us? Would all our time and strength be occupied by these things? So we deliberated how after graduation, after joining society we might express our faith.[14]

Such mundane yet pressing obligations as work and family—mainstream adult concerns—stood in contrast to the spiritual possibilities and social concerns that preoccupied them as university students.

As personal, cloistering, and potentially selfish pursuits, narrow fixations upon work and family also challenged directly the particular faith they had been developing. Mostly graduates of the class of '86 and class of '87, these friends had been maturing intellectually, socially, and spiritually as Hong Kong had been changing. They looked to the future with great anticipation, with questions about direct elections, human rights, and the rule of law. They sought ways to live out their faith beyond the confines of the church, with the gospel applied as a way to cope with social change. Those issues brought them together in fellowship to talk during their time as students. Would there still be a way to be involved in the conversation after they left university?

> And then we concluded that if we still wanted to have that kind of interest, we wanted to fulfill our holistic faith, why separate? It would be difficult if each of us faced these things separately; individually it would be hard to hold onto the mission and vision which we had in the university. So we

---

[14] Author's interview with Mr. Fu, August 25, 1998.

agreed we needed to have an organization. That would give each of us the necessary momentum. And a group effort gives group momentum to fulfilling that kind of mission and vision.[15]

Friends joined in fellowship founded an NGO to satisfy needs that could not be met by any individual member's religious and secular affiliations. While collectively they shared in Christian faith, they did not hold any common institutional tie.

Founders of Concern for Hong Kong had been members of their individual secondary school fellowships and then churches long before arriving at university. They had come together in university fellowship, moreover, from at least two university campuses. Even on an individual level, no one institution completely integrated any person's interests; neither church nor university nor fellowship alone had been sufficient to meet his or her developmental needs. Concern for Hong Kong as their own joint invention combined the strengths as well as the potentials of each of these three familiar institutions: university, church, and fellowship. As Mr. Fu elaborated, the new organization would maintain the university's function of stimulating members' social conscience by feeding their intellects, encouraging them to pursue knowledge about Hong Kong's political and human rights interests. At the same time, Concern for Hong Kong would serve as a platform for influencing Christians in Hong Kong's churches, spreading the viewpoint that social concern should be an integral part of faith, and disseminating their knowledge of the special place they called home. Finally, the organization would provide people with fellowship: members holding similar viewpoints on holistic Christianity and sharing interest in Hong Kong's democratization could shore up their strength and offer support to each other.

By combining the strengths of university, church, and fellowship, Concern for Hong Kong offers its members a way to align their intellectual, religious, and social selves. That said, Concern for Hong Kong does not replace a single one of the institutions that informs its multiple functions. Instead, it adds another commitment option to the already (over) committed individual. In his book on the fate of American community, *Bowling Alone*, Robert D. Putnam remarks that the work of building social capital, such as volunteering for community projects, assuming civic responsibility, or working in a local organization, is taken on by

---

[15] Author's interview with Mr. Fu, August 25, 1998.

a committed minority, in his case a generational cohort, while the vast majority reaps the benefits of its labor.[16]

The NGO serves individuals who are seeking unity across the various aspects of their lives. For Mr. Fu, who chose the profession of teaching as a way to express his viewpoints and so influence society, his time is divided among many responsibilities.

> Because time is limited, it's a hard life. You need to give time to your work; you cannot be lazy in your job. You need to give time to your family; you are responsible for giving not just money but time. And also I am a Christian, I have a church life. So, it's hard.[17]

But the NGO he helped found is "a calling from God to do something": to know the world and live in this world. Speaking as if to bring me around to his point of view, he adds,

> There are other members, and we are joined together—not just me, lonely, to walk this road. And one needs more exposure about the society, knowledge that will make your work more meaningful and give you a wider perspective to know what is happening in the society that influences your students.[18]

Solving one's own adult problems by starting up an organization creates an opportunity for like-minded others to find a solution to their own similar problems through that same organization. Mr. Fu's desire to sustain his involvement in wider societal developments, and stay true to his understanding of Christian faith, led him to found Concern for Hong Kong. Other Christians exposed to a similar religious and political context followed suit, becoming members or staff of Concern for Hong Kong. In a postindustrial, increasingly well-educated and bilingual Hong Kong, middle management is the work destination of college graduates, much as it is in Europe and the United States. Christian NGOs like Concern for Hong Kong offer an alternative post in middle management. But how do people come to find this alternative? And of what consequence is it to have this alternative? In other words, what difference does the NGO make?

---

[16] Robert D. Putnam, *Bowling Alone: The Collapse and Revival of American Community* (New York: Simon & Schuster, 2000), 132.

[17] Author's interview with Mr. Fu, August 25, 1998.

[18] Author's interview with Mr. Fu, August 25, 1998.

The Way to Alignment

By offering an environment for people to pray together, work together, break their fast together, and march together, all in the name of God and his purpose, his values, and his calendar, the Christian NGO in Hong Kong extends the time frame and widens the terrain for being Christian. Sensitive to contradiction and hypocrisy, Hong Kong Christians readily avoid certain problems. Time and time again they articulate movement: running away, exiting, quitting, getting out, standing up, participating, protesting, joining, networking, and moving on. This particular institution affords some resolution of contradictions faced by these converts to a demanding way of life. Even if for such individuals the NGO exposes them to further contradictions, as another option in a vast inventory of choices it encourages an ever-wider perspective on what can be achieved through faith.

For years, Faith sought a position with Concern for Hong Kong. Like her boss, Mr. Fu, Faith started down her professional path as a schoolteacher. Yet, when she was barely settled into her post at a kindergarten, she abruptly abandoned her chosen field. It took almost a decade for her to realize her calling. In between, while working for a public university, Faith decided that Christian NGO work was different from anything else. Such work nourished her conscience.

> In 1989, before June 4, I received my diploma to be a kindergarten teacher. At the time I was not concerned about society. I didn't know what it meant to be political. But after June 4, I changed my life. I prayed to God that I be concerned about our country, our society. I decided to quit my job (*chihjīk*) and enter the NGO field.
>
> But in 1989 the Christian NGO field held few options—only three organizations were known to me: Center for Reflection, Student Christian Movement, and Concern for Hong Kong. There were no other choices, no positions. I prayed constantly. And then my pastor, at a summer camp, asked me for the first time, "What do you do? What's your job?" I answered, "I just quit my job!" He informed me of a staff appointment in his church organization and asked, "Are you interested?" I told him, "Yes, I'll try it!"[19]

After six months with this Christian organization, however, Faith left her post and instead joined the Hong Kong Christian Patriotic Democratic

---

[19] Author's interview with Faith, June 27, 2007.

Movement.[20] She worked there for three years, then took time off to travel through Australia, Africa, Europe, and Asia. Upon returning to Hong Kong, Faith worked at one university and completed a management degree at another. Finally, Concern for Hong Kong had a position open. She left her job at the university and has been with Concern for Hong Kong ever since. Within ten years, Faith changed not only her job but also the direction of her professional path five times: from kindergarten teacher, to church staff, to NGO staff, to university staff, and back to NGO staff.

Much as Christian converts express struggle in resolving the conflict between worldly, material temptations and Christian demands for pure, simple living, Christians like Faith indicate that abandoning the inequity and hypocrisy of the mainstream working world by doing the work of the faith-based NGO is a mixed blessing. As Faith described, the mainstream workplace fails to maintain the values of society, let alone Christian society, making it unbearable for the individual striving to align principles with practice:

> Supported by the Hong Kong government, the university has abundant resources. Because there's seemingly no limit, one professor took 15,000 sheets [30 reams] of paper. Too many! What did he do with them? Outside the university there are many poor people. During my time at the university the unemployment rate was 9.8 percent! Since the Handover back in 1997 joblessness has reached 14.5 percent, every year increasing by 1–2 percent! It's unfair that professors use resources for their family, for themselves.
>
> And I was working in the department of sociology. Outside, in the press conference or paper, sociologists show they have done so much to benefit society. But they're just concerned how many [stock] shares they've bought, how much their house is worth, how much money they earn. I'll tell you something funny: when I married in 1998, one professor asked, "What gift can I give you for Christmas?" I joked, "Give me an apartment; you have too many flats." He felt embarrassed, and ran away (*yangau chihjīk*). So this is what I'm talking about.[21]

But then NGO work demands constant striving to uphold obligations and abandon desires, a dilemma experienced traditionally by Catholic

---

[20] Not to be confused with Szeto Wah's organization. Former teacher, trade unionist, prodemocracy activist, and legislative council member Szeto Wah headed the Hong Kong Alliance in Support of Patriotic Democratic Movements in China until his death on January 2, 2011.

[21] Author's interview with Faith, June 27, 2007.

(notably Jesuit) clergy in a much more hierarchical and contained social world. More comparable still were the devout lay Catholics of medieval Milan, the Humiliati. Reacting not to poverty but to privilege, the Humiliati, who were literate capitalists, often of noble blood, chose a lifestyle of austerity for themselves and modeled an alternative Christianity in a wealthy, vibrant city.[22]

Faith is in an uncomfortable position: she grows truly concerned about society because the work she has chosen for herself requires that she know society. Reading newspapers, editing books, and watching the news are for Faith a necessary part of her workday, of her service work. Thus informed to assume others' perspectives, Faith sees and feels everything.

> In this NGO field I know my situation, I know my society, I know whether citizens are being lied to. Like with the Hong Kong government promoting Article 23 of the Basic Law: "It's good for you, it protects you!" It's a lie. When LegCo passes this law, we'll have no freedom of the press, no freedom to voice out against the government. We encourage citizens: "You have a right to fight!"[23]

In 2007, Concern for Hong Kong celebrated its twentieth anniversary. Faith, not a founder but a paid staff, worked to put together a commemorative book about her NGO. Originally intended to sustain the Christian development of a handful of friends beyond the environment of the university campus, the organization served to educate Faith. She had wanted an alternative to middle-management positions in various academic institutions, and she found one in working to educate Christians with Concern for Hong Kong.

Like Faith, Rachel recognizes hypocrisy in the working world. She has worked in journalism, corporate public relations, and education, each time coping with the gap between ideal and real. But as a Catholic, her options for response have directed her toward the Diocese Commission. After graduating from the university, Rachel first worked as a journalist. From this professional vantage she could see inequity and injustice, but her job did not compel her to challenge the system. Rachel's next job was in public relations for a large corporation. Again

---

[22] Rodney Stark, *The Victory of Reason: How Christianity Led to Freedom, Capitalism, and Western Success* (New York: Random House, 2006), 121–22.
[23] Author's interview with Faith, June 27, 2007.

she assumed a position that provoked her discomfort, but her job did not invite resolution. In fact, it required toleration.

> As a corporate staff you are very well protected, you get very good benefits. Because the nature of the job is to beautify, cover up, it really made me sick! You think: Why do big companies have money to employ people to run around just doing some sponsorship program, just trying to project a good image, when, indeed, they are doing things bad for society? I started to think about this relationship.[24]

Image making is not limited to the work of the mainstream marketplace. It can corrupt the work of the religious and produce personal dissonance within the structure of the religious marketplace, too.

Father Yi realized a moral dilemma when he accepted the role of representing the Hong Kong Diocese of the Roman Catholic Church at a critical time in its history. As official spokesman of the diocese in consultations on the Basic Law in the early 1990s, his position required that he engage the media, political groups, and wider society. Like many others, Father Yi had been moved by the spirit of the 1989 movement for democracy. On more than one occasion within the span of a month in late spring 1989, a million Hong Kong people (more than 15 percent of the total population) gathered in the streets to support calls for democracy not only in China but in Hong Kong. In the 1980s, when society seemed united around its own quest for justice, Father Yi was thrilled to act as spokesman at the behest of the diocese as well as to participate on his own in organizations like the Hong Kong Alliance in Support of Patriotic Democratic Movements in China. This loose amalgam—said to include over two hundred groups representing more than 60,000 social workers, teachers, civil servants, and political and religious organizations,[25] local union leaders, and legislators rather than members of parliament appointed by the British-born governor—initiated a signature campaign. Members demanded right of abode in Britain for all Hong Kong residents, full democracy before 1997, and a bill of rights. Of the demands successfully secured (which would become bones of contention with the Chinese leadership in Beijing) were a swifter course for direct democracy and the Hong Kong Bill of Rights Ordinance.

---

[24] Author's interview with Rachel, August 19, 1997.

[25] James L. Tyson, "Hong Kong Keeps the Torch Alive," *Christian Science Monitor*, July 20, 1989.

But already by the early 1990s, China had regained a sense of control over its domestic and international politics. Hong Kong people, Father Yi included, only gradually figured this out. According to Father Yi, however, the Catholic Church quickly adjusted to a more conciliatory stance with the leadership in Beijing, leaving him oddly out of step with his employer and unable to erase the impression that he personally was "not so friendly with China." As he explained,

> Somehow I became the shield of the church, a fence facing society. I came to understand what is inside the church and what is outside in society. And there was a discrepancy between what I had to say and what the church really thought or supported. When I spoke, I spoke according to the principles of Catholic teachings, which attracted people and made them believe the church. I established a beautiful image of the church—which it was my duty to do; as spokesman I have to build up a good image of the corporation. But then the image turned out not to be the reality the church itself wanted.[26]

In a vivid echo of Rachel's experience in the corporate world, Father Yi experienced dissonance in representing to the public a beautiful image of his corporation, the Hong Kong Diocese of the Roman Catholic Church.

As one who was not appointed to speak for himself, all Father Yi could do when his own documented position diverged from that of the diocese was to resign from his post. He elaborated,

> Had I not been spokesman for the diocese, I could still have spoken. But because I had been accepted by the media as spokesman, when I became aware that the church did not support what I said, I had to shut up. Otherwise I'd be telling lies. I just resigned (*chihjīk*) from being spokesman. That solved the whole problem for me.[27]

With Cardinal John Baptist Wu Cheng-Chung's passing in fall 2002, Joseph Zen Ze-Kiun, designated successor since 1996, rose to lead the Hong Kong Catholic Diocese. By summer, Bishop Zen had reforged the Catholic Church's association with the local prodemocracy movement by agreeing to speak at the annual June 4 commemorative vigil. Father Yi, himself restored to the position of spokesman for the diocese, publically announced this commitment.[28]

[26] Author's interview with Father Yi, August 7, 1998.
[27] Author's interview with Father Yi, August 7, 1998.
[28] Ambrose Leung, "Priest Has Blessing in Pro-Democracy Group," *South China Morning Post*, February 17, 2002.

For a lay Catholic like Rachel, an alternative source of inspiration exists within that same religious structure, although it is one that Father Yi describes as creating conflict similar to his own. Since its members assume a position between church and society, the Diocese Commission, as part of the church facing the general society, risks being disowned when it does not follow the Catholic Church. Certainly members like Paul, as he expressed in chapter 3, exercise caution about joining. But the pull of the organization on politically minded Catholics in Hong Kong is powerful. In a voice similar to that of Mr. Fu, cofounder of Concern for Hong Kong, Rachel articulates the hope and thrill that the collective offers:

> I have a group of friends who were involved in the student prodemocracy movement, although later on they gradually moved out. We would discuss how to be involved in society. Not in a very rigorous way; not talking about it all day long. But in our daily conversations, sometimes, we would think about that.
>
> And why I decided to join the Diocese Commission was by invitation of a friend. "Why don't you help us out?" So, then I joined, just as a member. And after two years they needed a chairperson, and I concluded it was time for me to do something.[29]

Chairing the Diocese Commission in a voluntary capacity means laity apply to a new organization skills developed in the professional world. As Rachel tells it, she is a "management kind of person." Used to running an office and overseeing a staff, she first studied her chosen organization, considered its interests, assessed her fellow volunteers, and resolved to heighten its impact. Doing this required questioning how things had been done in the past, caucusing among members to gauge support for initiatives, and facing frustration and disappointment when work did not proceed as expected.

At the Alternative Handover's July 1 Bazaar, for example, the Diocese Commission's physical absorption under the tent of Women Aware infuriated Rachel. The bazaar, a carnival-atmosphere daytime event that took place after the Handover's emotional observation in Statue Square the night before, drew a few hundred people. NGOs invited Hong Kong citizens to spend their day off visiting booths and tents that declared NGO concerns and generally advertised these organizations. Recounting to me her reaction then, Rachel pointedly asked staff,

[29] Author's interview with Rachel, August 19, 1997.

"How come you don't have your own logos? At least you should have a sign, right? We don't have either! If you don't show your [organization's] involvement, you become invisible." But then we went and handed out our postcards with a prayer saying that we don't see July 1 as an end, and that we as the Diocese Commission encourage people to stop their helplessness, to work for the poor and oppressed, to continue this work as Chinese Catholics.[30]

Applying the skills she had acquired in corporate Hong Kong, Rachel as chair of a faith-based NGO serves a totally different agenda; rather than assembling blinders for people to wear and accept a rosy reality, Rachel works to tear down the blinders. By revealing injustices, she, like Faith in educating Protestant evangelicals, encourages fellow Catholics to participate in society and thus to apply their faith in real life. Whether or not she succeeds in rousing their attention, she gains an opportunity. Participating in discussion enables Rachel to know what people think about an issue, and, she adds, "I get a chance to have some sort of reflection."[31] The NGO is not simply a surrogate for Rachel's service to God but also, more generally, a surrogate for religious life. Rachel exercises through the NGO the ritual of self-reflection and the application of religious teachings in real life—in other words, the individual and collective requirements of Catholic belief. Seemingly, all that is missing is prayer. No longer enthusiastic about prayer as she was when a teenager, Rachel does not miss it in her NGO work.

The NGO experience combines advocacy work and thus education of public and self with religious life. Whether through assigned tasks, responses to news developments, or spontaneous office conversations, NGO staff are stimulated and challenged. For Harriet this conflation of work and religious experiences, with her education undergirding both, requires self-correction. Trying to find a personal fit is not always easy within an NGO with a broad range of interests. She meets this organization, not unlike how Weber's ascetic/confessor finds Foucault's authority/listener. Harriet, like Rachel a journalist for a time, and an editor with several Hong Kong publications before completing a master's degree in politics at the University of York in England, was hired by Karen at Women Aware first as a publications secretary. Then Karen asked to extend her responsibilities to cover for the executive secretary,

---

[30] Author's interview with Rachel, August 19, 1997.
[31] Author's interview with Rachel, August 19, 1997.

an administrative position for internal management. Harriet responded by asking Karen whether she could modify her job description to specify publications and promotions. But Karen soon discovered that the combination was too much for one person.

In addition to managing work roles, Harriet found herself torn in other ways, too. The NGO encouraged her to consider what work she aspired to carry out even as it delegated tasks. Women Aware, while distinguishing itself as an organization seeking gender equality particularly for grassroots women inside and outside the church, facilitated networks of activity around broader concerns, including human rights and the July 1 Handover. Housed within the NGO was Network '97, a short-term, funded initiative whose purpose was to bring together NGOs in Hong Kong in anticipation of shared concerns after Hong Kong's return to Chinese sovereignty. Sometimes the work of Network '97, strictly Fiona's responsibility, overlapped with that of Harriet and Women Aware. In one example of this organizational ambiguity, Harriet passed along work to Fiona that their boss, Karen, had actually intended for Harriet. After the initial confusion, however, this situation sparked for Harriet clarity of personal purpose.

> If you ask me my agenda, actually it all depends on Karen. Sometimes she says that because one of the missions of her—of Women Aware—is to deal with social concerns on top of everything else, I have to deal with them. Whatever Karen is thinking is what I shall do. I really have no idea myself. That's why I think it would be better to do my own assignment: women's rights and gender equality. In future, I think my own scope will concentrate here. What I'm really interested in personally—although I'm not any feminist, or I have very shallow knowledge of women's rights—is human rights and gender equality.[32]

Harriet, while sensing in the NGO friction for which she is partly responsible, still sees her employment there as a godsend. So often her impulse has been to run away, to leave an uncomfortable situation.

> The church is full of dogmatic doctrines, interpretations of the Bible which really cannot convince me. I'm not an obedient person. I'm not an obedient daughter, I'm not an obedient Christian, and I'm not an obedient staff. Frankly, if I hadn't joined this organization I might soon have left the church. The doctrines or authority imposed by my church set me on a dead

---

[32] Author's interview with Harriet, August 13, 1997.

end road; my only alternative would be to run away. I always do that. But Women Aware is offering some exits (*chēutlouh*) for my thinking.[33]

Rather than exiting (*chēutmùhn*) at the first opportunity, Harriet finds at Women Aware avenues for her ideas about faith that are not tolerated and that discourage her membership elsewhere.

> Through Women Aware I can make better choices. This organization impresses upon me that since I only have to be loyal (*jùngsàm*) to the law of God, I don't have to be loyal to a person just because he uses the name of God. Learning more about feminist theology gives me ways to reinterpret my own religion. And then I get to know God in another way, one which is more comfortable and much easier for me to accept, which is truer than what I learned about the church on my own. So, I really get something here.[34]

Like Harriet, Benedict came to the NGO with professional experience. In his case, that experience was social work. But after three years as a case worker, his service work did not fulfill him as when he first started it. Participating in seminars and workshops at Center for Reflection, Benedict found that his Christian identity had come to mean much more to him. He began thinking about finding a job related to his faith, but he had no idea he would find a job with the Center. Reconnecting with a friend through one seminar, however, enabled his career move. As Benedict recounts,

> Around March of 1995 I joined a seminar about the upcoming [LegCo] election. There I met an ex-colleague of mine. A number of us participants had a discussion afterwards, and I told her I may want to find a job in a Christian organization. She knew that Center for Reflection had a vacancy. I thought, "Well . . . why not? Let's give it a try." So I came to see Reverend Hap. He had a short discussion with me, and then I was employed.[35]

The work at Center for Reflection, so broad in scope and responsibility, challenged Benedict. Employed as organizer and liaison with other NGOs, he concentrated on human rights, democracy, and social justice issues in Hong Kong. In addition, Benedict worked with civic educators to develop citizenship curriculum specifically for Hong Kong. At the same time, he edited a number of books each year. That was the initial

---

[33] Author's interview with Harriet, August 13, 1997.
[34] Author's interview with Harriet, August 13, 1997.
[35] Author's interview with Benedict, August 15, 1997.

agreement. Soon Center for Reflection placed Benedict in charge of organizing gatherings and courses, the in-house programs of the Center.

His heavy workload at the Center, as well as his enrollment in courses on feminist theology at Women Aware, showed Benedict a ray of hope. He discovered a different choice in the matter of living out his Christianity, one that allowed him to be himself rather than negate his previous existence as an engaged member of Hong Kong society. Working for an NGO could, as Paul and Father Yi hinted, involve sacrifice, danger. But for Benedict, who wanted to be a concerned Christian, the choice felt right. And was he the right person for the job? Laughing, Benedict said, "I was never the person." But he managed.

> Working here is like being a skillful juggler. You throw so many balls into the air, you can't catch them all at once; so you have to throw one high in the sky and catch those coming down. Particularly in the first year: when I had just married, I was still in the final stages of writing my master's thesis, and adapting to my new work environment.
>
> Now, with the routines down, I consider what more I can do. One thing I want to try to do is build networks so we can mobilize more Christians to participate in protests and other kinds of social action. Courses and gatherings in our in-house program are ways to get in touch with people who at least have some interest in the messages we send out. They may not immediately make that big leap and join our marches and protests, but they come to know about our work. And even if we cannot draw them in, we can try to make them appreciate what we're doing, not become someone who opposes us.[36]

Prompted to clarify what the Center is teaching, versus what most churches are teaching, Benedict pauses before explaining that the difference lies in learning a certain way of being Christian:

> Because they think they are peacemakers, they are people who don't create struggle, church leaders teach Christianity in a way that being a Christian has nothing to do with encountering injustice in the society. We are trying to tell people to be concerned Christians who reflect and act with conviction. In short, maybe we are trying to convey how to be a Christian.[37]

Center for Reflection affirms Benedict's vision of being Christian. Benedict's quest for alignment rests in realizing his true Christian self as he

---

[36] Author's interview with Benedict, August 15, 1997.
[37] Author's interview with Benedict, August 15, 1997.

decides to work with like-minded others. In this example, as with the Catholic volunteer Rachel, working for an NGO helps to achieve personal goals. Even when reflecting on the organizing component of his job, the thrill of collaborating with others, Benedict admits that struggle might not be for everyone; it is, however, good for him. "What I am sure," he declares, "is I'm doing it for myself."

WIDENING THE WAY

By enjoining its members to occupy the ample space between church and state in Hong Kong, the NGO broadens religious experience. It widens the way one can be Christian as it turns voluntary membership into a direct route to civil society. A video compilation of one NGO's various projects and partnerships explicitly communicates this stance. In the 2004 video disk (VCD) "Another World Is Possible: Civil Society Education for Youth," Karen states that civil society education is the responsibility of the church because the church is not four walls separating itself from society but is a part of society offering hope. The program directs students, as youth the pillars of society, to act out a particular identity of citizen. More than a membership drive, then, civil society education (whether packaged as such or not) carried out by the NGO passes along a skill set for others to employ as it suits their seemingly unique selves.

Sitting in the seat occupied by her pastor and mentor until she replaced him at Center for Reflection, Karen implicitly communicates a second function of the NGO. In addition to instructing Christians on how to practice their faith beyond the confines of a church building, she demonstrates the relationship of the Christian to the NGO. Karen has chosen the NGO as an expression of faith beyond the church building; she has left behind the leadership of one NGO, Women Aware, to lead another, Center for Reflection. Having liberated herself not only from one set of four walls but also the mentality of four walls, she acts as an example of the fluid, developmental Christian finding ways to align, realign, or maintain alignment of work, belief, and self.

The digital recording in which Karen features opens with an all-male band churning out its music. The sound is decidedly discordant, not unlike the feeling many Christians describe in their lives. The lyrics are impatient, critical, again echoing the sentiments more mildly communicated by Christians frustrated by mainstream work and worship: "No more words / No more nonsense / Use time to wear away all accusations." Superimposed are the Chinese characters representing four concepts:

contention, resignation, dissatisfaction, and reform. Interspersed with footage of the band are iconic images of Hong Kong: high-rise housing, foot traffic, road traffic, but also smiling, active school kids speaking into microphones and moving in unison. This is the "Youth Civil Society Education" project VCD put together by Center for Reflection.

Through its civil society education project, Center for Reflection meets young people in their own environment of Christian and secular schools. There the Center extends its skill set by orchestrating collective activities geared toward developing experience and reflection among the younger generation. One student experiences social marginalization by assuming the identity of one who is underemployed; she must then account for her thrift, answer for her supposed laziness, or actually go without a meal. Another learns what it is like to communicate issues; artists instruct him to express in abstract form, and teachers encourage him to organize his own school assembly and signature campaign. A third experiences politicization; she investigates government policies on the environment and the government response to student mobilization in Tiananmen Square 1989, and so realizes which issues matter to her. Along with such lessons, young people learn to use microphones, perform in front of cameras, and conduct interviews just as NGO staffers themselves do in their work lives. In these ways, they are prompted to reflect on their own experiences and the experiences of others.

Other NGOs, outwardly secular and staffed with professional social workers, provide civic education programs in a marketplace where government and school administration appear to shun sensitive issues like Chinese history from June 4 to the present or Hong Kong's path of political development. One such staff member, Mr. Gung of the Boys' and Girls' Clubs Association of Hong Kong, explained that the use of experience and reflection to enhance critical thinking is a common feature of his organization's civic education curriculum, too. In this case, critical thinking means individual, self-reflective thinking. Young people learn that if they have the right to vote, they can choose not only which candidate to support but whether or not to vote at all. As association is voluntary, so, too, the decision to participate or not is strictly voluntary.

Mr. Gung's secular NGO is not bent on shaping a form of citizen; its goal is not indoctrination, a distinction Mr. Gung makes in relation to mainland China. Here he employs language that does not fit communist or contemporary China but harks back to an imperial past, where subjects, rather than citizens, were made:

In providing civic education to our clients we do not have a position on what an ideal citizen should be. It is very different from civic education in China. They have an ideal: a subject should be cultured, educated, should have . . . I forget. But we do not have any ideal stereotype.

We do not mold our children. We help them with the methods: how to interview others, what's brainstorming, what are problem-solving skills, what's group discussion. We teach them such skills, and then encourage them to summarize their learning in a booklet or a VCD or on a home page. On their own they explore about themselves and try to form their own impression, if any.[38]

The point of comparison and contrast for Boys' and Girls' Club of Hong Kong might better be Center for Reflection, rather than China. Despite sharing an emphasis on experience, reflection, and critical thinking, the secular NGO's approach differs from civil education in Hong Kong as developed by Christian NGOs. That Mr. Gung allows for student choice in trying to "form their own impression, *if any*" (emphasis added) suggests a position of intentional neutrality. In contrast to Boys' and Girls' Club, Center for Reflection touts its political agenda. Sitting in the general secretary's office at Center for Reflection in 2004, Karen explains in a filmed interview for the "Youth Civil Society Education" VCD the benefits realized through the Hong Kong civic education project:

In the beginning many NGO friends were not quite aware that what they themselves were doing is part of education. The schools also did not see what the small organizations were doing out there in the community. Neither saw they could work to make a bridge, to let students really have new experiences through participation. After trying this way in the past few years, we both feel very excited. Some schools, after participating with nongovernmental organizations, feel that we can really cooperate. More exciting still are those children—the students themselves. They actually indicate to us that they have a degree of moldability. They are very much ready to act out the identity of citizen.[39]

NGOs, themselves formed through the simple possibility of choice and thus capable of restraining the state, do not simply underscore the voluntary basis of young people's place in society. They, like so many self-proclaimed civil society organizations the world over, prefer a certain form of citizen in formation:

[38] Author's interview with Mr. Gung, Boys' and Girls' Club, August 28, 1998.
[39] Karen, "Another World Is Possible: Civil Society Education for Youth" VCD, Center for Reflection, 2004.

> In our beliefs and acts we hope to encourage [other] believers, encourage Hong Kong citizens to continue moving Hong Kong toward the values of justice, democracy and human rights, etc. At the same time we feel that participation is itself educational material—also a very important educational resource. We very much hope to bring these experiences into schools, to churches, make believers understand that what we say about justice and democracy is not a matter of abstract values or concepts but a kind of change [achieved] through our participation together.[40]

Citizens demonstrate change not only, for example, through individual testimony to the cause of June 4 justice, with personal pledges to join in mass demonstration and candlelight vigil. They also evidence change through awkward, collective attempts, such as that of the four high school students who founded JPERS, a volunteer team. JPERS is both a personal and purposeful acronym. The letters stand for the first initial of each founding member's English name. At the same time, founders communicate their common intention to be justice and peace keepers, a purpose already claimed by many Catholics—the fact of which these students appear innocently unaware. The question of originality aside, their filmed interviews convey a sense of how groundbreaking is the social and spiritual path to small group affiliation, a phenomenon that was commonly experienced by adult NGO participants when they themselves were in school. Regardless of whether schoolmates, teachers, church leaders, or government officials have already registered a similar group, students work to found, name, sustain, and propagate their own.

Finally, through the lens of Doctor Loi we see that initiative of moving into the public sphere extended into adult life. Doctor Loi became Christian not through infant baptism but through Protestant fellowship as a student. As a grown man he searched to find a liberal form of Christianity but found in Hong Kong neither liberal church nor publications to satisfy him. After taking courses through seminary and NGOs, poring over books and Internet sources, he signed on with the Boston-based Unitarian Universalist Association. But still he did not stop. Hoping to know others in Hong Kong with similar questions and doubts, Doctor Loi in 2004 organized at Center for Reflection a forum for liberal Christians. As Doctor Loi explains it in an online article he penned for the Unitarian Universalist publication *Hot Rice*,

[40] Karen, "Another World."

> My original plan was to establish a Hong Kong Liberal Christian Fellow-
> ship and did not dare to push for a UU group, fearing that many Christian
> participants might not be comfortable with a non-Christian religion. But
> there were also a few non-Christians in our group and hence we ought to
> be more inclusive, accommodating non-Christians as well as Christians.
> UUism seemed to be a good candidate.[41]

Not long after, he launched the Spiritual Seekers Society, a fellowship
and action group for those curious about Unitarian Universalism.

While Spiritual Seekers Society members hold biweekly meetings at
Center for Reflection to support one another in the quest to understand
faith, they also gather occasionally to infuse wider Hong Kong society with their particular perspective on political and social issues. At
the end of 2005, they demonstrated for universal suffrage and participated in the Religious Blessing Session of the International Day Against
Homophobia Parade. Fourteen months later, the group produced a written response to a program broadcast on television concerning homo-
sexuals in Hong Kong. Pleas for minority tolerance, press freedom, and
extension of education to children constituted their agenda. In 2009
the group achieved its goal of formal membership in the International
Council of Unitarians and Universalists and renamed itself the Unitarian
Universalists Hong Kong.

Exit, Voice, and Loyalty

The fluidity required for finding fit, whether religious, professional, or
personal, through a middle-management post in an NGO stands in sharp
contrast to the experience of work that has long been structured and
controlled on the Chinese mainland by the Chinese Communist Party
(CCP). Loyalty as blind obedience to the CCP, as journalist Liu Binyan
recounts in his autobiography titled *A Higher Kind of Loyalty*, guided
government judgments of citizens well into the 1980s, or the era of Deng
Xiaoping.[42] Once the CCP secured power and through it the interests of
the Chinese people in 1949, small group study of Marxist texts (how Liu
and his revolutionary peers in the communist underground developed

---

[41] Doctor Loi, "UUs Organize in Hong Kong," *Hot Rice: The Newsletter of
Asian/Pacific Islander Unitarian Universalists and Their Allies* 2, no. 2 (2006).

[42] For a 1990s update, see Amy Hauser, "The Chinese Enterprising Self: Young,
Educated Urbanites and the Search for Work," in *Popular China: Unofficial Culture*

a personal commitment to communism) came under party leadership. Independently upholding the principles established in Marxist texts was not recognized as an expression of loyalty but, instead, contradicted the self-abnegation required by Marxism. In fact, independent study became suspect as submission to group, or loss of self, became orthodox. Likewise, seeking movement in job placement generally raised suspicions, signaling as it did the taint of the original sin of self-interest. Liu writes,

> Any young worker's request, to transfer to another place of work or to go to a university—in other words, anything suggestive of personal gain, even if it did not conflict with the collective interest—was condemned as a sign of bourgeois individualism, and harshly repressed.[43]

As opposed to classical liberal thought, communism dictated that society could not be found via individualism but was strictly achieved through the group.

Yet through the work of Liu Binyan, we gain a window onto the ordinary people whose conviction, resolve, and innovation this Chinese investigative reporter and communist party member asserts embody a higher, although unrecognized, kind of loyalty in the People's Republic of China. Like Liu himself, these ordinary people are punished for their truth telling. But by deciding within his appointed profession of journalism to report their stories, Liu advances the idea that loyalty to nation, to people, to party cannot be confused with the political loyalty demanded by individual representatives of the party. Such higher loyalty (*jùngsàm*) is in evidence among religious innovators in Hong Kong, too. We hear it in the interview with Harriet, when she proclaims that the law of God, rather than that of individual religious leaders, guides her. More generally, such loyalty to Christianity is expressed when individual Christians interpret the holy book and remain committed to their faith, when they voice out (*chēutsèng*) a prophetic alternative and exit (*chēutmùhn*) any particular, organized formation of Christians.

The choice of words to capture Hong Kong Christians' experience is uncanny for its demonstration of the political economist Albert O. Hirschman's categories of response to the gap between ideal and real; exit, voice, and loyalty each represents a distinct human response to

---

in a Globalizing Society, ed. Perry Link, Paul Pickowitz, and Richard Madsen (Lanham, Md.: Rowman & Littlefield, 2002).

[43] Liu Binyan, *A Higher Kind of Loyalty* (New York: Pantheon, 1990), 65.

the actual and often frustrating experience of institutional affiliation, whether economic, political, or social.[44] For Hirschman, loyalty might sooner prompt voice than exit, as when an individual takes it upon himself to change rather than abandon an unsatisfactory situation for the better. For members of an organization, exit as resignation (*chìhjīk*) spells surrender, abandonment, a point of no return. For ordinary citizens, exit as emigration (*yìmàhn*) might be the path of last resort, communicating to others indifference if not outright betrayal.

But if we in this reflection on Hong Kong Christianity suspend our judgment, refrain from automatically privileging the NGO as a vessel, and instead appreciate the individual finding himself within the group, as Georg Simmel suggested, we can see that NGO membership in the Hong Kong Christian context encourages a loyalty such that exit can in fact be a further expression of religious commitment. The Lutherans of Germany, the Puritans of England, and countless charismatic sects breaking with the mainline churches all demonstrate exit that holds tenaciously to a religion that inspires. Beckoned by the wealth of options in Hong Kong's religious marketplace, Hong Kong Christians regularly commit the sin of bourgeois individualism, for which Liu Binyan was repeatedly punished, expelled from the Chinese Communist Party, and in 1987 exiled to the United States.

SPOTLIGHT ON FELICIA

FROM STAFF MEMBER TO BOARD MEMBER TO VOLUNTEER

As represented in the case of Doctor Loi, who stays in Hong Kong and remains a member of his Alliance Church, exit is a way to set up a liberal church in Hong Kong and further express personal loyalty to the Christian teachings as he establishes a church open to non-Christians. This exit, moreover, represents not a break from the NGO but both practical and personal realization of its lessons. Doctor Loi finds society via his

---

[44] Albert O. Hirschman, *Exit, Voice and Loyalty* (Cambridge, Mass.: Harvard University Press, 1970). On exit as outmigration, see Khun Eng Kueh, "Negotiating Emigration and the Family: Individual Solutions to the 1997 Anxiety," *The Annals of the American Academy of Political Science, The Future of Hong Kong*, ed. Max J. Skidmore (September 1996); Shu-Yun Ma, "The Exit, Voice, and Struggle to Return of Chinese Political Exiles," *Pacific Affairs* 66, no. 3 (1993); and Wei-Chin Lee, "Read My Lips or Watch My Feet: The State and Chinese Dissident Intellectuals," *Issues and Studies* 28, no. 5 (1992).

individualism, demonstrating that Christianity supports civil society as a pathway and foundation for public life, not by requiring entry but by inviting entry and exit. In doing so, the work of the NGO develops the person and so gives collective definition to choice as well as commitment.

Achieving such a longitudinal perspective on membership requires more than just periodic updates. The wider social and political reality of Hong Kong must make membership an experience of commitments, shifts, and exits. The institutional support of organized, free, yet competitive religion must make it so. Individuals themselves must make choices and take actions to make it so. In the years since Felicia graduated from university, in her NGO she has taken up and passed along the roles of salaried staff, volunteer board member, and independent, occasional volunteer. Despite their variety, these voluntary commitments never exhausted the available options. Other, more long-standing ways to express faith present themselves in Hong Kong's rich religious marketplace, compete for people's consideration, and challenge individuals to define themselves through the particular affiliation and its demands. A thoughtful convert to Catholicism whose involvement in Catholic groups attracts attention within the community, Felicia has received encouragement in her development. One more-traditional option suggested by others, for example, has been for Felicia to become a nun. She understands this role to encompass a regular routine of living and working involving prayer, obedience, and obligation that would not suit her: "Although my style is a disciplined person, but I don't feel I have to be a person like that."[45]

When approached for the staff position with the Diocese Commission, Felicia was likewise hesitant. As she tells it,

> I became a full-time staff apprehensively, but came to feel it was really my calling. In the process of working, I later felt that some other work relating to social justice or social ministry was important if we wanted to encourage more Christians to be involved in the work of justice and peace. One such work was the formation of theological education. So I went to California and continued my studies, something I'd been encouraged to do since I graduated from seminary in 1997. During my time away, the Diocese Commission kept asking me whether I would come back to work for them. After thinking it over, considering my age and working style, I concluded I should instead serve in another way. Not working as a full-time staff, a

[45] Author's interview with Felicia, June 30, 2007.

frontline worker having to go to NGO meetings all the time, but as a volunteer. In volunteering I've found more space, more flexibility in deciding what kind of work I really want to devote myself to. I can also work with other Christian groups I've enjoyed cooperating with in the past. I can choose for myself.[46]

Of course, not all exits from the NGO yield innovations, just as not all exits from the church yield innovations. Harriet, who explained to me that she was not an obedient daughter, nor an obedient Christian, nor an obedient staff member—that she was loyal only to the law of God—disappeared from the NGO scene by 1998. Another young woman seeking answers of personal faith and social concern replaced Harriet at Women Aware. Passing the torch in a profession that demands the suitability of workers beyond mere educational attainment, as I will explain in the next chapter, challenges NGO founders and dedicated community members like Felicia, who recognize the problem of finding more Christians to involve in work that they believe matters.

[46] Author's interview with Felicia, June 30, 2007.

— 5 —

Passing the Torch

Rally at Star Ferry Pier, Tsim Sha Tsui (photograph by Lida V. Nedilsky, 1998)

The compelling dynamics of individual choice and commitment that form the backbone of *Converts to Civil Society* as a study both of real people and of theoretical ideas about engagement in the public sphere were vividly expressed in the earliest interviews. While working in the offices of Center for Reflection in the summer of 1997, immediately before her move to England to study art, Agnes mentioned the particular burden of NGO work that consumes staff and challenges others to commit to an NGO's program. In addition to her day job at the Center, Agnes volunteered with and served as an executive committee member of Women Aware. In those capacities and within a friendship circle dating back to her days as a university student, she applied her professional skills as a writer and editor. She squeezed this work into her free time over evenings and weekends, as she testified:

> I help with the journal *Liberation*. And, occasionally, if at Women Aware they have a book they are going to publish, I may help write an article or translation. Yes, sometimes it's exhausting doing so many things. Yet my experience with the Center, Women Aware, and groups like them is that we don't have many resources: not only in terms of money, but also people. We find familiar faces in doing work for nearly a decade. Where are the newcomers? It's important to train more people to share the tasks and responsibilities.[1]

Sustainability is clearly an issue for Agnes: sustainability not only of her own energy level and involvement but also of any organization to which she dedicates herself. How is the NGO as an expression of religious commitment sustained in so individualized and personally exacting a system? The NGO, like the Catholic order or the Protestant sect, is an invention of human beings working out their problems and meeting their needs. Neither timeless nor fundamental to human life, it instead expresses life in a particular context. For Hong Kong Christians, their particular context is dominated by political transition as well as by personal transformation based on the choice to commit to a demanding form of life. Depending so much, as the NGO does, on a combination of spiritual, religious, philosophical, and political commitment from its personnel, open recruitment or establishing a pipeline of trained staff is impracticable. Instead, as described in the previous chapter, NGOs rely on formal and informal structures to identify candidates appropriate for positions that demand initiative.

[1] Author's interview with Agnes, August 15, 1997.

Church-related institutions that initially draw in young people for conversion also function as support structures for the continued vitality of Christian NGOs. One example, Chung Chi College of the Chinese University of Hong Kong, guides new staff and young interns who have initiative. According to Professor Tung, not only religious affinity but also political and philosophical alignment explain Chung Chi's connection to faith-based NGOs. In the context of NGO founding during the late 1980s, Hong Kong Christians, including theology faculty, debated what role Christians should take leading up to Hong Kong's return to Chinese sovereignty. The fault line dividing Christians hinged on anyone's answer to the question of whether to maintain a critical, prophetic voice or to assume a conciliatory position with regard to China and Chinese churches. Faculty at Chung Chi College sided with the advocates of prophetic voice, in turn facilitating, from Professor Tung's perspective, the supply of student interns and future staff of NGOs.

> At Chung Chi they provided an atmosphere cultivating discussion, so students could consider issues from different sides rather than care about the official position of the institutional church or its leaders. Because of this liberal attitude, they supported democratic views. The majority if not all faculty of Chung Chi were in favor of direct elections in 1988, the earliest that the Democratic Alliance was calling for, and, in really tense situations like the Tiananmen Massacre of 1989, sided with student demonstrators.
>
> That affected students. Although some came from conservative churches, and some from churches not agreeing with this line, they came already committed in terms of being members of Christian communities. If graduates were not already political activists or social activists themselves, they became more sympathetic to social and political activities. Really looking for such opportunities to work, people like these Chung Chi graduates supply most of the staff for Center for Reflection, for Women Aware, even for the [Catholic] Diocese Commission.[2]

Chung Chi's role in channeling like-minded students to NGO destinations is more complicated than Professor Tung admits. While NGO staff and members including Agnes, Wilson, Noah, and James graduated from Chung Chi, among faculty at Chung Chi some studied under NGO founders like Reverend Hap. NGO founders including Reverend Hap, Reverend Gwong, and Karen have taught courses at Chung Chi and at other schools of theology, as well as directly through churches. Moreover, among NGO staff interviewed across the years, institutional

---

[2] Author's interview with Professor Tung, July 29, 1998.

affiliation has gone far beyond Chung Chi College to include other colleges at the Chinese University of Hong Kong, as well as Shue Yan University, Lingnan University, Baptist University, the Hong Kong Polytechnic University, and the University of Hong Kong.[3]

Although incomplete, the professor's rendering of the process by which individuals move from university and church to NGO suggests two central factors. On the one hand, disturbances like the assault on prodemocracy demonstrators and supporters in and around Tiananmen Square on June 4, 1989, push Christian students and faculty to realize their own purpose in life and so demand more from education under exceptional circumstances. On the other, turnings like the more predictable change in status from secondary to tertiary student pull believers onto higher levels of religious formation and intellectual growth as a matter of course. As James recounted in chapter 2, the Tiananmen Square Incident as an unpredictable disturbance urged him to change his life and seek justice. At the same time, becoming a Catholic and later a university student compelled him to handle these two separate changes in his status as if related. Distinguishing himself from those students intent on securing a degree in business and entering a pipeline to employment and promotion, he instead pursued religious studies and self-discovery at Chung Chi College. James's response to disturbances and turnings in his life illustrates how, by helping address the individual's problem of purpose, these two dynamics at once generate individual commitment and sustain the community of voluntary members.

DISTURBANCES AND TURNINGS

The process by which commitment transcends one generation holds practical implications for all those people who find inspiration from their freely entered commitments. Consequently, how to sustain commitment is a question neither new nor strictly academic. The seventeenth-century Puritans, whose model of community so influenced colonial America, built their world on the idea of covenant. Only individuals who voluntarily entered into a promise with God to realize the true church, and so regenerated their personal commitment, counted among visible saints, the elect, and therefore full members in communal religious and political

[3] Only the Hong Kong University of Science and Technology, established in 1991, was not represented as a formative, educational institution among the people interviewed for this study.

life. As original members began to have children, a significant issue in the development of both adult individuals and their religious community, a practical problem presented itself to the Puritans: How should the church handle the matter of baptized children, those incapable of testifying to their spiritual regeneration? New England clergy who gathered in Boston at the Synod of 1662 answered with the half-way covenant, a formula for securing partial membership and partial privilege without compromising the religious community's command for every individual's regeneration of personal commitment to God and to each other.

As articulated in a late nineteenth-century elaboration of the creeds and platforms of Congregationalism, written two centuries after the Puritan settlement of New England, baptism by true Christian parents solved the problem at least until children reached adulthood:

> Church-members who were admitted in minority, understanding the Doctrine of Faith, and publickly professing their assent thereto; not scandalous in life, and solemnly owning the Covenant before the Church, wherein they give up themselves and their children to the Lord, and subject themselves to the Government of Christ in the Church, their children are to be Baptised.[4]

Then, by revealing to the congregation their spiritual transformation, adult regenerates could confirm owning the covenant themselves. In this way, God granted children the means to accept salvation, unless in resisting the means they refused it.[5]

Yet, as baptismal records show, many churches greeted with reluctance the half-way solution offered by the Synod of 1662. If they accepted it in principle, they appeared slow in implementing the reform in practice. Considering that by the late seventeenth century "at least half those who owned the covenant had reached an age where one would expect them to have children," such reservations begged the question of why more did not seek baptism for their children.[6] Rather than use the half-way covenant, individuals continued to rely on regenerative membership

---

[4] Williston Walker, *The Creeds and Platforms of Congregationalism (1893)*, cited in Ross W. Beales, "The Half-Way Covenant and Religious Scrupulosity: The First Church of Dorchester, Massachusetts, as a Test Case," *William and Mary Quarterly* 31, no. 3 (1974): 465.

[5] Perry Miller, "The Half-Way Covenant," *New England Quarterly* 6, no. 4 (1933): 694.

[6] Robert G. Pope, "The Half-Way Covenant: Church Membership in Puritan New England" (1969), as cited in Beales, "Half-Way Covenant," 467.

inspired by contemporary disturbances as the means for entry. In other words, the second generation experienced its own religious fervor, in its own time, and under its own conditions of stress.

The above academic discussion of turnings and disturbances in America's religious history shares three important parallels with the case study of religious and political commitment in post-1997 Hong Kong. First, like the Puritan example in which focus on personal commitment to Christianity cuts across space and time, raising the question of regenerative membership and scrupulosity, *Converts to Civil Society* takes a longitudinal approach to the study of voluntary commitment. Hong Kong Christians insist on entering into a relationship with church and God on individual initiative, even if they had been raised within Christian households. Moreover, they choose an additional set of standards to guide them in their development as Christians: involvement and often employment in the NGO, an organization that demands selflessness through service, for example via a middle-management position without much in the way of financial compensation or promotion. In so doing, they establish exacting conditions difficult to sustain by voluntary membership.

Second, that a context of disturbance encourages the next generation's observance of strict standards of religious membership deserves investigation, considering Hong Kong's particular historical context. While any polity faces challenges on economic, social, and political fronts, Hong Kong in the aftermath of its return to Chinese sovereignty faced several disturbances. Heightened by the uncertainty of what it actually meant to be reunified with China under the Chinese Communist Party in a one country, two systems model, these disturbances assumed epic proportions.

In fact, on July 2, 1997—within a day of Hong Kong's official return to Chinese sovereignty—crisis hit this financial center with the floating of the Thai baht. Hong Kong experienced economic destabilization, with a regional currency meltdown that saw the value of South Korean, Philippine, Malaysian, Indonesian, and Thai currencies substantially depreciate with respect to the U.S. dollar. Just in one month, between early December 1997 and early January 1998, Indonesia's rupiah plummeted from approximately Rp 3,700 per U.S. dollar to Rp 8,000 per U.S. dollar.[7] Hong Kong felt the effects of the general economic

---

[7] "Memorandum of Economic and Financial Policies of the Government of Indonesia" (Washington, D.C.: IMF, January 1998).

slowdown. Residential property prices dropped by 40 percent in early 1998 compared to their third-quarter 1997 peak,[8] while the stock market lost more than 30 percent of its value.[9] The depth of Asia's financial despair generated more than fiscal woes. When overseas Chinese living in Jakarta, Indonesia, became targets for physical attack in May 1998, Hong Kong people realized that extreme economic hardships had merged with violent social discontents. At Star Ferry Pier, depicted in the photo heading this chapter, men, women, and children gathered to denounce the atrocities.

Within the same period, 1997–1998, Hong Kong people experienced a brief but intense health crisis with avian influenza (H5N1), or bird flu. Reports that three Yuen Long chicken farms had lost considerable livestock were followed by news that four people had died across a period of eight months; health concerns of bird-to-human viral transmission ensued. In late December 1997, Hong Kong suspended imports from mainland China, while the PRC imposed an indefinite ban on live chicken exports. With direction from the Centers for Disease Control, in Atlanta, Georgia, as well as the World Health Organization (WHO), based in Geneva, Switzerland, Hong Kong followed up a strategy of closing its border with the mainland with an initiative to cull all commercial poultry within its territory. Public workers and even civil servants came out in force to gas or slit the throats of 1.3 million birds, including geese, ducks, chickens, pigeons, and quails, whether locally bred or imported live from the PRC. By early February 1998, it proved safe to lift the ban on Chinese importation of poultry; yet bird flu raged elsewhere in Asia. In subsequent months, H5N1 outbreaks across China, Vietnam, Laos, Kampuchea, Thailand, Indonesia, South Korea, and Japan required culling 25 million birds. The Hong Kong SAR's handling of bird flu raised questions there of transparency and efficiency as well as government accountability.

Problems of defending boundaries merged with problems of defining them with the right-of-abode debates in 1998–1999 and again in

---

[8] Sanjay Kalra, Dubravko Mihaljec, and Christoph Duenwald, "Property Prices and Speculative Bubbles: Evidence from Hong Kong SAR," *IMF Working Paper 00/2* (Washington, D.C.: IMF, January 2000): 3.

[9] Staff of the International Monetary Fund, "Chapter III: International Financial Contagion," *World Economic Outlook* (Washington, D.C.: IMF, May 1999): 73.

2002, and the anticult panic of 2001. In the first case, the High Court's interpretation of Hong Kong's Basic Law stating that families divided at the border between PRC and SAR had the right of reunification and abode was overturned by the National People's Congress Standing Committee in Beijing. Children in Hong Kong without right of abode were soon denied entry into schools. The Hong Kong Diocese of the Roman Catholic Church, overseeing the education of a significant portion of Hong Kong youth, entered the debate when Cardinal John Baptist Wu called on schools to defy the education ban. His successor, Coadjutor Bishop Joseph Zen, appealed to the diocese's three hundred schools to keep open their doors and affirm the right of unity of the family in Hong Kong. Pressure of this kind may very well have led to the government's eventual capitulation, abandoning its closed-door policy on schools at the end of 2001. More than a policy issue, however, the right-of-abode debate tested Hong Kong's legal sovereignty after its High Court's ruling on the Basic Law was opened to reinterpretation by the central government. The arrangement of one country, two systems was again tested in 2001 when certain representatives of the Hong Kong legislature, taking cues from China's Religious Affairs Bureau, moved to draft a definition of religion versus cult along the same lines as that of the PRC. Coupled with a push to enact an antisubversion law (Article 23 of the Basic Law), this invitation to engage religious leaders in formalizing the meaning of religion raised concerns about diminishing religious freedom and Christianity's loss of privilege in the Hong Kong SAR.[10]

Spring of 2003 brought another health crisis: the outbreak of severe acute respiratory syndrome, or SARS. In early April, fatalities due to SARS numbered seventeen; by midmonth, the number rose sharply to eighty-one. And when at May's end officials finally lifted the WHO-imposed travel ban to Hong Kong, the SARS medical crisis had infected 1,750 residents and taken nearly three hundred lives. Although government measures included the closing of schools, housing estates, and business activities, while commercial and personal interests cancelled conferences, expos, and celebrations, again questions emerged from the public concerning transparency and accountability. As information surfaced regarding the mainland government's underreporting of SARS infections within its own borders, people in Hong Kong questioned

[10] Lida V. Nedilsky, "The Anticult Initiative and Hong Kong Christianity's Turn from Religious Privilege," *China Information* 22, no. 3 (2008).

whether their Hong Kong SAR government delayed its communication with the public so as to respect the information blockade by China's leadership. Many wondered whether the Hong Kong SAR regime understood itself accountable to the PRC or to its own people.

Concurrent with the SARS outbreak of 2003 and peaking with the heat of July, Hong Kong's government initiated definition of the political crimes of treason, sedition, subversion, and secession in relation to PRC sovereignty. Chief Executive Tung Chee-Hwa's push to secure approval of an amended Article 23 by a legislative council only partly determined by direct election incited public outcry. Residents complained that the process, as well as the product, threatened basic civil liberties, the common law system, Hong Kong democracy, and Hong Kong autonomy. As one local newspaper reported, religious leaders openly opposed the proposed legislation:

> In a statement, signed by more than fifty prominent figures from the Anglican, Methodist, Baptist, Presbyterian and Catholic churches in their personal capacities, church leaders vowed that Christians would unite and uphold social justice in opposing the implementation of Article 23 of the Basic Law, which aims to ban acts of treason, subversion and sedition. . . . [One Protestant leader, Reverend Yam] said Christian churches would be under threat if the laws were enacted, as it could affect links between local churches and their mainland counterparts. Other concerns raised by the clerics include a "chilling effect" on their missionary works.[11]

By official counts, July 1 demonstrations that year numbered half a million people. Within a week of the demonstrations, on July 7, 2003, Chief Executive Tung through spokesman Donald Tsang Yam-Kuen announced the shelving of the offensive legislation. By September 5 that same year, he withdrew this legislation from consideration. And on March 10, 2005, Tung resigned from his position of leadership, making way for his designated successor, Donald Tsang, to automatically assume the job of chief executive. Essential for preserving citizens' interests in light of the public's 2003 battle on Article 23, July 1 demonstration organizers in 2007 promoted universal suffrage in the election of all legislators and the Hong Kong chief executive.[12] As Hong Kong's

---

[11] Ambrose Leung, "Christian Leaders Issue Rare Call for Protest on July 1: The Groups See the New Security Bill as a Potential Threat to Religious Expression," *South China Morning Post*, June 21, 2003.

[12] For elaboration on the various mechanisms used to determine representatives

transition to a post-1997 order, or one reunified with China, is yet ongoing, disturbances have been a regular source of renewed attachment to religious scrupulosity among existing believers.

Finally, while disturbances provoke some Christian NGO workers to deliberate whether to bring children into such an unstable world, more often than not Christians in Hong Kong NGOs readily enter parenthood. In so doing, they mark a transition to a new role, or what anthropologist David Mandelbaum calls a turning, in their lives. The life cycles of Hong Kong NGO workers reorient toward rearing the next generation.[13] Domestic workers from the Philippines and Indonesia, hired to shop, clean, cook, and supervise family members young and old, help free Hong Kong men and women to be committed Christians. But such help cannot solve the fundamental problem of Christian commitment: growing preoccupation with private rather than public concern. As Mr. Fu explained in chapter 4, starting a family introduces a new struggle against self-centeredness. Not limited to a focus on the individual person and his or her pleasures, self-centeredness in this instance means a focus on the well-being of the family unit to the exclusion of society's well-being (not unlike the critique of family under radical communism in Maoist China). Affecting as it does Christian formation, the influence of family demands the convert's reflection and judgment. And like the Puritans, who, prompted by a new generation of potential believers, reexamined their doctrines of personal choice and commitment, Hong

---

in Hong Kong government, as well as the religious response to one in particular, see Lida V. Nedilsky, "Institutionalizing the Representation of Religious Minorities in Post-1997 Hong Kong," in *Marginalization in China: Recasting Minority Politics*, ed. Siu-Keung Cheung, Joseph Tse-Hei Lee, and Lida V. Nedilsky (New York: Palgrave Macmillan, 2009), 215.

[13] Life cycle research, where gendered and social psychological considerations prevail, circumvents this question of family socialization of the next generation of activists. Male activists, although admittedly shaped by sibling example or spousal relations, appear free of private commitments and ready to sacrifice for the general cause. Conversely, while addressing the impact of raising children, research on the life cycles of women attends less to women's wider commitments. In both instances, children are charges rather than companions in development. See David Mandelbaum, "The Study of Life History: Gandhi," *Current Anthropology* 14, no. 3 (1973); Donatella della Porta, "Life Histories in the Analysis of Social Movement Activists," in *Studying Collective Action*, ed. Mario Diani and Ron Eyerman (London: Sage Publications, 1992); and Susan Geiger, "Women's Life Histories: Method and Content," *Signs* 11, no. 2 (1986).

Kong Christians likewise deliberate their children's potential to live lives of their own choosing.

SUCCESSION AND THE ORGANIZATIONAL PIPELINE

Disturbances and turnings, as vehicles of change in the lives of individual Christian converts, together underscore the indeterminacy of organizational succession for the Christian NGO in Hong Kong that depends on the convert for its own wherewithal. NGOs cannot rely on the training of a cohort of workers to simply take up where the older generation left off. At the same time, each generation expects to leave its own mark on the organization as well as on society. In the NGO sphere, the dynamism sparked by disturbances and turnings therefore encourages innovation of the sort that enables widening initiative.

For example, the East Asian financial crisis signaled by the Thai baht's plummet in value on July 2, 1997, developed over time and had unexpected repercussions. Within a year, the precipitous depreciation of the Indonesian rupiah coupled with rising incidence of bankruptcy and capital flight, inflating fuel and food prices, and burgeoning unemployment rates to create a climate of intense suffering in that country. This implosion of Indonesia's economy ended the thirty-two-year rule of Suharto and prompted a new president, Bacharuddin Jusuf Habibie, to urge his mostly Muslim population to weather the economic storm and implement personal austerity measures by fasting at least twice weekly. The impact of Indonesia's fall was felt in Hong Kong, some 2,030 miles (or 3,270 km) away.

Reports in mid-May 1998 that angry rioters and renegade soldiers had gang-raped ethnic Chinese women in Indonesia sparked members of Women Aware and those in their network to stage a rally and postcard drive on August 17 at Star Ferry Pier in Kowloon. The group of mostly women volunteers raised two banners and erected a display of newspaper articles resembling a memorial, propped up as it was like a tablet honoring the dead. While journalists photographed the banners and video documented the rally, a prerecorded informational played over loudspeakers. Middle-aged women in gray T-shirts moved among the crowd, inviting people to sign postcards addressed to President Habibie and donate money to cover postage. Individuals then dropped their postcards into a clear plastic box. According to newspaper reports, scoured by organizers in the days after, rally efforts yielded over three thousand signed postcards and donation in the amount of HK$16,000 as people contributed far more than the HK$1.20 required for postage.

Organizers demonstrating at Star Ferry Pier intended both to underscore women's solidarity with the victims of rape and to distinguish their own protest from those of the previous month, when Hong Kong's opposing political parties led separate vigils and submitted petitions urging the central government in Beijing to apply diplomatic pressure on Indonesia to protect its ethnic Chinese minority from human and civil rights violations. At least one of those late July petitions for accountability, staged outside the Indonesian consulate general, ended with a barrage of eggs and chants of "hang them."[14] Fiona, no longer working for Women Aware by 1998 but now spokesperson for a related group and an employee of an international NGO, expressed her intention to join an upcoming demonstration organized not by a political party but by women and NGOs. When asked what it would mean if media presented the issue as a matter of Chinese solidarity, Fiona answered,

> While problematic, that's certainly likely. Fellow participants are also likely to be there because of the Chinese connection. I'm working into the statements the point that the solidarity being expressed is not just Chinese, but women supporting women against domination by soldiers, men. The particular circumstances (Indonesia, Chinese women) are not important to me.[15]

Womanhood, not nationhood, was the basis of solidarity in this instance. And yet the rally represented another distinction.

Within its own Christian NGO universe, Women Aware's participation in the rally evidenced the dynamic innovations possible for both organization and members when the torch of leadership is passed from one individual to another. As one participant unaffiliated with Women Aware put it, the event at Star Ferry Pier showcased new people coming in to address women's issues in a way less ideological and more theatrical than had dominated past activities.[16] It brought together around an issue of current import different generations of what she referred to as activists.[17] By staging the demonstration in a public, open, high-traffic

[14] Simon Ng, "Protestors Hurl Eggs in Anger," *Hong Kong Standard*, July 27, 1998.

[15] Author's interview with Fiona, July 22, 1998.

[16] Author's interview with Cecilia, August 21, 1998.

[17] Adelyn Lim, "The Hong Kong Women's Movement: Towards a Politics of

place like Star Ferry Pier, all ages and genders came together. Familiar and unfamiliar faces in the crowd included staff from Women Aware, with new allies forged through the NGO's current leadership and recent projects among working-class women, like those from a public housing estate in Tsing Yi where Women Aware collaborated with female clergy (including Reverend Gwong) to address issues of domestic violence. "Just see what umbrella you are opening," Women Aware staff member Queenie explained, and you get the particular composition of groups for a particular demonstration.[18]

Except for the administrative assistant, the entire staff at Women Aware had changed from just the previous year. With Harriet gone, a young woman named Nicky soon joined. While still a philosophy and theology major at Baptist University, Nicky read on the door of one professor's office an advertisement for a course on feminist theology offered by the Christian NGO. The flyer reminded her of how a teacher from secondary school had once sparked her interest when mentioning social concern and Women Aware. Nicky registered and paid for the course but also accessed the NGO's library of feminist literature. She finished her studies in May, and by June Nicky was working at Women Aware, eager to glean more on the topic of feminism.

> Because my father lived and worked in Indonesia, I grew up in an all-female household, one of four sisters. Whereas my grandparents on my father's side berated my mom for having only useless girls, she—an immigrant from China who did not get the chance to attend school—tends to boast about having a university-educated daughter. That's what matters to me. My mom knows I'm working for a women's group, though she probably has no idea what that means.[19]

Even the familiar faces in the NGO community now fulfilled different roles from those of the previous year. In addition to Fiona finishing up her work at Women Aware at the end of 1997, Karen had vacated her post as the organization's general secretary to continue divinity studies in the United States. An important link to the senior women advocates in the public spotlight, Karen still exerted a force through Women

---

Difference and Diversity," in *Women's Movements in Asia: Feminisms and Transnational Activisms*, ed. Mina Roces and Louise Edwards (New York: Routledge, 2010).

[18] Author's interview with Queenie, August 4, 1998.

[19] Author's interview with Nicky, August 6, 1998.

Aware that drew together different generations. This was due in part to her effort to find a replacement for herself at Women Aware. Reaching out to Queenie, the recovering Catholic who had led the crowd in song on the eve of Hong Kong's return to Chinese sovereignty June 30, 1997, Karen found a temporary solution. Queenie filled in for her mentor through the post of executive secretary for the mostly Protestant organization. In turn, Fiona filled in for Queenie as spokesperson of a group Queenie had cofounded in 1995 with the support of Women Aware to assist Hong Kong people struggling to be open about their sexual orientation. Although not present at the rally herself, Karen enabled Queenie's initiative and helped staff it for an emphasis on women rather than Christians.

Queenie's approach to the demonstration, opening up the particular umbrella she did for the Star Ferry Pier postcard drive, hinged on speaking the same language as her allies, in this case women who were not necessarily Christian. As someone raised Catholic, who had graduated (like Fiona and Felicia) from Sacred Heart Canossian College, Queenie could speak like a Christian. But in the context of working within a coalition, and to her relief, she need not:

> I myself am not a very Christian person, although Karen keeps emphasizing I am a very spiritual person. I'm a better Christian than some [famous Christians in Hong Kong]! Admittedly it is weird: although I accept Jesus as a very great leader, I do not accept him as my savior. You have the chief woman at Women Aware not believing in Christ.
>
> At first it was awkward, but now that I've adopted the Christian language, the ideology, it's easier. As long as you speak their language they think you are the same. The worst part is they'll ask which church you go to![20]

Having accepted the torch from Karen to lead Women Aware in 1998, Queenie carried it until a sense of hopelessness and stress got her thinking about what next to do.

By spring 2000, demoralization and disappointment framed Queenie's recollection of work at Women Aware over the previous two and a half years: from inability to rectify family reunification, which the government jeopardized by its handling of the right-of-abode issue ("we are not a city of rule of law anymore"), to frustrated attempts at demonstrating Christian repentance through prayer after the culling of

---

[20] Author's interview with Queenie, August 4, 1998.

more than a million birds ("a little too much impact on our soul!"), to impotent efforts at reflection beyond mere memorialization on the tenth anniversary of June 4 ("when it came to reflection, everyone became a dead dog"), to personal failure to normalize Catholic participation in Protestant-based Women Aware ("we are not Northern Ireland, but at the very low level you get all this conflict").[21] What appeared simple to achieve and obvious to support ended up impossible and contentious, such as with the issue of mainland Chinese children of Hong Kong parents trying to exercise their right of abode in Hong Kong.

> To us the thing was very simple; children should have the right to stay with their parents. But police allowed progovernment organizations to use extremely loud loudspeakers repeating one sentence: "Support the government." It so overwhelmed that everybody became deaf. Even though we had some very loud musical instruments, we could hear nothing: bang, bang, bang, but no sound. How symbolic! You tried to raise your voice and yell, but no one listened. Instead, they used a bigger voice.[22]

For Queenie, it was like a big war; and the human rights organizations, organizers of NGOs, students, liberal individuals, and, in the end, even the Catholic Church lost the war. Exercising a principled voice in the public sphere seemed hopeless in Hong Kong. Within the year, in 2001, Queenie returned the torch she had secured from Karen and moved on.

For Queenie, giving up leadership at Women Aware did not mean abandoning civil society. In 2004 she ran for and won election to the position of district councilor, representing as her constituency the entire population of one geographic district. In her new capacity she neither generated policies nor wrote laws nor even made decisions. Instead, she facilitated dialogue between citizens and their civil servants. Her leadership guided and so enabled others' initiative. Whereas in NGO work she had selected her concerns and chosen her sides, distinguishing between the deserving and undeserving, the work of representation required concern for everyone: from those living in government-subsidized public housing estates, to those in low-rent buildings, to those in high-rent developments. "You have to listen to what they say. And, of course, one thousand people have one-thousand-and-twenty opinions."[23] Echoing her approach to working among committed Christians at Women

---

[21] Author's interview with Queenie, April 5, 2000.
[22] Author's interview with Queenie, April 5, 2000.
[23] Author's interview with Queenie, July 3, 2007.

Aware while at the same time criticizing the attitude of NGO advocates toward the public, Queenie elaborated her strategy of cooperation thus:

> You cannot just have your own opinion and talk down to everybody, because no one will be talked down to by you! Only thing you can do is speak their language and negotiate a solution where everyone feels happier or less unhappy. That already is success.[24]

Responding to other people's concerns, Queenie now took greater interest in questions of land use and public access to spaces, Hong Kong's old districts and their experience with urban renewal, and the relationship between personal responsibility and democracy. Sharing physical space fostered democratic norms, as she humorously described in a 2007 interview toward the end of her four-year term in office:

> An architect was determined to design a pet park for us on a strip of land near the harbor. When it came time to consider management of the space, the government worried: "We have a pet park, we have grass, but how are we going to manage that? People are going to let the dogs mess it up!" In talks we suggested, "Why don't we provide them with bags? We'll have signs begging them to put the poo into the bags and the bags into the rubbish bin. We must try our best to show the government, show the world we are mature people." It didn't take long before all the poo was being tidied, demonstrating that ordinary citizens are not barbarians. They can behave themselves. They can be responsible for their society, for their city. Even the chief of the Department of Leisure and Culture was amazed.[25]

In her shift from NGO work to the work of district councilor, Queenie redefined democracy. Her meaning shifted from one of representing the unrepresented to that of ensuring continued space for self-representation and self-agency of citizens. In her mind, this set her apart from other politicians:

> When the guys in LegCo talk about universal suffrage, I say, "You talk about whether I support you, and you have my vote, and then you don't care." What I care about is building platforms so people can speak and decide what is going to be in this city. Let people be responsible for what they say and do. Like this pet park. When Hong Kong people take responsibility for management or development of their whole city we have real democracy; because people can make their own decisions, right?[26]

---

[24] Author's interview with Queenie, July 3, 2007.
[25] Author's interview with Queenie, July 3, 2007.
[26] Author's interview with Queenie, July 3, 2007.

Lessons in democracy likewise followed Reverend Hap as he moved beyond the NGO. When Reverend Hap retired from Center for Reflection in 2000, positioning Karen at the helm, he continued teaching courses and preaching sermons well into the 2000s before taking on one last project, whose vision he explained in 2007.[27] Having spent the years after his retirement circuit riding like the clerics of old—responding to invitations to preach at one church one month, another church another month—Reverend Hap grew fully aware of the challenges and limitations of local churches. Moreover, he felt exhausted. "I have been around since 1977. That's thirty years. Constantly meeting people, I get very tired, both psychologically and physically. So you understand, can't you?"[28] Settling down to attend to the needs of one local church would meet his own needs as he modeled against hopelessness. "When you hear so much, 'Local churches are impossible, local churches are hopeless,' then of course I say, 'Let me show you that might not be the case.' So that's why I'm here."[29] He returned to a congregation to try his hand at creating a model local church.

By "model local church," Reverend Hap means one internalizing the message that Christians are on this earth together to serve the world. Reorienting church time to general time, and reorienting leadership and initiative from the minister to a group of members, a wider circle of church people, known as a corporate ministerium, enables God's servants. Reverend Hap had come upon a church in chaos. Founded in 1927 but built on a colonial missionary legacy going back to the 1840s, the church had seen so many transitions in leadership that, despite a sustained church history, members of the congregation functioned without theological grounding. Even worship lacked order. It moved, instead, with the rhythm of a whimsical congregation, what members compared to a family. Reverend Hap's job was to help congregants learn order and purpose and so realize the model local church.

> I tell them, "The church is not a family. It should be a servant of God in this world." If you ask me what that model is like, I say it's about gradually

---

[27] Within that organizational structure—demanding intense commitment, vision, and drive—Center for Reflection, like Women Aware, faced a problem of succession. When Karen decided to retire, the Center found but a temporary solution in promoting Wilson to executive secretary.

[28] Author's interview with Reverend Hap, June 18, 2007.

[29] Author's interview with Reverend Hap, June 18, 2007.

becoming a servant of God in this world. Don't ask me how to serve, because it is the church's business to answer. While I can give a few pointers, I only motivate.

And in order for the church to solve its own problem of purpose it has to be a truly worshipping community. Only in worshipping God can you have the sense of worshipping God outside [knocks on the wall of his church office]. I see worship as equipping them to serve God once they disperse and go back to their own family. If you equip them, this service will grow out naturally.[30]

And what does worship accomplish, precisely? How does it affect the person's being, equip man and woman to serve? Some would say that doing is a sign of being.

Exactly! We often say that Jesus worked miracles. You have to ask: How come he could do that? Now I begin to understand. Jesus could work miracles because he was constantly experiencing interior communion with God. In the Bible we have one story: A woman wanted to be healed. So she wanted to touch Jesus. And she was healed. Jesus discovered the power just came out. Jesus didn't do anything. He simply was present with those people in need.

And so the inner self is more important than the outside doing. Both are very important! But if you constantly ask, "What do we do?" I wonder whether that's enough. We should equip our interior. Our inward journey will make the outward journey more meaningful, more fruitful![31]

In Reverend Hap's reflection on his turning from NGO director to church senior pastor, much like Queenie's account of her turning from NGO executive secretary to district councilor, leadership means cultivating in yet another arena the skills necessary for Hong Kong people to be free and responsible citizens. Sustainability of the NGO purpose comes, it appears, from individual agendas both inside and outside the NGO, and might not even involve personal commitment to or membership in the NGO itself. Passing the torch, therefore, should not just be understood in the limited sense of straightforward organizational succession.

Not only are organizational succession and congregational leadership delicate conditions to nurture and sustain if one wants to encourage public action, but also religious freedom itself requires effort and innovation to maintain. One final example of the passing of the torch

[30] Author's interview with Reverend Hap, June 18, 2007.
[31] Author's interview with Reverend Hap, June 18, 2007.

through the organizational pipeline appears in the response to a disturbance that directly threatened Christianity in Hong Kong: the initiative of 2001 to define evil cult and ban Falun Gong in Hong Kong. In the course of engaging the debate, Christianity turned from a position of privilege to accept its vulnerability in the post-1997 Hong Kong context, and so changed the terms of its engagement in the public sphere.[32] It did this through a combination of actions and enlightenments out of self-interest just as much as out of principle.

When, after a bold demonstration in Tiananmen Square by some 10,000 believers, Beijing leadership officially banned Falun Gong as a threat to PRC national security in July 1999, the movement to proclaim openly commitment to Falun Gong resurfaced in Hong Kong. Employing the same spaces as demonstrators before them, Hong Kong practitioners of Falun Gong placed display boards at Star Ferry Pier depicting in graphic photos the violence suffered by practitioners on the mainland at the hands of public security agents. Practitioners' international meeting in January of 2001 included a march to the central government's Liaison Office to beseech justice on behalf of those physically violated and killed. Within a month, Ye Xiaowen, director of China's Religious Affairs Bureau, appeared in Hong Kong, publically criticizing the dangers inherent in the contemporary Falun Gong movement as well as the historical abuses by Christian missionaries in China. Hong Kong leaders in both the executive and legislative branches of government immediately responded with public recognition of Hong Kong's cult problem. The Home Affairs panel of LegCo initiated a meeting of religious representatives to clarify the meaning of religion to reserve the protections offered by Article 32 in the Basic Law concerning freedom of religion only for religions and to exclude cults.

This push to define cult in contradistinction to religion incited discussion among NGO members and staff and a widening array of Christian interests in Hong Kong to define Christianity, defend the private sphere of religious belief, and secure the line separating Hong Kong from China in the one country, two systems formula. In all these actions, NGOs reinforced the cultural practice of moving back and forth across the boundary separating private and public spheres, pulling in more people with each effort. Upon being solicited for help, Karen at Center for Reflection first directed Home Affairs to invite denominational heads

---

[32] Nedilsky, "Anticult Initiative."

to its February 2001 meeting to define religion versus cult. After the meeting, Bishop Joseph Zen of the Roman Catholic Church, the general secretary of the Hong Kong Christian Council, and Karen came out together in official opposition of any such definition. Participation, the three argued, suggested capitulation to outside pressure to attack Falun Gong in Hong Kong, as well as violation of the separation of church and state via tapping religious leaders to define political terms. Second, Karen met with two representatives of Falun Gong to gain an understanding of their own position. Third, she mobilized a dozen Protestant leaders, not limiting the group to mainline churches already familiar at Center for Reflection but including also evangelical and Pentecostal representatives new to dialogue with the group and with the government. Fourth, Karen collaborated with the Diocese Commission, with Faith at Concern for Hong Kong, and with several other NGO offices to compose a petition and mobilize a signature campaign through *Ming Pao Daily News* rebuffing government efforts to draft an anticult law for Hong Kong: "We are worried about the issue that the Hong Kong government intends to enact an anti-cult or mental manipulation law . . . [and] call upon every believer to actively express your opinion."[33]

Like the opinions expressed by Queenie's constituents, responses within the wider Christian community varied markedly. They included at one extreme the call to widen the net to include other so-called cults, specifically Jehovah's Witnesses and Mormons. In the middle were Christian leaders who expressed indecision and the need for further reflection. And at the other extreme, those practiced in the public sphere called on fellow Christians to actively oppose any ban on cults. Such differences were overshadowed, however, by the common recognition that religious belief in Hong Kong was neither fully understood by arbiters in the courts or media nor beyond the scope of violent suppression by the intolerant. Christians betrayed, in fact, a common concern that their own faith (not a matter of rational thought or rational behavior) was vulnerable to prosecution as well as persecution. Such enlightenment opened the way still wider for defining Christianity as more tolerant and engaged after Hong Kong's reunification with China than when it was a religion privileged under the colonial administration of Britain. In turning away from religious privilege and addressing their religion's vulnerability head-on,

[33] "Invitation of Signatures to Oppose the Enactment of an 'Anticult Law.'" For publication in *Ming Pao Daily News*, June 2001, draft copy obtained by author.

not only because theology directed it but because self-interest and political circumstances necessitated it, Christian NGOs drew still more faithful into the realm of civil society. In June 2001 the office of the chief executive announced that it had aborted its initiative against cults.

SUCCESSION AND THE HOME

By shaping conversations and experiences in the home, disturbances and turnings play their part in forming the younger generation's relationship to the Christian NGO and civil society in post-1997 Hong Kong. For Christians and their non-Christian colleagues in the NGO field documented in this book, early recollections of growing up in Hong Kong of the 1960s and 1970s conjure factors that directed them onto their own distinct paths of development. As elaborated in chapter 2, converts to Christianity grew up in an environment of radical economic, educational, and religious development. Postwar baby boom Hong Kong was a space for individuality and choice that parents born of the prewar generation simply could not enjoy, though their hard work had secured it for their children.[34] More than that, as accounts of converts attest, where children literally squeezed themselves into a government-issued apartment room with four or five siblings, grew up with parents who had not themselves had access to formal schooling and so took their children's education as a basis for mature decision making, and ventured off to what was typically a church-run school, young people often sought and found in religious community both refuge and themselves.

Today, these same people, now not only adults but in many cases parents, work at their middle-management jobs, enjoy the fruits of at least a university education (and often a master's, professional, or Ph.D. degree besides), and have no more than two children. Despite this measure of success—or, as Mr. Fu in chapter 4 suggests, because of this measure of mainstream stability and success—today's adults seeking to be true to their chosen faith feel strained as well as conflicted by the roles they have assumed. Encouraged in work and faith to look beyond family and children's interests to take on the additional concerns of the wider society, they recognize that family as a conservative institution poses obstacles to social concern and any transformative agenda they contemplate as Christians. This normal yet life-altering turning, starting

---

[34] Lui Tai-Lok, *Four Generations of Hong Kong People* (*Seidoih Hèung-góngyàhn*) (Hong Kong: Step Forward Multimedia, 2007).

a family, presents a distinct set of concerns. Yet the decision to have a family provides another opportunity for demonstrating commitment. Having a baby opens entirely new possibilities and hopes.

MAKING TIME FOR FAMILY

Not every couple wants to start a family by bringing a new life into the world. Faith, the proud mother of a little girl, explained that her husband, rather than she, wanted a baby. So at thirty-three years of age she considered it. Then she prayed. If she had one, she would have one; if she did not, then that would be okay. Faith displays images of her daughter, whose name in Chinese means "peace from God," everywhere in her office; pictures adorn the desk, walls, and computer screen. Believing that a sibling would be good for her child, Faith seriously considered having a second. But with her husband in a new job, a mortgage, and a sense of instability, she told him she did not need a second baby. Like many parents in the United States, Faith found another way to enjoy the promise of young life: through World Vision, Faith supports four children in Africa and mainland China.

She had worked for a church organization, a political campaign, and a university, as well as the NGO Center for Reflection, before joining Concern for Hong Kong. So when Faith first began her new job, she logged long hours and focused solely on her professional commitments. Since having a child in 2004, staying at Concern for Hong Kong has ensured freedom and flexibility to close the office early or miss a day of work if her daughter is sick. Her boss understands, and her modest salary does not seem so bad because there are no strings attached with their consequent pressures. Her husband, in contrast, works from 8:30 a.m. until 10 p.m. Of course, Faith attends meetings some nights, and finds it time consuming to plan for occasional weekend events like the July 1 prayer vigil and protest march of 2007. Her daughter knows enough now to ask her mother each morning whether she has a meeting that night. Faith wants to spend as much time with her as she can, knowing that these are the years her daughter needs her mother most. Moreover, playing with the domestic helper is no substitute for doing homework with her mother and learning from her generally. Most nights, however, Faith comes home tired. She considers switching to part-time work or even retiring young, but continues.[35]

[35] Author's interview with Faith, June 27, 2007.

Luke and his wife have one son and another baby on the way when Luke relates his experience of family. With the pressures and promise of an additional member joining his household, Luke scrambles to complete his advanced academic degree. Working as a full-time staff member during a period of leadership transition at the Protestant evangelical NGO that has employed him for much of his adult life relieves many of his concerns, since he can continue the research and writing necessary for his dissertation. Even in the office Luke is permitted to read his books, and his work time is flexible. Of course, it helps that Luke's research relates to this organization: what he studies and what he writes have applications at work and for the young people he engages on university campuses. Despite finding this comfortable fit, Luke recognizes he needs to switch to part time if he is to finish his dissertation before his next child is born.

The winding path of the intellectual might not be what Luke's wife wants for their children, especially since as a social worker she tends toward the more realistic and practical. Luke, on the other hand, reaches out for ideas and inspirations. He found a gem of a book in the sale bin of a bookshop. A manual of sorts, the book, written by a Catholic priest, explores the role family can play in expanding civil society. Luke's current interest in Catholicism, including both its element of spirituality and the struggles of liberal theologians with the Catholic Church's legalism, relates to and informs his life. This sale bin find is especially eye opening for Luke, who associates the institution of family with the establishment and maintenance of rules. He says, "Introducing as it does a liberal conception of family, with a liberating and political potential for family, the writing of this Catholic priest offers something scholars completely ignore."[36]

LEARNING TO PRAY

Wending up the hill to the Catholic cathedral for a Mass celebrating the thirtieth anniversary of the Diocese Commission's founding, Rachel arrives just in time to catch and join the march of the cross nearing its final station. Rachel bemoans the chanting, recalling an occasion that same spring when she and her husband decided to take a walk at the Peak before lunching together. She had heard a similar singing of hymns and remembers being bothered by it. Then she realized it was a group

[36] Author's interview with Luke, July 15, 2008.

of Catholic regulars who walk with Cardinal Zen every Easter Monday. Rachel's apparent impatience with her church is almost normal. Asked whether she ever brings her teenage son with her to church, she replies,

> He comes sparingly; he has his own ideas about religion and God that he's working through. Of heaven he thinks it is a rather creepy place: "You have to be there forever, and be always happy. Yet how can you know happiness if you are never sad?"[37]

Rachel is close to her only son. As he tells it, his mother calls him every day to check on him. And they always have dinner together, since his father is normally out late for work. Do they go to church together? Rachel interjects, saying that this is her failure. She grew up closely tied to the church. Through Catholic schooling, through a circle of friends who did everything together and were committed Catholics, she experienced not just Catholic Mass but Catholic community. She wishes that her son knew something of Catholic fellowship, since it is a different kind of friendship one can have through Catholic community than one has through school or work. When a couple of her schoolmates recently returned from San Francisco for a visit to Hong Kong, they all went to church together. It made Rachel happy, that feeling of community, with everyone there together. She hopes that her son will come to appreciate these things, too. When asked whether he is Catholic, Rachel's teenager responds by specifying that he believes in Jesus Christ and he believes in God. The New Testament speaks to his beliefs. Even today he tells the truth 97–98 percent of the time, he announces very seriously. But the Old Testament, he asserts, is not believable, as it does not make sense that God tells Joshua that he can have a kingdom, and then Joshua destroys existing ones. Why should this be acceptable to God?[38] What makes still less sense, he says, is the false promise of total peace and happiness that some seek. If one has always been ensured of happiness, then one will not know how to make oneself happy. One will not be able to appreciate happiness. It is the same with freedom.[39]

---

[37] Author's interview with Rachel, June 17, 2007.
[38] Author's interview with Rachel and son, July 8, 2008.
[39] Author's interview with Rachel and son, July 8, 2008.

WHEN MY CHILD IS BIGGER

The religious calendar of Hong Kong in the twenty-first century includes not only the colonial-era observance of Christmas, Boxing Day, Good Friday, Easter Sunday, and Easter Monday but also June 4 (the anniversary of the 1989 Tiananmen Square Incident) and July 1 (the anniversary of Hong Kong's 1997 handover from British to Chinese sovereignty). These last two dates, occurring in the heat of summer, are occasions of public demonstration rather than private prayer or community celebration. Not to overstate the contrast, June 4 and July 1 as public demonstrations involve demonstrating the love, hope, and joy experienced through the right to gather in huge numbers and exercised through the freedom of speech in Hong Kong. NGO parents often include their children in celebrating these anniversaries, trying to pass on the love of democracy to the next generation.[40]

Already Jefferson and Fiona have introduced their infant son, whose name in Chinese means "life of the universe," to the social activist lifestyle; one year old in summer 2008, he attended both the June 4 candlelight vigil and the July 1 demonstration. For June 4, Fiona's father also participated. They showed off the baby to friends who for years have been reuniting at the vigil. But July 1 was sweltering. Fiona's mother and father both accompanied the trio into the crush of marchers. Joining late in the afternoon at 4:30 p.m. to avoid the heat of the sun, Fiona carefully hydrated her infant so he would not suffer heatstroke. They avoided not only sun but also loudspeakers. "Other parents bring their children," Fiona commented, "so my son isn't a novelty at this event."[41] But his presence added something fresh and exciting to these two familiar and anticipated anniversaries. In 2008 Jefferson attended the June 4 candlelight vigil for the nineteenth time. Having never missed a single commemoration of the Tiananmen democracy movement's violent end, Jefferson and his family on this particular occasion were photographed by *Apple Daily* newspaper laying a bouquet of flowers at the memorial.

But as the culmination of countless meetings, preparations, and smaller orchestrations, June 4 or July 1 commemoration feels like a

---

[40] Hong Kong organizers claim that mainland Chinese university students studying in Hong Kong, tourists who happen to be in Hong Kong, and tourists intentionally visiting for the dates (excluding mainland performers who engage in official observance of July 1 reunification) consider these two events to be demonstrations and willingly participate.

[41] Author's interview with Fiona, July 4, 2008.

workday rather than a holiday for many NGO personnel. Faith, as full-time staff at Concern for Hong Kong, finds she must wait until her daughter grows before pulling her into the crowd.

LVN: Will you take your daughter to go for a demonstration?

Faith: When she's bigger. Because you know this July 1 I must organize programs. I cannot go back from Hong Kong Island to the Kowloon side and fetch her from home! And marching is demanding! So, once she grows up a little bit, I'll tell my husband to bring her and meet me.

LVN: Why? I understand you take her together to church with you to pray. But why take her for demonstrations?

Faith: Why? I want her to know that Hong Kong has no democracy. I want her to learn to fight for her rights. When Hong Kong returned to China in 1997, human rights were reduced. We must fight for direct elections for the full Legislative Council and then for the chief executive.[42]

At no more than three years of age, the children of Faith's boss at Concern for Hong Kong, Mr. Fu, joined their father to demonstrate. The younger daughter, transported in a stroller for the evening event, participated when just a baby. Now, with the younger in primary school and the older already thirteen, they express interest in joining the June 4 candlelight vigil as well as in watching television news. In fact, such is the case not only with Mr. Fu but with other members of Concern for Hong Kong. Because the parents know what happens in society, so too do the children. Faith agrees with this approach to parenting and wants to help her child know the significance of June 4, July 1, Hong Kong news reports, and Hong Kong government policies. She promises her four-year-old daughter the chance to march next July 1.

Luke's son is two years old in 2008, and very lively. Luke has certain expectations for him, which are communicated through the Chinese name chosen for him. "My son's name means he speaks to hope," Luke explains. "It means to bring hope to the world."[43] Luke takes his toddler to church with him, where he participates in Sunday school by playing with the other children but also learning to pray. Luke wants his child to be considerate and respectful toward others. For example, he teaches his son that he cannot simply expect to be served by but must also serve

[42] Author's interview with Faith, July 7, 2008.
[43] Author's interview with Luke, July 15, 2008.

their domestic helper. Exposure is Luke's greatest responsibility to his son. When he gets a little bigger, his son will accompany him to some of the places Luke leads college students for exposure: the tough side of Hong Kong—neighborhoods like Sham Shui Po and Tin Shui Wai. These are places where new immigrants settle, with high rates of poverty, suicide, and domestic violence. Luke elaborates,

> Sham Shui Po is today what Mong Kok used to be before its redevelopment. This issue—planning and community impact—increasingly draws into public life today's young people. It's not the black-and-white/which-side-are-you-on engagement that defined my generation. I was shaped by Tiananmen Square. But the young people of today were only one or two years old when the People's Liberation Army tanks rolled into Tiananmen and crushed the demonstrations for democracy. Young people today don't know anything about it. But they do have an interest in what is changing within Hong Kong itself.[44]

That the political awakening of today's Hong Kong teenagers stems from something other than Tiananmen Square does not mean that Hong Kong's struggles fail to work on their young hearts and minds. Instead, just as their parents grow in their understanding of citizenship and its responsibilities, so too do their children grow.

As Wilson cooks up one dish after another in his home kitchen, his preteen son eagerly handles the cleaver to chop scallions and garlic, helps wash the rice, and inspects the live shrimp for dinner. With Wilson sautéing the vegetables, his son, named to embody the place between heaven and earth, describes his understanding of his father. What is most important in his father's life? He considers the question, and after some thought answers: family, friends . . . health, life . . . money. His father's hobby being photography, he explains, money is important in order to have the other things, like to buy a camera.[45] And how does his father communicate what is important to him? Wilson himself answers, "I show what I believe in through my actions."[46] His son reflects on this and says he observes through his father's actions that the government is important to him, as well as the ethnic minorities, and being fair. Is it important to his father to support the government? "No, it is not a matter of supporting the government," Wilson interjects. His

[44] Author's interview with Luke, July 15, 2008.
[45] Author's interview with Wilson and son, July 5, 2008.
[46] Author's interview with Wilson and son, July 5, 2008.

son then elaborates: his father believes that when the government is not doing what is right for the people, then he must say something about it to make things right. Does he want to act by his father's example, or do other, maybe additional, motives guide him? Yes, he agrees with his father, but he is often doing his own thing with friends, concerned about the small things rather than big things. But the big things can affect him now or in the future, so he knows he should care. He has gone to rallies, and he has learned about the ethnic minorities in Hong Kong, and he now carries his own plastic water bottle, rather than contributing to Hong Kong refuse and global pollution.

For his part, Rachel's teenager, on the verge of university exams and entry, eagerly talks about elections. Touring Taiwan with his parents in 2008, he accompanied his father on visits to party headquarters for the Kuomintang and Democratic Progressive parties, respectively. Ma Ying-Jeou struck him as a man of intelligence, ability, and will to fight corruption, and the 78 percent voter turnout to choose the national leader of the Chinese world's first real democracy inspired him. He even had his own taste of citizenship the previous December with the 2007 Hong Kong Legislative Council runoff between former Chief Secretary for Administration Anson Chan Fang On-Sang and former Secretary for Security Regina Ip Lau Suk-Yee. He volunteered for Anson Chan's campaign, stuffing envelopes and such work after completing his school day. Anson Chan won with 57 percent of the vote, and at the victory celebration Rachel's son had his picture taken with both former Chairman of the Democratic Party Martin Lee Chu-Ming and newly elected LegCo representative Anson Chan. As the youngest volunteer for the campaign, he stood out that night. But being involved in a political campaign, getting onto the street corner and then moving into the square, comes with painful life lessons, too. At a street rally for his candidate, much like at the Beijing Olympic torch procession in South Korea where demonstrators against violence in Tibet met Chinese advocates, he sometimes felt physically overwhelmed by supporters of the rival candidate. Neither a competitive election nor a democratic political system guarantees civility.

NOT FOR ME TO SAY

While it is clear that, like most parents, Hong Kong's committed converts to Christianity guide their children in replicating their own principles and practices, they also reveal a reluctance to control or even predict their children's personal commitment. Faith addressed her daughter's political and spiritual development, and the implications of that development:

LVN: If your daughter has no interest in Hong Kong's political development, what then?

Faith: If my daughter doesn't even know at least her basic rights, her human rights, and doesn't want to fight, then that's her foolishness. It is out of ignorance that she doesn't care about society. But if she knows and then she doesn't want to fight for her rights or gives up the fight, then that's okay. This is her right. As her mother I must give her this chance to know and decide.

LVN: And if she doesn't believe in Jesus Christ, what then?

Faith: I can't do anything about it. I've given her the chance to believe, taken her along to believe, but if she doesn't believe, then there's nothing more I can do. I cannot force her.

Offering a half-way covenant of her own, Faith sees this dual obligation to afford opportunity and thwart ignorance as her basic parental responsibility. But it is not for her to decide her daughter's faith. Likewise, she judges herself powerless in determining whether her daughter eventually responds to the call of civil society as Faith responded when the Tiananmen movement shattered her political ignorance. Yet, when asked whose children if not her own child will continue the push for Hong Kong democracy, Faith recognizes in her daughter something of herself that cannot be generalized to Hong Kong citizens at large nor to the Christians Faith attempts to educate through Concern for Hong Kong.

My daughter knows I'm very interested in watching television news. She will watch along with me and ask, "Who is that?" and I tell her, "That's the chief executive. He is a very bad guy!" After that, the next time she watches news with me she will say, "Oh Mommy, why is he a bad guy?" I tell her he lies and makes bad policies that favor rich men. So I analyze the news for her. But I add, "Don't you say this in school!"[47]

Luke's son refers to hope; in fact, his name means "to bring hope to the world." While such a name communicates serious expectations, Luke admits there's very little he as a parent can or should control that the boy himself must ultimately decide. Instead, he wants his son to explore, discover. Does discovery include religious discovery? Will Luke's son grow up Christian, or will he enjoy the space to choose faith much as

[47] Author's interview with Faith, July 7, 2008.

his father did before him? Luke first considers, then announces, that he wants his son to grow up concerned about others, not self-centered: "I want my son to have justice in his heart. If as a boy he grows up to admire Buddha, for instance, if he can articulate why a certain religion is meaningful to him, then that is fine. He doesn't have to simply follow my lead."[48] Wilson, too, communicates that whether his two children share his concern for social justice, and follow him into the church, into the NGO, out into the square, depends upon their personal decisions, interests, and choices. What if his children refused to attend church with him? Whatever. What if his children attended Catholic church? Whatever. What if his children attended Islamic mosque? Whatever. What if his children did not believe in God? It's their decision.[49]

Wilson and his wife and children attend church together, and his children participate, infrequently but on their own volition, in certain Center for Reflection activities. His daughter, whose name reflects "the ideal of highest achievement," has indicated to Wilson some interest in his work and at least one issue the Center has handled in a post-1997 Hong Kong. In 2007 she voluntarily joined the civic education program, seeing it as an opportunity for her to develop and make new friends. But for the most part she would rather be less serious. When sometimes Wilson remarks on a sermon they heard in church, she tells him not to be so serious in his conversation. And when told that a trip to Taiwan with her father involved changes to their itinerary (Wilson, at a time of staff resignations, had to lead a four-person tour of church people affiliated with Center for Reflection to the southern city of Kaohsiung to familiarize them with developments among the faithful there), she could not hold back the tears. She had imagined being in Taipei, with opportunities to participate in activities around pop idols and other Taiwanese celebrities. As a teenager, the news threatened to spoil her dream vacation.[50]

HOPE FOR THE FUTURE

While in discussing the future they reveal judiciousness formed of a mix of practical reality and liberal parenting philosophy, in naming their children parents betray hopefulness well beyond the bounds of reason. Life of the Universe, Highest Achievement, Hope to the World, Peace from

---

[48] Author's interview with Luke, June 28, 2007.
[49] Author's interview with Wilson, July 5, 2008.
[50] Author's interview with Wilson, July 5, 2008.

God, and Between Heaven and Earth all are names carefully chosen to communicate to parent, child, and public the expectation of good things to come. Rachel's son recalls fondly listening to his mother's rendering of Bible stories and Aesop's fables; four or five years old at the time, he learned much from his mother this way. In so doing he gives his mother a chance to offer her own mild praise. Rachel describes telling him the story of *Journey to the West*, the classic Chinese tale of the monk and the monkey king who journey together to India to retrieve Buddhist sutras. As the story goes, the monkey king, a disciple of the monk, at one point faces a monster disguised as a beautiful maiden in order to harm the monk. Suspecting this much, the monkey king uses his staff and martial arts to dispel the apparition. Instead of receiving praise or thanks, however, the monkey is told to leave the monk. At this, Rachel's son broke down in tears. He recognized the injustice done to the monkey, Rachel finishes proudly by way of explanation.[51]

As Fiona explains, in being a social activist she has developed (as most people in her line of work do) a negative, critical view of the world around her. But with the birth of her first child, with this baby's entry into her world, she finds hope. She expects good things to come because he now exists. He may change things for the better: not just her mood, but the world itself. Jefferson, too, has such feelings, she adds. His greatest wish is that his son grows to be a truly good man, who cares for the environment and is concerned for the poor. But, if after years of attending demonstrations, their son refuses to go, Fiona acknowledges, "It is his choice."[52]

If the children of committed Christians do not follow the example of committed Christians and converts to civil society, then who will? And what will be the consequence for society? Every generation, Wilson states, has its problems. This generation may be very comfortable, self-centered, but it will be responsible for dealing with its problems. Of course, it will not be able to solve all of them. That would be impossible. His son and daughter have to make their own choices but at the same time understand that they are responsible, that their actions have consequences for others. But the world will be better. He is confident about this.[53]

---

[51] Author's interview with Rachel and son, July 8, 2008.
[52] Author's interview with Fiona, July 4, 2008.
[53] Author's interview with Wilson, July 5, 2008.

JULY 1, 2007: *Jàngchéui Pouseun*

STRUGGLING FOR DEMOCRACY IN HONG KONG

The ten-year anniversary of the July 1 Handover promised to bring together NGO founders, staff, and members once again. Since 1997 both Paul and Rachel had attended July 1 demonstrations practically every year; they measured their children's growth in the photographs taken each year; they judged Hong Kong's democratic development with the demands as well as the size of one march after another; they lamented Hong Kong's continued lack of democracy and challenged the assumption that Hong Kong people were not prepared for such a responsibility as universal suffrage. Paul, who recently stepped down from a visionary role with the Diocese Commission's executive council to be a volunteer following the lead of others, discussed with Rachel over lunch on June 29, 2007, what the plan was to be for that anniversary day. The march was scheduled to begin at 2:30 in the afternoon on Sunday, July 1, preceded by a prayer meeting involving Cardinal Joseph Zen, ministers of Protestant churches, and leaders of faith-based NGOs. Rachel immediately expressed her reluctance to attend the prayer meeting:

Rachel: You know, I never attend the prayer meeting. I always join the rally, only. I don't want any prayer meeting. I think it's too . . . it's . . .

Paul: A gesture only?

Rachel: I think it's just like Mass, too self-serving.

Paul: But for Catholics, or Christians, we have to pray before we do. Maybe we feel comfortable as a consequence, can supplicate on behalf of God, something like that.

Rachel: What I mean is maybe our fellow Christians or Catholics think that if they first say a prayer it transforms the march into a mission, it's then something very serious.

Paul: I think with the prayer meeting the march is more communal, because we start off pursuing the same objective. And all of us are Christians, so we have a sense of community, a sense of belonging. And then afterwards we move to join the march. Without the prayer meeting we just act as individuals to join the march. It's not very attractive: either we have no objective, or our objectives are not the same as those of the people around us.[54]

---

[54] Author's interview with Paul and Rachel, June 29, 2007.

The people who gathered in 2007 for Hong Kong's tenth July 1 demonstration certainly appeared more diverse and numerous than those who assembled in Statue Square the night of June 30, 1997. Numbering in the tens of thousands, they represented the accumulation of participants across time. But rather than a constant and predictable growth, their numbers ebbed and flowed. Again, the event was not billed as a celebration. In fact, mainline Protestant churches referred to this particular July 1 as "Hong Kong Sunday." At the church where Reverend Hap presided, worshippers considered the Handover's anniversary as a chance to achieve a new understanding of what Hong Kong was and what Hong Kong needed.

The readings selected for the occasion were meant to be difficult to hear, the sermon a test of humility. Reverend Hap asked,

> Why does Jesus say, "It is not enough for you to honor me and say you'll come with me"? Why does he reject people who say they are willing to follow him? Because Jesus knows what it would mean to follow him. To follow him means to find no relief, to find no place to hide, to find no home. That is what happened to those men who followed him. Following Christ was an extreme demand upon each man and upon him. We cannot forget that for him it meant the passion and death and rebirth, things we cannot imagine. For him it meant the pain, the agony, the suffering, the humiliation, the test of commitment. Such commitment is beyond us. We're human.[55]

The demand for ourselves, Reverend Hap preached, is not to be sacrificed on a cross, but to be generous with others: to be concerned about the poor, to be concerned about the marginal, to not be self-centered or even family centered, but to reach out to strangers and other people. To be Christian is to do those things that do not make sense to us in our daily lives. That in itself is a struggle. That is enough to show our commitment.[56]

The assembly in Victoria Park, starting point for the march just as it is the site for the annual June 4 candlelight vigil marking the anniversary of Tiananmen Square, filled in 2007 with representatives of the invisible, the marginal, the unrecognizable, the ineligible, and Christians, who accepted the call to do that which did not make sense in their own daily lives. Under a white canopy, Karen, Faith, the general secretary of

---

[55] Author's field notes paraphrasing sermon of Reverend Hap, July 1, 2007.
[56] Author's field notes paraphrasing sermon of Reverend Hap, July 1, 2007.

the Hong Kong Christian Council, various ministers, and lay Christians gathered together with Cardinal Joseph Zen, Paul, Felicia, Rachel (who had chosen to attend along with her husband and son), and many others, whether they were Protestant or Catholic, to participate in singing the prayer of Saint Francis: ". . . that I may not so much seek to be consoled as to console / To be understood as to understand / To be loved as to love . . ."

They then moved out from their sheltered corner of the park, on a day when predictions of heavy rain did not materialize, to join with other groups assembled on the wide open playgrounds that dominate the southern end of Victoria Park. Thanks to organizers' experience handling the comings and goings of countless small groups, volunteers raised a platform upon which singers at microphones entertained the crowd, while organizers lined up demonstrators like an army of discrete regiments to move out onto Hennessy Road. Queenie sang that day, too. As she recounted in an interview a couple of days after the demonstration,

> I just went there and sang three songs, and then went back to my position (on Hennessy Road). That's more important, because we collected some money (for our campaign fund) at this event. Now they have new people (working the demonstration), so let the young people do it. I know I'm not going to work with them because I'm in another position now, and I know I'm never going to go back.[57]

Standing in the crush for forty-five minutes before any regiment could move, practically the only way to assess the extent of the surrounding crowd was by the number of soccer fields organizers had indicated as divisions.

But as organizers directed them to step forward, individual groups were visible arraying themselves. The Confederation of Trade Unions joined to protest the deterioration in working conditions. A crying panda bear with black rings around his eyes, symbolic of workers' exhaustion under longer hours of labor, decorated their banners and signs. Nearby, a group of construction workers donning hard hats led a burro, a beast of burden they had made of papier-mâché. With arms and faces painted white and black rings around their mouths and eyes, calling to mind Jefferson's liberal use of lipstick on the night of the Handover, a phalanx

[57] Author's interview with Queenie, July 3, 2007.

of some seventy female Indonesian migrant workers wearing aprons and head scarves awed those standing around them. Even children marched on behalf of their schools, demanding the recycling of their lunch boxes. Carrying an enormous sculpture of empty plastic containers that resembled an iceberg, like other voiceless segments of the population, schoolchildren too young to vote communicated their own political platform.

Despite the critical stance each group assumed and the vulnerability implicit in their presence, the lively carnival atmosphere that brought them together buoyed everyone's spirits. Inspired, one pastor exclaimed, "Next year I have to organize my church! The church will have a banner, and we will have drums!"[58] And in the context of all these groups, such expressions of commitment were readily understandable; standing among those assembled there seems so much more to do, so much yet to say, and so individuals decide to turn toward the public sphere as others turn toward Jesus. A worker with a faith-based international NGO, an ethnic Chinese from Indonesia, commented that there were so many different voices it was confusing what the place was about. But the combination of interest groups and political parties in attendance indicated that one popular forum existed for bringing together elected representatives with citizens as well as noncitizens, those with limited voting rights and those with none at all. The small groups carried banners that expressed interests: the need to uphold labor laws, the need to change social policies, the need to demonstrate tolerance of minority populations, the need to seek justice for asylum seekers and refugees, the need to take action against pollution of the environment. Under these banners they met face to face with politicians of certain colors, elected district councilors including Queenie and LegCo members, under the common banner of *Jàngchéui Pousuen*, Struggle for Universal Suffrage.

At the far end of the demonstration, where it tapered off around Admiralty, a performance art installation—that had been developed and previously performed in Mong Kok highlighting the issue of racial discrimination toward ethnic minorities—drew considerable attention. On the sidewalk outside Pacific Place shopping mall, a young man covered in ochre paint reached out for the hands of passersby streaming from two directions, the mall and the march. He challenged them to overcome their hesitation and touch him, accept him as he was. Karen gleefully shook hands, thanking him for the experience, while others drew back

[58] Author's field notes of Reverend Chan, July 1, 2007.

and shook their heads instead. Wilson was notably absent. Just ten days earlier he had shared his own and his daughter's involvement in this project through an outreach excursion into the neighborhood of Sham Shui Po offered by Center for Reflection. Wilson had even employed his photographic skill to document the common journey of Nepali, Pakistani, Chinese, Christian, and non-Christian youth.[59] Yet, acting as an individual with the freedom to assemble or not assemble, he had chosen to sit out this particular demonstration.

Visible from the second level of a double-decker trolley, one massive group brought up the rear of the demonstration. Their colorful uniforms and precision formation brought to mind a different July 1: the official celebration rather than alternative commemoration of Hong Kong's return to Chinese sovereignty. There, beautiful costumes and polished performances featured Cantonese opera singers and a lion dance. The effect of seeing this last group inspired even more emotion than encountering either the white-faced, black-eyed Indonesian domestics or the man whose basic humanity could be affirmed with a handshake. How came it to be that such a group crossed boundaries and joined an opposing march? Misguided assumptions soon modified. Elderly ladies dressed in bright yellow pantaloons and tops, each woman's head capped by a tiny headdress, expertly performed on percussion while dancers in equally bright uniforms kept steady pace behind. A marching band in royal blue raised shiny trumpets into the air, measuring time with the sharpness of every synchronized step. And there, finally, appeared the banner that rose above the practiced splendor: Falun Dafa. The spiritual and exercise group Falun Gong, banned in mainland China for offering a system of morality alternative to that of the Chinese Communist Party, brought up the rear so that it connected with the larger demonstration without compromising either its own integrity or that of another group. Its objectives would not be confused for another's.

"You know," Reverend Hap had said two weeks prior, "in the Bible we have one story: A woman wanted to be healed. So she wanted to touch Jesus. And she was healed. Jesus discovered the power just came out. Jesus didn't do anything. He simply was present with those people in need."[60] From a theological perspective such as that presented by Reverend Hap, the Christians who gathered at the July 1 demonstration

[59] Author's interview with Wilson, June 21, 2007.
[60] Author's interview with Reverend Hap, June 18, 2007.

may have been present through each one's communion with God. From another perspective, sensitive to the cause and effect of official rhetoric such as Reverend Hap's sermon from the pulpit, individual Christians had followed the direction to do what was for each uncomfortable and in contrast to his or her everyday actions. But a sociological perspective attentive to the long-term, dynamic development of individuals and groups reveals that practiced skills, extraordinary despite their everyday presence, account for such a demonstration.

SPOTLIGHT on Reverend Gwong

Shepherd of the Community of Believers

In order to sustain both the particular conception of true Christian and the public role of Christians in Hong Kong, leadership has been a torch passed from one committed individual to another. By employing, modeling, and guiding the development of everyday skills necessary to be free and voluntary members of any association, NGO leaders, church pastors, and budding politicians have drawn fellow believers, fellow citizens, and future citizens into a place where they, too, can initiate actions relevant to their interests and aspirations. The sustained principle of respect for the individual's potential to think, feel, and grow forms the foundation of community. While posing challenges to sustainability, such an unstable basis for regeneration adapts as it responds both to predictable, personal turnings and to unpredictable, general disturbances.

Upon retiring in 1998, Reverend Gwong had the option of moving into a home for retired ministers. But being a city person, she did not want to sit in a kind of prison, trapped in some remote place. Likewise, having spent her adult life directing the development of individuals and churches—whether as a teacher (1954–1963), college tutor (1964), school chaplain (1966–1977), secretary for mission education with one missionary organization (1977–1981), or general secretary of her church (1981–1998)—Reverend Gwong did not want to stop guiding and supporting Christians after her retirement.

Attending programs at Center for Reflection, Women Aware, Concern for Hong Kong, and similar NGOs; guest preaching; teaching courses at Chung Chi College and China Graduate School of Theology—she continues to work with individuals to support congregations, and through congregations to nurture individuals. Like Reverend Hap, Reverend Gwong preaches at a different church every week. "I'm still a minister,

I'm still preaching, that's my job. Many people ask me to preach, so it is by invitation. I go by choice."[61] She chooses small churches, because with thirty to forty members they cannot hire a minister; without her they cannot receive Holy Communion. In contrast with her own denomination, where they "do things very properly, very orderly," these independent churches have just one man leading and serving. "That person has a tough job. He may be theologically decorated but not yet a minister. In theological studies nobody tells him what theologically to do; he has only studied what's up there [ideas], not what's down here [practices]."[62] Still enjoying teaching, she treats church members like her students:

> I want to make them think, make them respond. But it's not the church culture to say anything. They just want to leave. They're in church an hour and that's enough. I always say you want to be a 168-hour Christian, for every hour in the week. It's not about saying alleluia all the time, not about praising the Lord. It's about how you think, how you feel about what's happening, how you behave: being, like Christ, a mountain for people.[63]

In Hong Kong, the opportunities exist to establish a form of life based on choice as well as commitment. Possessing not only a variety of churches but also a variety of conceptions of Christian faithful, Hong Kong's open, competitive, religious marketplace puts the onus on individuals to realize their potential. For Reverend Gwong, her entire adult life story reads like a road map of emerging options. At every turn, she presents the torch to young and old with the stubborn hope that someone will take it. Few, unsurprisingly, are capable of seizing that torch directly and unflinchingly. Yet, whether by Reverend Gwong's actions or words, she touches enough people in different ways to ensure the opportunity endures. What this endurance means for Hong Kong since its convergence with China is the subject of the concluding chapter.

---

[61] Author's interview with Reverend Gwong, June 18, 2007.
[62] Author's interview with Reverend Gwong, June 18, 2007.
[63] Author's interview with Reverend Gwong, June 18, 2007.

— 6 —

The Question of Convergence

Outline of the Goddess of Democracy spray painted onto facade,
The Chinese University of Hong Kong, Sha Tin
(photograph by Lida V. Nedilsky, 1997)

As contemporary Hong Kong straddles the twentieth and twenty-first centuries, commitment to organized religious life reveals a complexity not unlike that also faced by the United States in the same period. All of the forces that make for a quest culture—modernity and its discontents, the rise of the expansive self, the role of the media, and global influences[1]—appear relevant in Hong Kong's context, too. In addition to these overlapping and general forces, one factor Wade Clark Roof employs to distinguish his own study of the United States from that of any other society is the cultural meaning of religion in the United States.[2] The experience of seeking, finding, trying, and transforming makes sense to Americans on a very personal level. It is not that individual actions like seeking are bound to happen to everyone, or that there is a linear pattern of change for those who do take a boundary-testing step. Rather, more and more members of general society experience in their lives some aspect of questing. Further, Americans increasingly relate to and tolerate the complexity of religious membership.[3]

As documented in the preceding chapters, Hong Kong's quest culture, while not identical, shares much in common with that of the United States. Circumstances and practices significant to fostering choice and commitment in religious life exist in Hong Kong. The wedding of industrial and urban development to a capitalist engine has meant that even in a Chinese society known for submission to group, especially family, the individual has found significant freedom. Families in Hong Kong have had to cope with migration and resettlement in a competitive employment environment. Along with benefiting from gradually greater access to higher standards of education, the younger generation has known ever-rising professional specialization that further pulls it away from the older generation's life experience. Taken together, these strains on family cohesion have enabled contemporary educated children to achieve social mobility and self-definition. Media outlets for private use, such as low-cost book publishers, newspapers, newsletters, VCDs, and radio programs, have also pushed individual development, self-expression, and

---

[1] Wade Clark Roof, *The Spiritual Marketplace: Baby Boomers and the Remaking of American Religion* (Princeton: Princeton University Press, 1999).

[2] Roof, *Spiritual Marketplace*, 59.

[3] As Roof argues and Robert D. Putnam's survey research in his most recent book confirms. See Robert D. Putnam and David E. Campbell, *American Grace: How Religion Divides and Unites Us* (New York: Simon & Schuster, 2012).

self-discovery. Among the ever-growing numbers of Hong Kong college students and young people, a constant array of choices and accompanying uncertainty in decision making combine to create a language of struggle, introspection, and striving that would sound completely familiar in the United States. Organized religion in Hong Kong has tapped into the possibilities presented by these trends of social change and individual transformation. Grounded in the territory's colonial past but also invigorated and diversified through global circuits of preachers, missionaries, and activists along with homegrown charities, schools, and political forums, Christianity plays a central role in supporting individual development there.

So what about that special ingredient unique to the place itself—the cultural meaning of religion in Hong Kong? In the United States in the 1960s, the synthesis of moral, religious, and civic values fell apart, creating a distinct historical context defining what was to come.[4] On a personal level, individualism, coupled with a loss of confidence in American society, increased as people experienced greater social mobility and less certainty. On a national level, Americans beheld the assassination of one president, John F. Kennedy, and, soon after, the political demise of another, Richard M. Nixon, in the aftermath of the Watergate scandal. Between these events, the Vietnam War provoked equally profound domestic struggle. Doubt gained a certain amount of legitimacy in all conversations, including the religious ones. Writes Roof,

> People still spoke of God but the talk no longer had the power to shape and to summon people's lives in ways it once did. Talk *about* religion was for some replacing the language *of* religion; speculating about God was easier, and in some ways more reinforced in the culture, than believing in God.[5]

Such norms of openly expressing uncertainty combined with a Christian culture centered on individual conscience and an ever more diverse religious marketplace to bring about reflexive spirituality.[6] Among Americans today, the onus rests on the individual to know truth, and the individual plumbs her own inner depths to access that truth.

---

[4] Roof, *Spiritual Marketplace*, 64. See also Putnam and Campbell, *American Grace*.

[5] Roof, *Spiritual Marketplace*, 65 (emphasis in original).

[6] Roof, *Spiritual Marketplace*, 65.

LESSONS FROM STATUE SQUARE

In Hong Kong, by comparison, belief in God as expressed through the language of individual commitment still constitutes the core of the convert's experience. Religion, specifically the colonial legacy of Christianity, exercises the power to shape lives and summon people. Rather than speculating about God, people who have chosen against the example or even wishes of family speculate about the institutional church, the religious community, and the religious self. Converts struggle with the inconsistencies and doubts of this world. And these doubts compel their further interest about and investment in faith here on earth. The religious experience of Hong Kong's believers continues to be grounded in groups. Whether in churches, fellowships, or, most recently, NGOs, people find themselves through voluntary association and then form groups compelled by their growing individualism. Such reflexive religiosity, involving give and take between the individual and the collective, preoccupies the believer with the personal and communal achievement of true (*janjingdīk*) belief. As Jefferson noted in chapter 4, Christians in Hong Kong do not blame Christ or Christianity for their doubts; they blame their churches. The NGOs that individual believers establish in collaboration with others like them help resolve some of the dissonance for such doubting Christians. This newest forum for organized religious expression, the NGO, has room even for those who deny belief, like Jefferson and Queenie. At least, it does for a time.

In a manner that increasingly fits the profile of American believers, Hong Kong Christians negotiate religious commitment. But in Hong Kong, believers keep striving for growth within organized religion. Converts, as novices who personally choose a faith, must work to actualize the role of being a true Christian. Finding in Hong Kong a marketplace rich with ideas for how to be a true Christian, and exposed if not immediately receptive to an array of alternatives to any particular denomination or theology's teachings, converts in fact continue to grapple with doubts, disappointments, questions, and quandaries. Called to reflect upon their progress through the process of introspective struggle (*jàngjaat*), they turn, then, to countless teachers for guidance. These teachers engage them through books, mailings, newsletters, websites, VCDs, newspapers, lectures, workshops, courses, conferences, rallies, protests, prayer meetings, vigils, and marches. They connect with them at Sunday school, on university campuses, in seminaries and Bible colleges, in

NGO offices, at churches, on ferry piers, in parks, and on streets. They direct them to seek and find employment that sustains their religious life and personal development within Christianity. But both teachers and pupils will eventually exit their current collective, responding to continued need for personal development as well as continued conflict with the self.

For the lifelong novice, the believer who doggedly seeks greater understanding, the path to correct belief looks daunting, the choices overwhelming. Often, as the only recognizable Christian within the immediate family, the novice cannot and does not turn to family members for guidance. Yet someone must offer guidance throughout the course of the quest. An authority on religion, whether in a religious or secular institution, a teacher or professor, a chaplain or NGO staff, can serve as a guide for the individual walking what looks to be a distinct and lonely path. Recall Felicia, who navigated her way from campus Catholic student group member, to lead staff of the Diocese Commission, to Catholic convert, to volunteer with both Catholic and Protestant NGOs. Interspersed with these Hong Kong commitments were two stints as a theology student in North America. James, first drawn to the authority of priests, turned to professors at Protestant Chung Chi College for lessons on how to be a good Catholic before seeking out Hong Kong's NGOs, including Women Aware, for further support. Doctor Loi, born to Congregationalists and receiving infant baptism, only became a Christian, he explains, through Protestant fellowship. From youth to adulthood he moved in group circles, shifting from fellowship to Alliance Church, and then seeking extra education at Baptist Theological Seminary as well as through courses at Center for Reflection while still a member of his church community. All this questing eventually led Doctor Loi to sign on to the Unitarian Universalist Association, set up an online discussion group, and then form his own local group. Ultimately, in 2009, he organized and assumed the presidency of the Unitarian Universalists Hong Kong.

In this quest for religious maturity, no single someone can satisfy all questions; nor can the institution contain the individual as does a vessel. In the accounts of Hong Kong Christians as converts to Christianity and civil society, no mention of a single leader, church, or organization resounds as having dominated anyone's development. Nor do converts express practical commitment to any one leader, church, or organization. Strikingly absent from individual testimonies about religious conversion and social concern, considering his religious prominence and media visibility, is mention of Cardinal Bishop Joseph Zen Ze-Kiun of the Hong Kong Diocese of the Roman Catholic Church. An outspoken advocate of secular democracy for Hong Kong's general polity, while at the same time a staunch defender of his sole authority when he was assigned to represent the Hong Kong Diocese,[7] Bishop Zen has not been singled out as an inspiration for social action, let alone conversion. While his support of groups like the Diocese Commission and causes like the right of abode sustains certain efforts for a socially concerned and democratic Hong Kong, his leadership does not mark the beginning or the end of these or similar actions. With the exception of Benedict, who along with his wife converted to Catholicism in 2003, most Catholics interviewed for this book converted well before Bishop Zen's rise to power. Even their participation in NGOs preceded his ascent first to coadjutor bishop in 1996, then bishop in 2002, and finally cardinal in 2006.

Among Catholics, moreover, religious as well as political participation transcends the Catholic world. Increasingly, individual Catholics collaborate with like-minded Protestants through their respective organizations. But with narrower choices in the religious marketplace and strict hierarchies within the church structure, Catholics turn, for example, to Protestant colleges for religious instruction and to Protestant NGOs for organizational membership. Rachel, Paul, and Father Yi at once recognize alternative sources of inspiration and are painfully aware of the conservative limitations of any organized religion, including the Catholic Diocese of Hong Kong. Counter to expectations, the Catholic Church does not function as a vessel for social concern in Hong Kong. Scholars find documenting this reality challenging if not troubling. Unless rooted in a recognizable and bounded community, that commitment to social concern, and thus connection to and investment in others, is ephemeral if not utterly absent.

Yet, new trends in self-conception invite close inspection of both religion and civil society. In the United States of the twenty-first century, the individual identifies on a personal level with a wide range of membership yet need not practice a communal form in any one religion. Through the

[7] Lida V. Nedilsky, "Institutionalizing the Representation of Religious Minorities in Post-1997 Hong Kong," in *Marginalization in China: Recasting Minority Politics*, ed. Siu-Keung Cheung, Joseph Tse-Hei Lee, and Lida V. Nedilsky (New York: Palgrave Macmillan, 2009), 221.

example of a self-described "Methodist Taoist Native American Quaker Russian Orthodox Buddhist Jew," evidence exists of the depth of committed belief rather than the depth of practical commitment.[8] For civil society, any depth of commitment—whether individual or group based, whether to belief or practice—has relevance not only for the scholar but for the society as a whole. Reverend Hap, senior pastor and NGO founder with thirty years' experience leading Protestant Christians in their quest for true faith, explores in his retirement the tension between committed belief and committed practice. Practice without worship, he discovers, is action without purpose, because it is action without communion with God. In living out the dynamic rituals that bring individuals together to confess their common humanity, to receive both individual and collective forgiveness, and then to redirect and inspire their actions outside the community of the church, he explains, believers act out the basic steps of skilled Christians. Queenie, someone who refuses religion yet recognizes inspiration in particular offerings from Catholicism, Protestantism, Buddhism, and Judaism, finds rituals equally important for citizenship. The rituals of communicating interests and negotiating differences in a geographic constituency bring together individuals, herself included, and shape groups that strive for some common good.

In both instances of discovery, for Reverend Hap as well as for Queenie, these same skills of entering and exiting, of finding both self and group, make a vibrant civil society. Our common historical reality begs the question, why should not the nature of civil society, like that of any other institution (family, religion, education), change according to the changing meaning across an aggregate of individuals? If Hong Kong at the turn of the twenty-first century is any indication, today's civil society is an evolution rather than a copy of the associational model of the mid-nineteenth century. In the unsettled context of the city, today's civil society assumes a more permeable, situational, and dynamic mode of membership. Here, individualism and solidarity constantly engage rather than compete with one another.

Another striking distinction in the context of Hong Kong's particular quest culture is the urgency added by Hong Kong's return to Chinese sovereignty. For three months in late spring 1989, the imminent political

---

[8] Robert Wuthnow, "A Reasonable Role for Religion? Moral Practices, Civic Participation, and Market Behavior," in *Democratic Civility*, ed. Robert W. Hefner (New Brunswick, N.J.: Transaction Publishers, 1998).

reunification appeared to promise a democratic future for both China and Hong Kong. Through journalists' video footage, banned in mainland China yet shown today in Hong Kong's classrooms via NGO programs in civic education like the one designed by Center for Reflection, young believers witness not an assassin's bullet taking down a president but the People's Liberation Army crushing its own people's movement for democracy. What happened to university students, state-owned factory workers, and ordinary citizens in and around Tiananmen Square June 4, 1989, had profound and personal consequences for individual Christians in Hong Kong. Again, many Christians embraced the biblical lesson of social concern well before June 4. Some even developed political consciousness prior to both conversion and this human catastrophe. But for NGO Christians interviewed for this study, the disturbance left serious doubts about China's political system that resembled those raised by Americans in the aftermath of the Kent State Massacre, when protesting university students were shot down by Ohio National Guards. As detailed in chapter 3, among clergy and lay Christians alike, individuals perceived the student movement as—to quote James, interviewed in 2000—"a kind of Jesus movement." These Christians in Hong Kong looked upon the educated elite student and the common worker occupying the public stage in Beijing as having bravely, selflessly risked the wrath of the state. When tanks rolled in from the surrounding suburbs into Tiananmen Square and people died, theirs was the ultimate sacrifice.

The specter of the Goddess of Democracy then fled Tiananmen Square in Beijing for Hong Kong, where she found shelter as well as visibility on university facades, conference tables, and bookshelves. Although Hong Kong served as the initial point of escape for leaders of the democracy movement, few stayed.[9] Those who did mainly continue to work toward change in mainland China, rather than integrating their goals with those of Hong Kong people. In most literature on 1989, in fact, apart from serving as an alternative model of economic development, escape is all Hong Kong appears to be good for. *Converts to Civil Society* reveals otherwise. Hong Kong Christians, feeling anger and frustration as well as grief, reached out for the goddess and for

[9] An important exception is Han Dongfang, who established an NGO, China Labour Bulletin.

God, and so found commitment rather than escape. As they explained, they felt called upon by God to judge the violent suppression of Chinese citizens as a grave injustice. In their eyes, their local churches, keen to avoid burning any bridges, whether with potential converts or the future sovereign, did not go far enough in offering censure. Consequently, converts to Christianity sought in the early 1990s an alternative to their churches for a source of moral guidance, fellowship, and information about democracy. Christian NGOs, mostly established in the late 1980s during Sino-British negotiation of Hong Kong's future, offered such an alternative. They tapped believers' potential for private struggle (*jàng-jaat*) in order to generate public struggle (*jàngchéui*) in their own square, Statue Square.

So much of the experience of discovery has been made possible by the freedom of speech, assembly, and worship in churches, Bible camps, fellowships, and NGOs that was enjoyed in the former British colony. Without democracy in Hong Kong itself, Christians today still wonder, what is the long-term prospect of security for religious believers and their continued development? Intent on pursuing a personal relationship with God, a small but significant minority of Hong Kong Christians have mobilized around NGOs to realize their true religious selves and fulfill a public role as members of civil society. Whether these believers complain about or accept the limits of the church, either way they realize they must go beyond the church to satisfy their complex needs. They join the NGO with skills already cultivated through the many small and large groups that make up their religious lives and in so doing maintain in postreunification Hong Kong commitment to their city's political development under a new sovereign. Once in the NGO, they engage in issues of social, political, economic, and religious concern including domestic violence in Hong Kong and violence against women of Chinese ethnicity in Indonesia, the ambiguity of Article 23 of the Basic Law and the ambiguity of terms like cult and religion, the right of abode of mainland children born to a Hong Kong parent, and the right to one person, one vote in selecting Hong Kong's chief executive. Everyday skills needed to be free that were introduced through the colonial legacy of Christianity are sharpened by historic events that for countless people add urgency to a personal quest. These skills are what Christians and non-Christians carry when they exit any particular institution in post-1997 Hong Kong.

The Question of Convergence

All this conveys worthwhile lessons beyond the experience of just one city, even if that city is a vital one like Hong Kong. Hong Kong's development of civil society raises in the post-1997 context the question of convergence.[10] After the more than 150 years of political separation of Hong Kong Island from the Chinese mainland required by the 1842 Treaty of Nanking that ended the First Opium War, the Handover of July 1, 1997, signaled political convergence. Distinct parts of a greater China unified to form the Hong Kong Special Administrative Region (SAR) within the People's Republic of China (PRC). Although it was not the democratic political convergence imagined by Hong Kong people when they filled the streets of their city in solidarity with mainland citizens during the 1989 Tiananmen Square demonstrations, for the next fifty years Hong Kong was guaranteed its separateness from the PRC, even as Britain surrendered its ultimate sovereignty to the central authorities in Beijing. Through the creative arrangement of one country, two systems (*yātgwok léuhngjai*), attributed to China's paramount leader and market reformer Deng Xiaoping, Hong Kong's guarantees of freedom of religion, speech, assembly, and press as well as direct participation in public life, rule by English Common Law, and a capitalist economic system would conceivably remain firmly in place. As laid out in Hong Kong's Basic Law, only its national defense and international diplomacy would be assumed by the central government.

Apart from and yet presumably bolstering political convergence is the matter of Hong Kong's cultural convergence with China. Culture change in China has been crucial in determining the timing of political convergence. Under Britain, Hong Kong people had grown accustomed to making their own choices in a marketplace of not only manufactured goods but also schools, professions, religions, and lifestyles. When they reverted to Chinese sovereignty, they faced Chinese leadership and Chinese populace, themselves altered. The PRC of 1997 and still more of 2007, despite a violent and oppressive past, is not the PRC of 1957 or 1967; China no longer functions as it did under Mao Zedong, with radical, mass, destructive mobilizations like the Great Leap Forward or the Great Proletarian Cultural Revolution. Politics, or the concern with siding with the proletariat and the Chinese Communist Party against

---

[10] Thanks to Joseph Tse-Hei Lee for framing the issue.

counterrevolutionaries of all stripes, no longer consumes its citizenry. Instead, profit, or the concern with accumulating private, material, and nonmaterial resources to further generate wealth, consumes it. Political struggle has been superseded by the struggle to succeed. Under the direction of Deng Xiaoping, China moved onto the capitalist road, merging with Hong Kong. The state has devolved responsibility and with it enabled individual agency as well as mobility to the point where it is now difficult for the state to maintain control of citizen initiatives despite the state's stubborn belief in control.[11] Both as they move within the spaces of cities and move from the countryside into the city, more and more Chinese are able to attempt if not achieve the realization of their personal aspirations.

At the same time, China's transformation has induced Hong Kong people to further develop Hong Kong civil society. Debates and lessons expressed in the public sphere underscore Hong Kong people's own preoccupation with the change in sovereignty, not as it decides allegiance and interest but as it offers choices of allegiance and interest. As recently as June 2012, public opinion survey results suggest a struggle exists within Hong Kong society between those who understand themselves to be an island, separated and shielded from the vicissitudes of the PRC, and those who view their self-identity like their home as a peninsula, connected firmly to the Chinese mainland. More intriguing, however, is the view, offered by the discussion of such survey results in the media and on the streets, that ambiguity and controversy in identity further shape Hong Kong.[12] When newspapers announced in January 2012 that "Hong Kong citizen" trumped "citizen of the PRC" and that the gap between the two identities had widened rather than shrunk after political convergence, the information provoked criticism from mainland

[11] Dorothy Solinger, *Contesting Citizenship in Urban China: Peasant Migrants, the State, and the Logic of the Market* (Berkeley: University of California Press, 1999); Kate Xiao Zhou, *China's Long March to Freedom: Grassroots Modernization* (Piscataway, N.J.: Transaction Publishers, 2009). See also Pitman B. Potter, "Belief in Control: Regulation of Religion in China," *China Quarterly* 174 (2003); Lida V. Nedilsky and Joseph Tse-Hei Lee, "Appeal and Discontent: The Yin and Yang of China's Rise to Power," in *China's Rise to Power: Conceptions of State Governance*, ed. Joseph Tse-Hei Lee, Lida V. Nedilsky, and Siu-Keung Cheung (New York: Palgrave Macmillan, 2012).

[12] Academic Robert Chang at the University of Hong Kong released survey results on identity issues on December 28, 2012, substantiating an earlier study by the Hong Kong Transition Project, Baptist University.

academics and officials that Hong Kong scholars were unscientific and that Hong Kong citizens were running dogs of British imperialism. In response, local pundits deliberated in newspaper editorials the principles of academic freedom and an informed citizenry, while protestors took to marching their pooches in front of the Liaison Office, the central government's Hong Kong outpost. A huge turnout at the summer's July 1 demonstration coincided with both a visit by China's departing president, Hu Jintao, and the swearing-in ceremony of Hong Kong's third chief executive, Leung Chun-Ying, who secured the votes of 689 members of a 1200-person election committee to assume office.

So much of what Hong Kong Christians understand about themselves as people of faith has been formed in response to what they understand or do not yet understand about China. In both instances, they take learning seriously and work on understanding better. To comprehend the convergence of the two worlds, this book ends by employing research by China scholars that relates to trends documented in Hong Kong. Chapter 6 investigates three pathways addressing the openness required of civil society, pathways evident in the Hong Kong case: (1) the pathway of a marketplace of ideas and individual struggle, (2) the pathway of voluntary association and individual agency, and (3) the pathway of Christian membership and individual conversion.

MARKETPLACE OF IDEAS AND INDIVIDUAL STRUGGLE

In Hong Kong's case, a vibrant marketplace exists for religious goods and services that fuels individual struggle among converts attempting to demonstrate true belief. Committed to realizing in word and deed their Christian identity, they find themselves struggling to resolve contradictions between church teachings and the actions of church representatives. Additionally, converts to Christianity involved in NGOs communicate struggle with the material world and its temptations. Like the Humiliati of Milan, they set themselves apart by choosing a demanding lifestyle, entertaining if not achieving sacrifice in a world of plenty. Finally, struggle as articulation of opposition to proposed government policies and actions, the type of contestation scrutinized by journalists and scholars anticipating political change through social movements, now constitutes an important part of being Christian in Hong Kong. Such struggle involves individuals in letter-writing and postcard campaigns, public prayer meetings, press conferences, and marches. This variety of struggle, sustained by competing ideas of what it means to be

Christian, pushes individuals who voluntarily entered into membership in a community of believers into the sphere of civil society.

One place to look for the roots of China's cultural convergence with Hong Kong and the potential for civil society there is in the marketplace of ideas where initiatives, expressions, and judgments compete. Instructive for appreciating civil society, China's market reforms potentially echo the conditions under which bourgeois individualism historically emerged and so may emerge in China.[13] Moreover, they may align China's economic policies and even its cultural conditions and practices with those of Hong Kong. Shifting from China's state socialism to capitalism as distinct economic systems involves more than just economic considerations and practices. Opening markets or freeing individual decision makers shifts the state's social orientation from positive to negative rights, or from guaranteeing that certain rights shall be achieved to freeing people to pursue the realization of rights and self-defined interests. On an associational level, this represents the turn from corporatism to civil society, from the state's recognition of identities and statuses to individuals' own discovery and pursuit of them.

Those who see a connection between capitalism's development in a postwar world economy and the growing visibility of civil society worldwide anticipate capitalism's beneficial social transformation of China. Whether to affirm or challenge such economic determinism, scholars knowledgeable of China's conditions offer clues to its reality. When the Chinese Communist Party gradually introduced state socialism in the early 1950s to achieve utopian ends, it moved to subsume and command all. In politics, manufacturing, education, worship, medicine, family planning, art, or discourse, the state saw matters of everyday life as public rather than private concerns. After Deng Xiaoping wrested power in 1978 from Mao's immediate and hand-picked successor, Hua Guofeng, he quickly introduced reforms meant to stimulate productivity by increasing individual economic responsibility through personal initiative and ownership. Begun in 1979 in China's countryside, market reform revealed a space not just vacated by a decentralizing state but

---

[13] While acknowledging the popularity of this view, China scholars Timothy Brook and B. Michael Frolic urge revisiting the concept of civil society now that China's case is available. See Timothy Brook and B. Michael Frolic, "Epilogue: China and the Future of Civil Society," in *Civil Society in China*, ed. Timothy Brook and B. Michael Frolic (New York: M. E. Sharpe, 1997), 199.

from which the state was pushed back after failures in grand collectivization and central planning.[14] Since then, institutions like the ration coupon, job assignment and with it housing assignment, work unit (*dānwèi*) affiliation, household registration, and inherited class status that once removed choice and freedom have largely disappeared. Urban economic reforms introduced in 1984[15] and emergent technology[16] continue to pry apart state and society as individuals working not only for private business but for alternative sexuality, independent media, and competing systems of morality gain agency. In pursuing private opportunities rather than seeking validation from the state, China's citizens continually establish their own spheres of purpose.

Yet, Deng never intended that socialism with Chinese characteristics be a wholesale transformation. Characteristically selective, his modernization agenda maintained the Leninist one-party state model and skirted the political risk of *glasnost* emphasized by Mikhail S. Gorbachev in the waning years of the Soviet Union.[17] Today the emergence of separate economic, political, and cultural spheres expresses the unevenness of openness in postreform China. From any one of these distinct spheres, citizens might challenge and check the state, reflecting the practices of democracy. At the same time, however, citizens testing the limits of openness in all aspects of their lives encounter unexpected and severe obstacles to their freedom. For instance, in contrast to the emergent marketplace of private economic interests, where communist officials and entrepreneurs both see an opportunity to profit and therefore formalize individual initiative, associational life is still heavily policed.[18] Rather than growing alongside the market, associations face

[14] Kate Xiao Zhou, *How the Farmers Changed China: Power of the People* (Piscataway, N.J.: Transaction Publishers, 1996).

[15] Kathleen Hartford, "The Political Economy behind Beijing Spring," in *The Chinese People's Movement: Perspectives on Spring 1989*, ed. Tony Saich (Armonk, N.Y.: M. E. Sharpe, 1990).

[16] Patricia Thornton, "The New Cybersects: Resistance and Repression in the Reform Era," in *Chinese Society: Change, Conflict, and Resistance*, 2nd ed., ed. Elizabeth J. Perry and Mark Selden (New York: Routledge, 2002).

[17] Under the banner of *glasnost*, Gorbachev released Andrei Sakharov from internal exile, permitted his publication of articles denouncing Joseph Stalin, and entertained his criticism in the Congress of People's Deputies that opposition parties and competitive elections were needed to end the Kremlin's monopoly on political power.

[18] Mayfair Yang, "Between State and Society: The Construction of Corporateness in a Chinese Socialist Factory," *Australian Journal of Chinese Affairs* 22 (1989).

restrictions that stunt this part of the private sphere. Such inconsistency generates its own struggles for purpose and meaning, as people wonder just when rules apply and for whom. Where different rules apply in different spheres of life, the ambiguity of civil society poses problems for China's citizens.

Take, as two examples, the experience of Falun Gong and of Catholicism in the 1990s. In a context of ideological abandonment and social abandon, Falun Gong gained popularity as a moral compass in postreform China. Inhabiting the space outside the bounds of China's state-sanctioned religions of Buddhism, Taoism, Islam, Protestantism, and Catholicism, Falun Gong's spiritual guides, books, videos, conferences, and exercise sessions went unregulated until their April 1999 mass gathering in Tiananmen Square demanded official recognition. Unhindered by the restrictions that kept religions like Buddhism marginal, Falun Gong as a *qigōng* or wellness group enjoyed a competitive advantage during the decade of its vibrancy.[19] Proselytizing openly in parks and at large-scale meetings in sports stadiums, its membership ballooned to number in the millions. But when 10,000 practitioners came together for a peaceful demonstration, the Chinese state apparatus moved to not only ban Falun Gong but completely erase its presence from society. Public officials and security personnel summoned members to denounce their belief, when belief was the very sign of commitment to their chosen form of life they felt compelled to announce. Physical struggle followed spiritual struggle, as many practitioners refused to give up on Falun Gong.

When one such practitioner died while in police custody, her daughter, Ms. Zhang, sought justice but found self-awareness. In the course of petitioning for her mother's death certificate, encountering indifference if not resistance from government officials, and meeting fellow petitioners who were being treated unfairly, Ms. Zhang struggled to resolve mounting frustrations. She ended up penning a handwritten essay of her own, titled "I Am Willing to Trust the Government, but Can the Government Convince Me?"[20] In solitary and dogged pursuit of bureaucratic recognition, Ms. Zhang developed a personal conception of justice and citizenship that underscored her lack of any real agency:

[19] So writes lay Buddhist Chen Xingqiao in an essay published by the Religious Affairs Bureau. In Ian Johnson, *Wild Grass: Three Stories of Change in Modern China* (New York: Vintage, 2005), 238.

[20] Johnson, *Wild Grass*, 272.

> I didn't quite understand Mother's act [of protesting]. On last April 25, I
> objected to the gathering [of Falun Gong demonstrators]. But after a long
> march to Beijing this time, I realized that a single person can do nothing to
> settle any problem. . . . Seeing the anger and sadness of other petitioners
> I am calm. I'm lucky because I know the reason why we can't make it.[21]

Her pursuit of posthumous justice exposed this nonbeliever to the very
same physical dangers and spiritual developments believers face.

In China, as elsewhere, the market creates disturbances which religion strives to address.[22] In doing so, it often exposes the tendency for
conservative and collective response. Existing groups exercise a hold on
individuals, such that community directs behavior, whether of a civil or
uncivil sort. China's Catholics, perceiving as threats to traditional values
the market as an arena and consumerism as a mindset, self-police their
members and guard their boundaries.[23] They interpret freedom of mobility associated with entrepreneurship as an assault on the self-enclosed
community of the parish.[24] More disturbing than the dangers of the
market are the tensions between the official and underground Catholic
Church, especially as demonstrated by the underground and the righteous
in China. These communicate incivility incongruous with civil society.
Hierarchical relations of power, all too engrained in the rural backdrop
of most Catholic settlements in mainland China, further polarize the two
faces of Catholicism there. The question becomes whether Catholicism
increasingly formed in an urban context might not eventually yield belief
and membership that are instead tolerant of difference.[25]

Where individuals and groups struggle with competing conceptions
of religion as well as with those who police religion's boundaries, a quest
culture has yet to be established in China's case. Questing involves mobility, experimentation, and reflection on individual self-fulfillment to gauge
fit with more than one supplier of religious values and interpretations.

---

[21] Johnson, *Wild Grass*, 273.

[22] For collapse of community as well as rebirth of religiosity in Taiwan under
urbanization and free market economy, see Robert P. Weller, *Alternate Civilities:
Democracy and Culture in China and Taiwan* (Boulder, Colo.: Westview Press,
1999); and Richard Madsen, *Democracy's Dharma: Religious Renaissance and
Political Development in Taiwan* (Berkeley: University of California Press, 2007).

[23] Richard Madsen, *China's Catholics* (Berkeley: University of California Press,
1998).

[24] Madsen, *China's Catholics*, 115.

[25] Madsen, *China's Catholics*, 22.

Converts in Hong Kong, who as individuals seek and so formalize a relationship with a community of believers, demand more than a market in ideas as products. They require the added services of alternative religious authorities and groups to guide them in resolving any questions and doubts about those ideas. From the examples of Falun Gong and Catholicism, boundaries between official and unofficial religions, groups and individuals, are still fiercely guarded in mainland China so that the marketplace of ideas is dangerous for the committed believer to navigate.

Voluntary Association and Individual Agency

Chinese society's gradual and uneven opening through market reforms follows decades of strident direction of all aspects of life by the Chinese Communist Party–ruled state. While justifiably eager to explore the liberalizing impact of these recent reforms, scholars must still address socialism's own legacy, its distortion of private initiative in China today and in the future.

Attentive to developments in Britain and continental Europe contemporaneous with the twilight of Mao's China, economist Friedrich von Hayek argued that institutions that compromise individual initiative profoundly affect culture. Specifically, the oversolicitude of government embracing the platform of social justice, organized labor, and the welfare state stymied development of voluntary association and stigmatized private actors as busybodies.[26] Devaluation of individual initiative eventually thwarted positive social change, for no government agency ever invented the likes of Alcoholics Anonymous.[27] Likening the social sphere to the economic, Hayek wrote,

> It is not true, as the argument in support of the various syndicalist or corporativist systems assumes, that anybody's interest is bound up with the interest of all others who produce the same goods. It may be much more important to some to be able to shift to another group, and these movements are certainly most important for the preservation of the overall

[26] Friedrich A. von Hayek, *The Mirage of Social Justice* (Chicago: University of Chicago Press, 1976), 152.

[27] Friedrich A. von Hayek, *The Political Order of a Free People* (Chicago: University of Chicago Press, 1979), 50. For a contemporary treatment of the subject, see David T. Beito, Peter Gordon, and Alexander Tabarrok, eds., *The Voluntary City: Choice, Community, and Civil Society* (Ann Arbor: University of Michigan Press, 2002).

order. Yet it is these changes which, possible in a free market, agreements between organized groups will aim to prevent.[28]

Given free choice, people associate with different partners depending on their particular and changing purpose.[29] Yet, as governments organize them in order to protect, promote, and edify specific segments of the population, they contain individuals in recognized membership and ignore their initiative to shift association.

Chinese intellectual and literary critic Liu Zaifu testified to the limiting tendency of socialist, compulsory association. In an article originally published in 1985, he posits,

> In the middle decades of the twentieth century, collective will took over and pushed individuality out. Consciousness was "nationalized" and "idealized." . . . All I'm saying now is that we need to restore the place of the individual's judgment, in addition to having national policies.[30]

Cautiously advocating on behalf of individualism, and thus betraying the sensitive, oppositional nature of his thoughts, Liu adds, "I have never been opposed to supporting the [Chinese Communist] party if one wishes. I'm just saying that the individual's own judgment should be the basis for the decision."[31] Limitations on membership in China's recent past have been the result of powerful mechanisms of control exercised by an authoritarian state.[32] Still today, the All-China Women's Federation, All-China Youth Federation, and All-China Federation of Trade Unions, as well as the fifty-five categories of ethnic minority and five official religions (including the Three Self Patriotic Movement and Chinese Patriotic Catholic Association, organs that govern Protestants and Catholics, respectively) continue to function as the sole official representatives of substantial segments of the population.[33]

---

[28] Hayek, *Political Order*, 92.

[29] Hayek, *Mirage of Social Justice*, 149.

[30] Liu Zaifu, "On the Subjectivity of Literature," (1985), translated by and cited in Perry Link, *Evening Chats in Beijing: Probing China's Predicament* (New York: W. W. Norton, 1993), 236.

[31] Liu, "On the Subjectivity of Literature," in Link, *Evening Chats*, 236–37.

[32] With the experience of historically authoritarian institutions, Taiwan and the People's Republic of China both know a closer association between voluntary association and state than is allowed by the Western concept of civil society. See Weller, *Alternate Civilities*.

[33] Despite their common history of British colonialism, countries like India, Malaysia, and Singapore evidence greater similarity with China than with Hong

Well before Mao's rise to power and the founding of the PRC, evidence shows the state's intolerance of the individual. In Nationalist China of the 1910s, the state judged individualism negatively. In the quest for national coherence, individuals were "loose sand" guided by concern for self-interest rather than the public good.[34] Even when individuals came together, for instance in self-governing institutions in the city of Shanghai, the negative judgment of state and society—everyday institutional and cultural constraints—presented setbacks that undermined the working practice and thus the foundation of real democracy.[35]

More recently, movements to occupy Tiananmen Square and other Beijing spaces in the 1970s, 1980s, and 1990s reveal a public sphere peopled by difference, not only in the sense of those coming from distinct sectors of society, regions, and levels of education, but also those realizing transformation in themselves through the course of their engagement in public life.[36] During the Cultural Revolution, Mao exiled his Red Guards from the cities to learn from peasants in China's vast countryside. Cut off from the constraints of party, school, and family, educated youth found they had more control over their own daily lives and learned to take initiative.[37] Eventually returning to the cities, these

---

Kong in regulating associational life. In postindependence India, for instance, state laws against mass conversion preserve Hindu religion, caste, and thus *Hindutva* or power in relation to Buddhism or Christianity. In postindependence Singapore and Malaysia, national policies of multiculturalism not only preserve but establish ethnic difference. Since the founding of the Hong Kong SAR, one step in the direction of formalizing religious difference has been to grant recognition to six official religions through representation in the election committee responsible for naming Hong Kong's chief executive. See Nedilsky, "Institutionalizing," 213–16.

[34] Bryna Goodman, "Democratic Calisthenics: The Culture of Urban Associations in the New Republic," in *Changing Meanings of Citizenship in Modern China*, ed. Merle Goldman and Elizabeth J. Perry (Cambridge, Mass.: Harvard University Press, 2002), 94.

[35] Goodman, "Democratic Calisthenics," in Goldman and Perry, *Changing Meanings*, 94.

[36] See Craig J. Calhoun, *Neither Gods nor Emperors: Students and the Struggle for Democracy in China* (Berkeley: University of California Press, 1994); Merle Goldman, "The Reassertion of Political Citizenship in the Post-Mao Era: The Democracy Wall Movement," in *Changing Meanings of Citizenship in Modern China*, ed. Merle Goldman and Elizabeth J. Perry (Cambridge, Mass.: Harvard University Press, 2002); and Patricia Thornton, "The New Cybersects," in Perry and Selden, *Chinese Society*.

[37] Goldman, "Political Citzenship," in Goldman and Perry, *Changing Meanings*, 163.

same young people applied organizational skills they had mastered as Red Guards in their own campaigns for greater freedom through the Democracy Wall Movement of 1978 and other post-Mao demonstrations for political reform. Likewise, the Cultural Revolution was a pivotal experience for religious leader Li Hongzhi, founder of Falun Gong. Li formulated an alternative, new religion to meet the needs of a changing society.[38] On April 25, 1999, members of his religious sect occupied Tiananmen Square and demanded official recognition. Everyday actions of budding individualism, an established competence, stood behind these initiatives.

Participation in the 1989 Tiananmen Square occupation over months yielded personal and societal transformations. On a personal level, people pressed to make statements and decisions grew to occupy ever more demanding roles, committed themselves (at least for a time) to bold and abstract causes, and even became heroes.[39] On a societal level, such change suggests that not all identities and group formations in China are directed by the state. Dynamism that begat diversity was eclipsed, however, by another reality. Those who ordered the public sphere were members of privileged and distinct groups recognized by the communist state: university students, established in the areas of scholarship on which the state depends for intellectual labor and the future well-being of the PRC, and workers in *dānwèi*, upon whom the state depends for physical labor as well the historic legitimacy of the CCP.

Continued transition to a market economy and thus liberalization in one sphere reveals attempts to negotiate state control.[40] More often than not, however, citizen-initiated groups succumb to the pressures of corporatism or insignificance. Along with international NGOs, such groups working to establish themselves face three possible scenarios: they are incorporated; forced to stay local, unofficial, and unorganized; or repressed.[41] Those intent on engaging the state risk its heavy hand.

---

[38] Thornton, "The New Cybersects," in Perry and Selden, *Chinese Society,* 250.

[39] Calhoun, *Neither Gods nor Emperors*, 21.

[40] Liu Xiaobo, "The Rise of Civil Society in China," in *Challenging China: Struggle and Hope in an Era of Change*, ed. Sharon Hom and Stacy Mosher (New York: New Press, 2007); Tony Saich, "Negotiating the State: The Development of Social Organizations in China," in *China's Deep Reform*, ed. Lowell Dittmer and Guoli Liu (Lanham, Md.: Rowman & Littlefield, 2006).

[41] Weller, *Alternate Civilities*, 128.

Rural tax lawyers and historic preservationists not formally aligned with state-sanctioned associations are two notable examples.[42] Like blind legal activist Chen Guangcheng, who fled house arrest in April 2012, they push stubbornly to advance their particular agendas and become vulnerable to hidden excesses by the security bureau, local party officials, and thugs.

Rarely is the heavy hand of the state as obvious to the wider public as when the individual and thus that person's relation to corporatist membership is of the highest rank.[43] Upon consecration July 7, 2012, at St. Ignatius Cathedral in Shanghai, Bishop Thaddeus Ma Daqin announced his resignation from the Chinese Patriotic Catholic Association (CPCA), the state-sanctioned governing body for the Catholic faithful in China. He was quoted by the *Washington Post* as saying,

> At this time I've been reflecting on what our loving mother church reminded me, once you assume your pastoral job ... your body and heart should be completely focused on pastoral things and evangelization. It is not appropriate to assume other duties anymore. So, from the moment of today's ordination, it is not appropriate for me to be a member of the Patriotic Association anymore.[44]

Although he was ordained with the approval of both Vatican and Beijing authorities, his exit from the CPCA did not come with the approval of Beijing authorities. He was not the religious figurehead China's leaders bargained for, and authorities immediately ordered his indefinite retreat and confinement for self-reflection, or struggle in the individual sense familiar in a politically orthodox People's Republic. Nor is Bishop Ma the standard-bearer of individualism that Hayek praises. Representing the institution of the Catholic Church, privileging the responsibilities of pastoral care over other roles, the bishop demonstrates the interplay between individual and community, the muted individualism associated with today's civil society.

Unlike the assembly of NGOs participating in the Alternative Handover in 1997 or Queenie opening up her umbrella of potential

[42] Johnson, *Wild Grass*.

[43] The purge of metropolitan Chongqing's party boss, Bo Xilai, from the Chinese Communist Party in September 2012 demonstrates involuntary exit at the highest level of political power.

[44] Leslie Hook, "China Detains Defiant Catholic Bishop," *Washington Post*, July 10, 2012.

allies for the rally at Star Ferry Pier in 1998, in China such insistence on individual judgment, as articulated by Liu Zaifu as well as by Ms. Zhang and Bishop Thaddeus Ma, can on its own be legitimate cause for harsh punishment. For advocating subjectivity in literature, Liu was placed under house arrest; Ms. Zhang spent three years in jail for appealing to the law on behalf of her dead mother, a Falun Gong practitioner; Bishop Ma remains in confinement to reflect upon his resignation from the only official representative body of Catholics in China, the CPCA.

CHRISTIAN MEMBERSHIP AND INDIVIDUAL CONVERSION

Research into Christian membership in the PRC today yields similar conclusions as research into the study of voluntary association in general; emerging market forces create conditions for membership at once grounding and perilous. To cope with bewildering opportunities and obstacles they find in the marketplace, young, urban professionals sample religion for the same reason they sample a McDonald's hamburger—as a symbol of cosmopolitanism.[45] They attend worship, ask questions, and buy books. Yet, through decades of state regulation, intervention, and repression, shortages of expert guides limit them in their journey. Even Christian membership poses risks, since the state continues to confine worship to registered church buildings.[46]

One convert to Christianity who communicates how conversion helps make meaning in reform-era China is Cindy, of the pseudonymous city of Nanfang. The fifth of six children, born in 1964 to a Nationalist Party official father and a mother who was the only child of an important capitalist, Cindy initiated her own professional and geographic mobility. While her law firm was entrusted with the task of defending activists prosecuted for their involvement in the Tiananmen Square prodemocracy movement, the firm's director advised staff against trying too hard in presenting a defense. Unable to bear the hypocrisy, Cindy quit her job in late 1989 and headed south. Her conversion to Christianity came afterward, when alone in Nanfang she succumbed to feelings first of self-doubt and then of depression. She said,

[45] Yang Fenggang, "Lost in the Market, Saved at McDonald's: Conversion to Christianity in Urban China," *Journal for the Scientific Study of Religion* 44, no. 4 (2005): 425.
[46] Yang, "Lost in the Market," 430.

In the past I could succeed no matter what I did. But now I failed no matter what I tried. I found nothing to hold up my life. I was like a walking zombie. I considered suicide. But I thought, life shouldn't be like that. I thought, there must be something that I should do and would never regret. But I did not know what it was.

In 1999 I got a phone call from a friend in Singapore, who suggested I read the Bible. I bought one and tried to read. Later I came to Nanfang to attend a psychology workshop. Another participant in the workshop was a Christian, who introduced me to the Timothy Training Course taught by an American named Tom. I took the course seriously, and read the Bible eagerly. During that period, all the past things passed through my head like on a screen. I realized that God protected me all along. I confessed all my sins, cried a lot to God. God is so good and loving. I experienced speaking in tongues. My heart had never felt so happy.[47]

Religious conversion, from Cindy's account, brings stability and peace within a context where she as an individual strives for a foothold; in urban Chinese societies, people face the risk of failing to flourish. They may even risk association with organized religion. But Cindy's conversion account gives no evidence of risking an internal struggle, of self-reflexive *jàngjaat* emerging from religious life. Christian converts like Cindy who mention Tiananmen Square in individual testimonies do not interpret it as a political incident. Instead, they describe it as a spiritual turning point, an event that triggers certain feelings and attitudes toward life.[48] But what those feelings and attitudes produce remains unclear. A striking difference between Cindy's conversion account and that of a Hong Kong Christian like Faith is the limited horizon Cindy communicates. Whether she is at the beginning of her development or stagnant, she lacks words with which to articulate the connection between her own awakening to Jesus and any awakening through Jesus to a sense of purpose.

Another development within Christianity linked to China's liberalization has been the spread of Christian culture fever (*wénhuà rè*) and with it the emergence of cultural Christians (*wénhuà Jīdūtú*). Whereas in the West the term cultural Christian is interchangeable with the concept of the nominal Christian, or one who is Christian in name but not in belief or deed, in China it refers to curiosity with or commitment to Christian values. The economic liberalization and opening up of the early 1980s generated new possibilities for investigation by both scholars and

---

[47] Yang, "Lost in the Market," 434–35.
[48] Yang, "Lost in the Market," 436.

a wider public. Market reforms' general liberalization invited people to consider the similarities and differences between Western and Chinese culture, including religion as a bedrock of culture.[49] But curiosity and commitment in the case of cultural Christians is not to be equated with a vigorous public role. Instead the paths diverge: an intellectual curious about Christianity is either a private believer or a public atheist, not a public believer.[50] As work on contemporary Protestantism, including the Three Self Patriotic Movement (TSPM), shows, save some role it plays in providing social service, Protestantism's public presence is severely limited. Book tables in TSPM churches may display approved texts, but no private bookshops, radio programs, or television shows present viable options, provide social or political commentary, or yield an alternative authority.[51] Why should anyone expect Protestants to succeed in articulating their own sense of purpose where other nonstate organizations have failed?

Instead, a new type of Chinese Christian, the *shìmín* or *lǎobǎn Jīdūtú*, civil or boss Christian, exhibits familiar purpose.[52] The rising market economy that revolutionized coastal cities also transformed the Catholic and Protestant Christians who live there. From fishermen and farmers, they became factory owners and other small business proprietors. From coastal town residents, they moved and became urbanites. And whereas they once cautiously practiced their faith underground, they now subscribe openly to religious membership. Even their interests have shifted toward ever-broader and more-complex concerns as they now engage in not only business but also public welfare and evangelization. Economically strong and politically competent, they approximate the Christian captains of industry of the American Industrial Revolution.[53] Yet, in emphasizing the identifiable and verifiable group, this new

---

[49] Yang Fenggang, "Between Secularist Ideology and Desecularizing Reality: The Birth and Growth of Religious Research in Communist China," *Sociology of Religion* 65, no. 2 (2004): 107–9.

[50] Ka Lun Leung, "Cultural Christians and Contemporary Christianity in China," in *Challenging China*, ed. Sharon Hom and Stacy Moser (New York: New Press, 2007).

[51] Daniel H. Bays, "Chinese Protestant Christianity Today," *China Quarterly* 174 (2003): 500.

[52] Chen Cunfu and Huang Tianhai, "The Emergence of a New Type of Christians in China Today," *Review of Religious Research* 46, no. 2 (2004): 185.

[53] Chen and Huang, "Emergence," 189.

variety of Christian harkens back to an earlier, prerevolutionary group form based on local ties and inherited statuses. Here, favors and ensuing allegiances among group members function as entangling commitments.

Alongside these other developments is the as-yet-barely-expressed potential for still more radical changes in Chinese Christian identity and culture. Urbanization brought on by economic growth and entrepreneurialism means rapid change from a long-standing agricultural life form rooted in the extended family to a recent and individualizing urban resettlement of mobile professionals. This physical mobility may appear a direct assault on the self-enclosed community of the parish, but even as people in the city often end up facing confusion and ambiguities, they secure alternative arrangements and contribute innovative solutions to religious life.[54] The example of Miss Xia, a rootless young woman in the big city, represents something special. Miss Xia is induced to faith. But her Catholicism is not grounded in the cloistered and antagonistic Catholic enclave; being neither the state-sanctioned Chinese Patriotic Catholic Association nor the underground church aligned with the Vatican and loyal to the Pope, her church is not about defending any share of the religious marketplace through the old vertical relationships of authority and dependence.

It is in Miss Xia that an alternative way appears where otherwise the path is set with pitfalls. Miss Xia shares more in common with Sheila, who crafted an idea of faith based on her own sense of self.[55] Or perhaps, like the Methodist Taoist Native American Quaker Russian Orthodox Buddhist Jew, Miss Xia represents, bound up in one woman, the medley of faiths certainly not foreign to the Chinese experience with religion. In either case, Miss Xia summons us to contemplate the importance of freedom not only in an individual but also in how it feeds individualism. But unlike either Sheila or the Methodist Taoist Native American Quaker Russian Orthodox Buddhist Jew, Miss Xia does not herself offer in words that sense of herself. Her voice cannot be used to articulate a general experience of religion and an innovation in social ties. She may not yet have the words.

[54] Madsen, *China's Catholics*, xxii.
[55] Robert N. Bellah, Richard Madsen, William M. Sullivan, Ann Swidler, and Steven M. Tipton, *Habits of the Heart: Individualism and Commitment in American Life* (New York: Harper & Row, 1985).

Conclusion

The question of convergence addressed in chapter 6 pulls observers of religious life away from the focus of *Converts to Civil Society*: Hong Kong Christians' individual choices and voices. Convergence draws attention to the patterns shared across individual lives, mutes the distinctions enabled by intimate investigation, and, in so doing, relates Hong Kong's Statue Square and China's Tiananmen Square movements. Just as taking such a big step back provides the wide scope to encompass two distinct Chinese societies, considering this one convergence invites the question of convergence for other squares entirely.

Consider this question in association with the Islamic world's Jasmine Revolution of 2011; Tahrir Square in Cairo, Egypt; or in 2013, Taksim Square in Istanbul, Turkey. In 2009 Al Jazeera English produced more than a dozen separate televised news episodes on the occasion of the twentieth anniversary of the Tiananmen Square demonstrations. Stories highlighted the political struggle within the CCP that was backdrop to Tiananmen, the government crackdown on Chinese citizens that ended in tragedy, and the Tiananmen Mothers' demands for justice after losing children to the crackdown. In addition, Al Jazeera conducted interviews with observers, leaders, and victims who had been in the Chinese capital the night of June 3, 1989. Their accounts of personal choices to act, to stay, to leave, to return, to face the police, to face in some distant future citizens free to vote candidates into office were accounts of a minority experience that already resonated with Al Jazeera's viewers in 2009. In an effect similar to that of the aftermath of the Tiananmen Square demonstrations, the aftermath of Arab Spring 2011 demands careful study of the nature of affiliation within Islam and Islamic-majority societies, with the goal of overcoming the limitations of a simplistic approach that pigeonholes Christian versus Muslim, Shia versus Sunni, Egyptian versus Tunisian versus Turk.

The lessons in *Converts to Civil Society* gleaned from attention to daily practices, utterances, and choices certainly apply beyond China. As Robert Hefner has written on Islam, analysis of ideas and institutions in the lives of believers, more so than of ideas and directives from religious leaders, attends to the realities of living in a modern, global world where people and their various products shift across political boundaries.[1] Such a vantage point requires an appreciation of the pluralism found within contemporary religious experience. The pluralism apparent in everyday experiences not only challenges settled authorities and solidarities,[2] but also highlights the basic fact that democracy cannot function without a civil culture and organization greater than itself.[3] Mythmaking about the cultural uniformity, calcified orthodoxy, and totalitarian religiosity of the Chinese or Islamic world gives way instead to scholarship of the intimate.[4] And so we are reminded of the need to appreciate the fine details, if we can only get close enough to see things as they are.

What scholars of China convey about individual members of Chinese society is thus significant. But the silence from China is almost deafening. Whether it is a silence generated by a society that cannot and does not articulate itself in this manner or one imposed by scholars documenting society within the limits allowed by the state, this silence spells a warning to anyone hoping innovation in China runs deeper than economic liberalization. Only as social scientific research gains acceptance in China itself and, like the best of journalism, allows investigation of China's religions on an intimate level can we begin to collect data on the entrepreneurial and complex membership possible in a diversifying religious marketplace. Research can give voice by allowing us to get close to people. But it cannot provide voices where none exist. No doubt

[1] Robert W. Hefner, "Public Islam and the Problem of Democratization," *Sociology of Religion* 62, no. 4 (2001).

[2] Hefner, "Public Islam," 495.

[3] Hefner, "Public Islam," 497.

[4] Robert W. Hefner, *Civil Islam: Muslims and Democratization in Indonesia* (Princeton: Princeton University Press, 2000).

the candor with which people speak in Hong Kong reflects the openness and practiced eloquence of the wider society. Only because Hong Kong people can speak—enabled as they are by the civil society they have created—can anyone document this least known and most telling form of life that sustains Hong Kong civil society. Only when we begin to hear from scholars of China the details and depth of voluntarily entered commitments will convergence be more than conjecture. It will be reality.

Glossary of Terms

Phonetic term[1]	English translation	Written term
baaisàhn	ancestor worship	拜神
chēutlouh	way out, outlet	出路
chēutmùhn	exit, go out	出門
chēutsèng	voice out	出聲
chìhjīk	quit, resign	辭職
dānwèi (Mandarin)	work unit	單位
duhklahp nàhnglihk	ability to be independent	獨立能力
gaauwúi	church, edification	教會
gìngyihm	experience, understanding	經驗
gwàiyì Yèhsōu	convert/turn toward Jesus	怪異耶穌
jàngchéui	(public) struggle	爭取
jàngchéui jihyàuh	struggle for freedom	爭取自由
jàngchéui màhnjyú	struggle for democracy	爭取民主
jàngchéui pouseun	struggle for universal suffrage	爭取博選
jàngchéui séhwúi faatjih	struggle for society ruled by law	爭取社會法治

[1] Terms are Cantonese unless otherwise indicated.

Phonetic term	English translation	Written term
jàngjaat	(private) struggle	爭扎
jonghèung	honor the dead	裝香
jùngsàm	faithfulness, loyalty, devotion	忠心
kautàuh	kowtow	叩頭
kyutji	decision to believe (in Jesus)	決志
lǎobǎn Jīdūtú (Mandarin)	boss Christian	老板基督徒
lihngnoih wùihgwài	Alternative Handover	另外回歸
luhksei	June 4 (Tiananmen Square Incident)	六四
náaihfán seuntòuh	milk powder believer, nominal Christian	奶粉信徒
pìhngfáan luhksei	reverse the verdict on June 4	平反六四
qìgōng (Mandarin)	breathing exercise-centered wellness	氣功
seunyéuhng	belief, faith	信仰
shìmín Jīdūtú (Mandarin)	civil Christian	市民基督徒
wándihng fàahnwìhng	stability and prosperity	穩定繁榮
wénhuà Jīdūtú (Mandarin)	cultural Christian	文化基督徒
wénhuà rè (Mandarin)	culture fever	文化熱
wùihgwài	the Handover	回歸
Wùihgwài lo. Yùhgwó lohk daaih yúh, jauh hóuwo!	It's the Handover, mind you. If there's a heavy rain, that's just fine!	回歸各. 如果落大雨就 好!
xiǎozǔ (Mandarin)	small group	小組
yangau chìhjīk	guiltily exit the scene	引疚辭職
yātgwok léuhngjai	one country, two systems	一國兩制
Yèhsōu sih Jyú	Jesus is Lord	耶穌是主
yìmàhn	emigrate	移民

Bibliography

Asad, Talal. *Geneologies of Religion: Discipline and Reasons of Power in Christianity and Islam.* Baltimore: Johns Hopkins University Press, 1993.

Attenborough, David. "Life in the Undergrowth." Series producer Mike Salisbury, 2/Entertain, BBC video, London, 2006.

Bankston, W. B., C. J. Forsyth, and H. H. Floyd. "Toward a General Model of Radical Conversion: An Interactionist Perspective on the Transformation of Self-Identity." *Qualitative Sociology* 4 (1981): 279–97.

Barmé, Geremie. "Confession, Redemption, and Death: Liu Xiaobo and the Protest Movement of 1989." In *The Broken Mirror: China After Tiananmen,* edited by George Hicks, 52–99. Essex: Longman, 1990.

Bays, Daniel H. "Chinese Protestant Christianity Today." *China Quarterly* 174 (2003): 488–504.

Beckford, James. "Talking of Apostasy, or Telling Tales and 'Telling' Tales." In *Accounts and Action,* edited by G. Nigel Gilbert and Peter Abell, 77–97. Hampshire, U.K.: Gower, 1983.

Beito, David T., Peter Gordon, and Alexander Tabarrok, eds. *The Voluntary City: Choice, Community, and Civil Society.* Ann Arbor: University of Michigan Press, 2002.

Bellah, Robert N. *Beyond Belief: Essays on Religion in a Post-traditional World.* New York: Harper & Row, 1972.

Bellah, Robert N., Richard Madsen, William M. Sullivan, Ann Swidler, and Steven M. Tipton. *Habits of the Heart: Individualism and Commitment in American Life.* New York: Harper & Row, 1985.

Bercovitch, Sacvan. *The American Jeremiad*. Madison: University of Wisconsin Press, 1978.

Berger, Peter L. *The Capitalist Revolution: Fifty Propositions about Prosperity, Equality and Liberty*. New York: Basic Books, 1986.

———. *The Noise of Solemn Assemblies*. Garden City, N.Y.: Doubleday, 1961.

Berger, Peter L., and Thomas Luckmann. *The Social Construction of Reality*. Garden City, N.Y.: Anchor Books, 1967.

Birnbaum, N., and Gertrud Lenzer. *Sociology and Religion*. Englewood Cliffs, N.J.: Prentice-Hall, 1969.

Brook, Timothy, and B. Michael Frolic. "Epilogue: China and the Future of Civil Society." In *Civil Society in China*, edited by Timothy Brook and B. Michael Frolic, 195–201. New York: M. E. Sharpe, 1997.

Brown, Deborah. *Turmoil in Hong Kong on the Eve of Communist Rule: The Fate of the Territory and Its Anglican Church*. San Francisco: Mellen Research University Press, 1993.

Calhoun, Craig J. "Introduction." In *Habermas and the Public Sphere*, edited by Craig J. Calhoun, 1–48. Cambridge. Mass.: MIT Press, 1992.

———. *Neither Gods nor Emperors: Students and the Struggle for Democracy in China*. Berkeley: University of California Press, 1994.

Casanova, Jose. *Public Religions in the Modern World*. Chicago: University of Chicago Press, 1994.

Chabbott, Colette. "Development INGOs." In *Constructing World Culture*, edited by John Boli and George M. Thomas, 222–48. Stanford: Stanford University Press, 1999.

Chan, Ming K. "Hong Kong: Colonial Legacy, Transformation, and Challenge." In *The Annals of the American Academy of Political and Social Science, The Future of Hong Kong*, edited by Max J. Skidmore. September 1996, 11–23.

Chen Cunfu, and Huang Tianhai. "The Emergence of a New Type of Christians in China Today." *Review of Religious Research* 46, no. 2 (2004): 183–200.

Cheng, May M., and Wong Siu-Lun. "Religious Convictions and Sentiments." In *Indicators of Social Development in Hong Kong, 1995*, edited by Lau Siu-Kai, Lee Ming-Kwan, Wan Po-San, and Wong Siu-Lun, 299–329. Hong Kong: Chinese University Press, 1997.

Cheng, Joseph Y. S. "Prospects for Democracy in Hong Kong." In *The Broken Mirror: China After Tiananmen*, edited by George Hicks, 278–95. Essex: Longman, 1990.

Chiu, Stephen Wing-Kai, and Lui Tai-Lok, eds. *The Dynamics of Social*

Movements in Hong Kong. Hong Kong: Hong Kong University Press, 2000.

Cohen, Paul. *China and Christianity: The Missionary Movement and the Growth of Chinese Antiforeignism, 1860–1870.* Cambridge, Mass.: Harvard University Press, 1963.

Coser, Lewis A. *Greedy Institutions: Patterns of Undivided Commitment.* New York: Free Press, 1974.

Coutin, Susan Bibler. *The Culture of Protest: Religious Activism and the U.S. Sanctuary Movement.* Boulder, Colo.: Westview Press, 1993.

Cunningham, Philip. *Tiananmen Moon.* Lanham, Md.: Rowman & Littlefield, 2009.

Degolyer, Michael E., and Janet Lee Scott. "The Myth of Political Apathy in Hong Kong." In *The Annals of the American Academy of Political and Social Science, The Future of Hong Kong,* edited by Max J. Skidmore. September 1996, 68–78.

Dutton, Michael. *Policing Chinese Politics.* Durham, N.C.: Duke University Press, 2005.

Dwyer, D. J. "Introduction." In *Asian Urbanization,* edited by D. J. Dwyer, 1–10. Hong Kong: Hong Kong University Press, 1971.

Eitel, Ernest John. *Europe in China: The History of Hong Kong from the Beginning to the Year 1882.* Hong Kong: Oxford University Press, 1895/1983.

Endacott, G. B. *A History of Hong Kong.* London: Oxford University Press, 1958.

Esherick, Joseph. *The Origins of the Boxer Uprising.* Berkeley: University of California Press, 1987.

Fantasia, Rick. *Cultures of Solidarity: Consciousness, Action, and Contemporary American Workers.* Berkeley: University of California Press, 1988.

Foucault, Michel. *The History of Sexuality.* Vol. 1, *An Introduction.* New York: Random House, 1978.

———. *The History of Sexuality.* Vol. 2, *The Use of Pleasure.* New York: Random House, 1985.

Geiger, Susan. "Women's Life Histories: Method and Content." *Signs* 11, no. 2 (1986): 334–51.

Giddens, Anthony. *Modernity and Self-Identity: Self and Society in the Late Modern Age.* Stanford: Stanford University Press, 1991.

Goldman, Merle. "The Reassertion of Political Citizenship in the Post-Mao Era: The Democracy Wall Movement." In *Changing Meanings of Citizenship in Modern China,* edited by Merle Goldman and Elizabeth J. Perry, 159–86. Cambridge, Mass.: Harvard University Press, 2002.

Goodman, Bryna. "Democratic Calisthenics: The Culture of Urban Associations in the New Republic." In *Changing Meanings of Citizenship in Modern China*, edited by Merle Goldman and Elizabeth J. Perry, 70–109. Cambridge, Mass.: Harvard University Press, 2002.

Habermas, Jürgen. *The Structural Transformation of the Public Sphere: An Inquiry into a Category of Bourgeois Society*. Translated by Thomas Burger. Cambridge, Mass.: MIT Press, 2000.

Hannigan, John A. "Social Movement Theory and the Sociology of Religion: Towards a New Synthesis." *Sociological Analysis* 52, no. 4 (1991): 311–31.

Harding, Susan Friend. *The Book of Jerry Falwell: Fundamentalist Language and Politics*. Princeton: Princeton University Press, 2000.

Hartford, Kathleen. "The Political Economy behind Beijing Spring." In *The Chinese People's Movement: Perspectives on Spring 1989*, edited by Tony Saich, 50–82. Armonk, N.Y.: M. E. Sharpe, 1990.

Hauser, Amy. "The Chinese Enterprising Self: Young, Educated Urbanites and the Search for Work." In *Popular China: Unofficial Culture in a Globalizing Society*, edited by Perry Link, Paul Pickowitz, and Richard Madsen, 189–206. Lanham, Md.: Rowman & Littlefield, 2002.

Hayek, Friedrich A. von. *The Mirage of Social Justice*. Chicago: University of Chicago Press, 1976.

———. *The Political Order of a Free People*. Chicago: University of Chicago Press, 1979.

He, Baogang. *The Democratic Implications of Civil Society in China*. New York: Palgrave Macmillan, 1997.

Hefner, Robert W. *Civil Islam: Muslims and Democratization in Indonesia*. Princeton: Princeton University Press, 2000.

———. "Public Islam and the Problem of Democratization." *Sociology of Religion* 62, no. 4 (2001): 491–514.

Hirschman, Albert O. *Exit, Voice and Loyalty*. Cambridge, Mass.: Harvard University Press, 1970.

Johnson, Ian. *Wild Grass: Three Stories of Change in Modern China*. New York: Vintage, 2005.

Jones, Catherine. *Promoting Prosperity: The Hong Kong Way of Social Policy*. Hong Kong: Chinese University Press, 1990.

Jordan, David. *Gods, Ghosts and Ancestors*. Berkeley: University of California Press, 1972.

Juergensmeyer, Mark. *Terror in the Mind of God: The Global Rise of Religious Violence*. Berkeley: University of California Press, 2000.

Jules-Rosette, Bennetta. *African Apostles: Ritual and Conversion in the Church of John Maranke*. Ithaca: Cornell University Press, 1975.

Kalra, Sanjay, Dubravko Mihaljec, and Christoph Duenwald. "Property

Prices and Speculative Bubbles: Evidence from Hong Kong SAR." *IMF Working Paper 00/2* (Washington: IMF, January 2000): 1–29.

Khun Eng Kuah. "Negotiating Emigration and the Family: Individual Solutions to the 1997 Anxiety." In *The Annals of the American Academy of Political and Social Science, The Future of Hong Kong*, edited by Max J. Skidmore. September 1996, 54–67.

Lam Wai-Man. *Understanding the Political Culture of Hong Kong: The Paradox of Activism and Depoliticization*. New York: M. E. Sharpe, 2004.

Lane, Kevin. *Sovereignty and the Status Quo*. Boulder, Colo.: Westview Press, 1990.

Langman, Lauren. "From Virtual Public Spheres to Global Justice: A Critical Theory of Internetworked Social Movements." *Sociological Theory* 23, no. 1 (2005): 42–74.

Lau Siu-Kai. "Social Change, Bureaucratic Rule, and Emergent Political Issues in Hong Kong." *World Politics* 35, no. 4 (1983): 544–62.

———. "Utilitarianistic Familism: The Basis of Political Stability." In *Social Life and Development in Hong Kong*, edited by Ambrose Y. C. King and Rance P. L. Lee, 195–216. Hong Kong: Chinese University Press, 1981.

Lau Siu-Kai and Kuan Hsin-Chi. *The Ethos of the Hong Kong Chinese*. Hong Kong: Chinese University Press, 1988.

Lawrence, Bruce. "Transformation." In *Critical Terms for Religious Studies*, edited by Mark C. Taylor, 334–48. Chicago: University of Chicago Press, 1998.

Lee, Rance P. L. "High-Density Effects in Urban Areas: What Do We Know and What Should We Do?" In *Social Life and Development in Hong Kong*, edited by Ambrose Y. C. King and Rance P. L. Lee, 3–19. Hong Kong: Chinese University Press, 1981.

Lee, Wei-Chin. "Read My Lips or Watch My Feet: The State and Chinese Dissident Intellectuals." *Issues and Studies* 28, no. 5 (1992): 29–48.

Leung, Ka Lun. "Cultural Christians and Contemporary Christianity in China." In *Challenging China*, edited by Sharon Hom and Stacy Moser, 252–60. New York: New Press, 2007.

Liebman, Robert, and Robert Wuthnow. *The New Christian Right: Mobilization and Legitimation*. New York: Aldine Publishing, 1983.

Lim, Adelyn. "The Hong Kong Women's Movement: Towards a Politics of Difference and Diversity." In *Women's Movements in Asia: Feminisms and Transnational Activisms*, edited by Mina Roces and Louise Edwards, 144–65. New York: Routledge, 2010.

Liu Binyan. *A Higher Kind of Loyalty*. New York: Pantheon, 1990.

Liu Xiaobo. "The Rise of Civil Society in China." In *Challenging China: Struggle and Hope in an Era of Change*, edited by Sharon Hom and Stacy Mosher, 109–22. New York: New Press, 2007.

Liu Zaifu. "On the Subjectivity of Literature," (1985). Cited in Perry Link, *Evening Chats in Beijing: Probing China's Predicament*. New York: W. W. Norton, 1993.

Luckmann, Thomas. *The Invisible Religion*. New York: Macmillan, 1967.

Lui Tai-Lok. *Four Generations of Hong Kong People (Seidoih Hèung-góngyàhn)*. Hong Kong: Step Forward Multimedia, 2007.

Ma Shu-Yun. "The Exit, Voice, and Struggle to Return of Chinese Political Exiles." *Pacific Affairs* 66, no. 3 (1993): 368–85.

Madsen, Richard. *China's Catholics*. Berkeley: University of California Press, 1998.

———. *Democracy's Dharma: Religious Renaissance and Political Development in Taiwan*. Berkeley: University of California Press, 2007.

Mandlebaum, David. "The Study of Life History: Gandhi." *Current Anthropology* 14, no. 3 (1973): 177–206.

Miller, Perry. "The Half-Way Covenant." *New England Quarterly* 6, no. 4 (1933): 676–715.

Mullins, Mark R. *Christianity Made in Japan: A Study of Indigenous Movements*. Honolulu: University of Hawai'i Press, 1998.

Myers, John T. "Residents' Images of a Hong Kong Resettlement Estate: A View from the 'Chicken Coop.'" In *Social Life and Development in Hong Kong*, edited by Ambrose Y. C. King and Rance P. L. Lee, 21–36. Hong Kong: Chinese University Press, 1981.

———. "Traditional Chinese Religious Practices in an Urban-Industrial Setting: The Example of Kwun Tong." In *Social Life and Development in Hong Kong*, edited by Ambrose Y. C. King and Rance P. L. Lee, 275–88. Hong Kong: Chinese University Press, 1981.

Nedilsky, Lida V. "The Anticult Initiative and Hong Kong Christianity's Turn from Religious Privilege." *China Information* 22, no. 3 (2008): 423–49.

———. "Institutionalizing the Representation of Religious Minorities in Post-1997 Hong Kong." In *Marginalization in China: Recasting Minority Politics*, edited by Siu-Keung Cheung, Joseph Tse-Hei Lee, and Lida V. Nedilsky, 211–35. New York: Palgrave Macmillan, 2009.

———. "Loneliness and the Re-socialization of Intellectuals in the First Decade of Post-liberation China." Master's thesis, University of California, Berkeley, 1994.

Nedilsky, Lida V., and Joseph Tse-Hei Lee. "Appeal and Discontent: The Yin and Yang of China's Rise to Power." In *China's Rise to Power: Conceptions of State Governance*, edited by Joseph Tse-Hei Lee, Lida V. Nedilsky, and Siu-Keung Cheung, 1–29. New York: Palgrave Macmillan, 2012.

Ngai, Jimmy Siu-Yan. "Tiananmen Days." In *New Ghosts, Old Dreams: Chinese Rebel Voices*, edited by Geremie Barmé and Linda Jaivin, 74–97. New York: Times Books, 1992.

Oi Ying. "Growing Space" *(Sihngjéungdīk Hùnggàan)*. In *Estate Reminiscence (Ngūkchyùn Naahnmòhng)*, edited by Victor Luk, 181–85. Hong Kong: Breakthrough, 1995.

Pattillo-McCoy, Mary. "Church Culture as a Strategy of Action in the Black Community." *American Sociological Review* 63 (1998): 767–84.

Pomphret, John. *Chinese Lessons: Five Classmates and the Story of the New China*. New York: Henry Holt, 2006.

Pope, Robert G. "The Half-Way Covenant: Church Membership in Puritan New England" (1969). *William and Mary Quarterly* 31, no. 3 (1974): 465–80.

Porta, Donatella della. "Life Histories in the Analysis of Social Movement Activists." In *Studying Collective Action*, edited by Mario Diani and Ron Eyerman, 168–93. London: Sage Publications, 1992.

Postiglione, Gerard. "The Decolonization of Hong Kong Education." In *The Hong Kong Reader: Passage to Chinese Sovereignty*, edited by Ming K. Chan and Gerard A. Postiglione, 98–123. New York: M. E. Sharpe, 1996.

Potter, Pitman B. "Belief in Control: Regulation of Religion in China." *China Quarterly* 174 (2003): 317–37.

Putnam, Robert D. *Bowling Alone: The Collapse and Revival of American Community*. New York: Simon & Schuster, 2000.

Putnam, Robert D., and David E. Campbell. *American Grace: How Religion Divides and Unites Us*. New York: Simon & Schuster, 2012.

Roof, Wade Clark. *The Spiritual Marketplace: Baby Boomers and the Remaking of American Religion*. Princeton: Princeton University Press, 1999.

Rudolph, Susanne Hoeber. "Introduction: Religion, States, and Transnational Civil Society." In *Transnational Religion and Fading States*, edited by Susanne Hoeber Rudolph and James Piscatori, 1–24. Boulder, Colo.: Westview Press, 1996.

Rudolph, Susanne Hoeber, and James Piscatori, eds. *Transnational Religion and Fading States*. Boulder, Colo.: Westview Press, 1996.

Saari, Jon L. *Legacies of Childhood: Growing up Chinese in a Time of Crisis, 1890–1920.* Cambridge, Mass.: Council on East Asian Studies, Harvard University Press, 1990.

Saich, Tony. "Negotiating the State: The Development of Social Organizations in China." In *China's Deep Reform*, edited by Lowell Dittmer and Guoli Liu, 285–301. Lanham, Md.: Rowman & Littlefield, 2006.

Scheiner, Irwin. *Christian Converts and Social Protest in Meiji Japan.* Berkeley: University of California Press, 1970.

Schell, Orville. "The Re-emergence of the Realm of the Private in China." In *The Broken Mirror: China After Tiananmen*, edited by George Hicks, 419–27. Essex: Longman, 1990.

Selden, Mark. *The Yenan Way in Revolutionary China.* Cambridge, Mass.: Harvard University Press, 1971.

Seligman, Adam B. "Between Public and Private: Towards a Sociology of Civil Society." In *Democratic Civility*, edited by Robert W. Hefner, 79–111. New Brunswick, N.J.: Transaction Publishers, 1998.

———. *The Idea of Civil Society.* Princeton: Princeton University Press, 1995.

———. "Individualism as Principle: Its Emergence, Institutionalization, and Contradictions." *Indiana Law Journal* 72 (1997): 503–27.

Shields, Jon A. *The Democratic Virtues of the Christian Right.* Princeton: Princeton University Press, 2009.

Simmel, Georg. "The Web of Group-Affiliations." In *Conflict & The Web of Group-Affiliations*, translated by Kurt H. Wolff and Reinhard Bendix. New York: Free Press, 1955.

Smith, Carl T. *Chinese Christians: Elites, Middlemen, and the Church in Hong Kong.* Hong Kong: Oxford University Press, 1985.

Smith, Christian. *Christian America? What Evangelicals Really Want.* Berkeley: University of California Press, 2000.

Snow, David A., and Richard Machalek. "The Sociology of Conversion." *Annual Review of Sociology* 10 (1984): 167–90.

Solinger, Dorothy. *Contesting Citizenship in Urban China: Peasant Migrants, the State, and the Logic of the Market.* Berkeley: University of California Press, 1999.

Stark, Rodney. *The Victory of Reason: How Christianity Led to Freedom, Capitalism, and Western Success.* New York: Random House, 2006.

Thornton, Patricia. "The New Cybersects: Resistance and Repression in the Reform Era." In *Chinese Society: Change, Conflict, and Resistance*, 2nd ed., edited by Elizabeth J. Perry and Mark Selden, 247–70. New York: Routledge, 2002.

Tocqueville, Alexis de. *Democracy in America*. Edited by J. P. Mayer. Translated by George Lawrence. New York: Harper Collins, 1969.

Unger, Jonathan, ed. *Associations and the Chinese State: Contested Spaces*. Armonk, N.Y.: M. E. Sharpe, 2008.

Walker, Williston. *The Creeds and Platforms of Congregationalism (1893)*. Cited in Ross W. Beales, "The Half-Way Covenant and Religious Scrupulosity: The First Church of Dorchester, Massachusetts, as a Test Case." *William and Mary Quarterly* 31, no. 3 (1974): 465–80.

Walzer, Michael. "Equality and Civil Society." In *Alternative Conceptions of Civil Society*, edited by Simone Chambers and Will Kymlicka, 34–49. Princeton: Princeton University Press, 2002.

Webb, P. R. "Voluntary Social Welfare Services." In *Chung Chi College, 25th Anniversary Symposium, 1951–1976: A Quarter Century of Hong Kong*. Hong Kong: Chinese University Press, 1977.

Weber, Max. "The Protestant Sects and the Spirit of Capitalism." In *From Max Weber: Essays in Sociology*, edited and translated by Hans Gerth and C. Wright Mills, 302–22. New York: Oxford University Press, 1946.

———. *The Sociology of Religion*. Translated by Ephraim Fischoff. Boston: Beacon Press, 1963.

Weller, Robert P. *Alternate Civilities: Democracy and Culture in China and Taiwan*. Boulder, Colo.: Westview Press, 1999.

———. *The Unities and Diversities of Chinese Religion*. Seattle: University of Washington Press, 1987.

White, Gordan, Jude Howell, and Shang Xiaoyuan. *In Search of Civil Society: Market Reform and Social Change in Contemporary China*. New York: Oxford University Press, 1996.

Whyte, William Foote. *Street Corner Society: The Social Structure of an Italian Slum*. Chicago: University of Chicago Press, 1943.

Williams, Rhys H., and N. J. Demerath III. "Cultural Power: How Underdog Religious and Nonreligious Movements Triumph against Structural Odds." In *Sacred Companies: Organizational Aspects of Religion and Religious Aspects of Organization*, edited by N. J. Demerath III, Peter Dobkin Hall, Terry Schmitt, and Rhys H. Williams, 364–77. Oxford: Oxford University Press, 1998.

Wolf, Arthur, ed. *Religion and Ritual in Chinese Society*. Stanford: Stanford University Press, 1974.

Wong Pik-Wan. "The Pro-Chinese Democracy Movement in Hong Kong." In *The Dynamics of Social Movement in Hong Kong*, edited by Stephen Chiu Wing-Kai and Lui Tai-Lok, 55–90. Hong Kong: Hong Kong University Press, 2000.

Wuthnow, Robert. *Christianity in the Twenty-First Century.* Oxford: Oxford University Press, 1993.

———. "A Reasonable Role for Religion? Moral Practices, Civic Participation, and Market Behavior." In *Democratic Civility*, edited by Robert W. Hefner, 113–29. New Brunswick, N.J.: Transaction Publishers, 1998.

Yang, C. K. *Religion in Chinese Society.* Berkeley: University of California Press, 1961.

Yang Fenggang. "Between Secularist Ideology and Desecularizing Reality: The Birth and Growth of Religious Research in Communist China." *Sociology of Religion* 65, no. 2 (2004): 101–19.

———. "Lost in the Market, Saved at McDonald's: Conversion to Christianity in Urban China." *Journal for the Scientific Study of Religion* 44, no. 4 (2005): 423–41.

Yang, Mayfair. "Between State and Society: The Construction of Corporateness in a Chinese Socialist Factory." *Australian Journal of Chinese Affairs* 22 (1989): 31–60.

Zald, Mayer, and Patricia Denton. "From Evangelicalism to General Service: The Transformation of the YMCA." *Administrative Science Quarterly* 8 (1963): 214–34.

Zald, Mayer, and John D. McCarthy. "Religious Groups as Crucibles of Social Movements." In *Sacred Companies: Organizational Aspects of Religion and Religious Aspects of Organization*, edited by N. J. Demerath III, Peter Dobkin Hall, Terry Schmitt, and Rhys H. Williams, 24–49. Oxford: Oxford University Press, 1998.

Zhou, Kate Xiao. *China's Long March to Freedom: Grassroots Modernization.* Piscataway, N.J.: Transaction Publishers, 2009.

———. *How the Farmers Changed China: Power of the People.* Piscataway, N.J.: Transaction Publishers, 1996.

Index